Developing Multicultural Educators

Second Edition

Jana Noel

California State University, Sacramento

WAVELAND
PRESS, INC.
Long Grove, Illinois

For information about this book, contact:
Waveland Press, Inc.
4180 IL Route 83, Suite 101
Long Grove, Illinois 60047-9580
(847) 634-0081
info@waveland.com
www.waveland.com

7

Contents

Preface

The layout of the second edition of the textbook *Developing Multicultural Educators* utilizes the same focus on identity development in multicultural education as in the first edition. The topics of the five chapters remain the same, and so does the Appendix. The second edition also maintains a pedagogical approach to multicultural education, with the continued inclusion of preliminary group and individual activities, guided discussion questions throughout the chapters, end-of-the-chapter reflective writings, and case studies. Changes in the second edition include updates to many references and statistics, new reflective writings, new discussion items, and several new identity stories.

The Preface of the first edition has been changed to become the Introduction to the book. It includes an expansion of my own identity story.

Chapter 1 includes a new section on community "funds of knowledge," discussing the theory and practice of connecting with a school's neighborhood community. It has an added reflective writing connected with community studies.

Chapter 2 has an extended and updated section on tracking and an entirely new section and reflective writing on the concept of "subtractive schooling." It also contains an updated checklist of "Possibly Racist Events," a list geared to initiate discussion. The checklist includes events that have occurred after the first edition of the book was published.

Chapter 3 contains some updated statistics and identity issues related to refugee and immigrant status.

Chapter 4 updates Gardner's multiple intelligences, adding his eighth intelligence, the naturalist intelligence.

Chapter 5 has added new identity stories illustrating the various stages of ethnic identity discussed in the chapter.

Acknowledgments

I want to thank Jeni Ogilvie, Editor for Waveland Press, for her assistance throughout the process of developing this second edition of the book. I would also like to thank the rest of the staff at Waveland who helped put this book into production. My appreciation also goes to the reviewers who at various stages of preparation of this book provided useful suggestions for improvements. Reviewers for the first edition included:

Janet S. Arndt, Gordon College
Aram Ayalon, SUNY-Potsdam
Harold Chu, George Mason University
Johanna Filp, Sonoma State University
Jo Gibson, Cleveland State University
Sandra Jackson, DePaul University
Mustafa Ozcan, Clarke College
Charles R. Payne, Ball State University
Francisco Rios, California State University, San Marcos
Louis G. Romano, Michigan State University
Jaime J. Romo, National University
Marguerite Terrill, University of Maine at Fort Kent
Brent Wendling, University of Central Oklahoma
June T. Young, Alabama A & M University

Reviewers who provided thoughtful comments as I was preparing the second edition included:

Marius Boboc, Cleveland State University
Don Bouchard, University of Southern Maine
Ed Coates, Abilene Christian University
Barbara O'Block, Calumet College of St. Joseph
Jose Vega, University of Wisconsin, River Falls
Benjamin Welsh, Ball State University
Russell Young, San Diego State University

And on a personal note, I want to give special thanks to my husband David Powell and to my parents Jim and Jan Noel, all of whom have given me love, support, and encouragement not only while I was working on this book, but in all my personal and professional endeavors.

Introduction

Overview of Book

Individuals' identities are shaped by the cultural, social, and historical background of their communities. We not only grow up in specific communities, we have the values, attitudes, beliefs, and traditions of those communities as part of the fabric of our characters. As such, our experiences have come within a particular cultural way of life, and our perspectives on the world have arisen out of the particular ways of our cultures and communities.

Being deeply woven into our characters throughout our lives, we may not realize the effects that these socially constructed beliefs and attitudes have on our daily actions and practices. Because our identities are embedded within the thinking, patterns, and traditions of societies, we are often unable to recognize that our identities are socially constructed within these frameworks. It's difficult to step outside our long-developing, socially constructed identities to understand our roles within these societies. If we have not been encouraged to actively examine the social construction of our identities, we are not likely to realize the effects that these beliefs and attitudes have on our daily actions and practices.

The approach to multicultural teacher education used in this text helps educators recognize this sociohistorical foundation for their identities and understand how the social construction of identities has shaped their perceptions, judgments, and understanding of the world. It does not take the usual approach of "telling about" multicultural education with hosts of definitions and demographics. For individuals who have not incorporated the issues of multicultural education into their own identities, being told about the need for multicultural education does not help them internalize the importance of the issues in the field. Readers do not necessarily internalize the importance of multicultural education when the texts do not actively ask their readers to make multicultural concepts a part of their own identities. This text, then, starts with each reader, not by telling but rather by drawing him or her in through his or her own experiences, by helping each person to see his or her own identity and world as socially constructed.

1

Relation of Socially Constructed Identities to Multicultural Education

The implications of seeing identity as socially constructed are that we learn that our identities are not developed in isolation. The cultures, traditions, history, media, institutions, practices, and stories of all people make up the society within which our identities develop and emerge. Our shared histories and societies act as shapers of our identities. Our identities, then, are made up of the lives and experiences of all people.

Many educators, though, enter a teacher education program or the teaching profession without recognition of the necessary connection of the identities of all people. When educators do not see their own identities as socially constructed, they do not see a shared sense of identity with others. They often see multicultural education as something that other people do or need. They have the misconception that, "If I were teaching students from my own background, I really wouldn't need to learn about multicultural education" (Marshall, 1994, p. 19). As one of my students wrote, "I intend to stay [in my community] and teach at a smaller school, so the use of multicultural education to me isn't very important." Students and teachers such as these have not made multicultural concepts a part of their identities. They do not realize that their socially constructed identities include the lives of all people, and they see no need to study multicultural education and see no connection between their lives and the lives of others outside their own communities.

The study of our socially constructed identities has several outcomes that strengthen students' connection to and incorporation of multicultural education issues into their own thinking about and preparation for teaching. First, when looking at identity as socially constructed, "one recognizes one's self as a member of various different subcommunities simultaneously" (Burbules and Rice, 1991, p. 404). For instance, when I taught at Montana State University, many of my rural and ethnically isolated Caucasian students disclaimed any similarities with Native Americans. They purposefully defined themselves in opposition to the way they perceive Native Americans. However, when talking with individuals from highly urban areas, these same students have proclaimed identities in opposition to what they view as urban values. In their desire to be identified as nonurban, they will go on to claim ownership of the very beliefs and traditions that are valued by many Montana Native Americans. Students come to realize, through this experience, that many factors in identity, for instance, rurality, are features that can be shared by many groups, regardless of ethnicity. They come to identify themselves not only as White, but also as rural, and they begin to allow that they may share some important values with those persons who identify themselves as Native American.

A second benefit of the identity development process is that "we can broaden and enrich our self-understanding by considering our beliefs, values, and actions from a fresh standpoint" (Burbules and Rice, 1991, p. 405). When individuals begin to reconsider their own beliefs as informed by the perspective of another culture, they come to see the "value of incorporating that perspective into a more complex and multifaceted framework of understanding" (p. 405). To continue the same example of my own students, they came to see their viewpoint as possibly not a view that was composed in isolation, but rather as one perspective of a framework of perspectives that is informed by many cultures around them and in their society. Their understanding of their own perspective becomes deepened. Following is an example from one of my students, as he displayed an extended understanding of how his perspective has been socially constructed through writing his reactions to watching an assigned video titled, "Transitions: Destruction of a Mother Tongue":

> I do hold biases against Indians as a whole. I mean I was raised almost to hate Indians. I have learned from my parents, my piers [sic] and some chance meetings with different Indian tribes that Indians are worthless. The only thing is that I have only learned one side of the story until now. . . . This film on the Blackfeet has confused me very much.

This unsettling of what we believe is certain about ourselves and about others is at the heart of the learning process in multicultural education. It allows us to see that our own identities have been constructed within certain communities, societies, and points of view, and it allows us to begin to recognize the other perspectives that exist in society.

Structure of the Book

This book is structured in a way to draw readers into the field of multicultural education through the study of the social construction of identities. It asks readers to continuously examine and construct their identities as they read and reflect on the ideas in the text. As a whole, the text is sequenced to draw readers further into reflections on identity, but each chapter may be considered useful for study on its own as well. The text draws on my experiences in teaching multicultural education, the experiences of other multicultural educators who have written about their experiences, from the literature of multicultural education, and from the psychological, philosophical, and sociological foundations of education.

Chapter 1, "Culture," is the starting point for this study of multicultural education. It makes the study personal since it asks readers to examine their own cultural backgrounds and the influences of those cultural backgrounds on their sense of who they are. This chapter also begins a look at the roles that schools and teachers play in the identity development process. Chapter 2 then challenges our sense of identity by bringing in the topics of "Stereotyping, Prejudice, and Racism." This chapter asks readers to examine the roles of these concepts within their own identities, and to look at how these ideas impact students. Chapters 3 and 4 ask readers to consider how identities are affected through "Immigration and Imposition" and "Classroom Orientations and Learning Styles." Through discussions of different patterns of immigration and imposition, chapter 3 explores the ways that individuals and groups form, maintain, retain, or reshape their identities after interaction with the dominant U.S. culture. Chapter 4 moves the discussion of identity construction into the schools, discussing the effects of the teacher's views of students who are struggling and describes the variety of learning styles and multiple learning intelligences that can help teachers better meet the needs of students. The concluding chapter, chapter 5, describes directly and clearly "The Identity Development Process" as laid out by multicultural educators. With the reading and reflecting undertaken by readers in the first four chapters, readers should be able to understand some of the reasons and mechanisms involved in the social construction of identity. They can see the process in action by reading comments from others engaged in the same process that they have just gone through. And most important, they should now be able to recognize the process of their own identity development in relation to multicultural education. These five chapters are the heart of the book. For readers who are eager to apply some of these ideas within their classrooms, the appendix, "Suggestions for the Multicultural Classroom," is included.

The structure of each chapter is also designed to draw readers into the field of multicultural education through the study of their socially constructed identities. Features of each chapter include the following:

1. Each chapter begins with an introductory section relating identity development to the specific topics of the chapter.

2. Each chapter then asks readers to engage in both individual and group preliminary exercises designed to draw out readers' awareness and attitudes about the topics of the chapter. These should help tie the readers' current levels of awareness and understanding with the content of multicultural education.

3. The major content of each chapter is the discussions of key topics, with continuous encouragement of reflections on identity development and multicultural education.

4. Reflective writings are suggested at the end of each chapter, asking readers to draw the connections between their identities and the field of multicultural education. These reflective writings are at different levels of reflection, including (a) summarizing material from the chapter, (b) reflecting on and drawing from one's own experiences, (c) synthesizing information into new ideas, (d) engaging in a critical analysis of schools and of society, and (e) designing ideas for practice in the classroom.

My Identity Story

I would like to present my identity story, an ever-evolving story, in hopes that it will serve as a model of the kind of effort and study that is required in the study of identity construction in relation to multicultural education. By laying out my struggles in studying identity, I hope that readers will get a sense for the efforts that are needed in such a study that is being asked of them by this book.

I came to the study of multicultural education without an understanding of the role of identities in the incorporation of multicultural principles. As a child and as an adult, I was always firmly entrenched in the dominant culture of society. It took my feeling like an "other," or an outsider, that caused me for the first time to begin to examine the society that shaped me and the factors that helped to form who I am.

I have had, as the saying goes, a wonderful life. My parents have been able to ensure that I have had a multitude of positive experiences. As part of a middle-class, White family, I had traveled around the United States and had been to a number of countries as a youth. I was successful in many academic and athletic endeavors. In looking at my background in specific, several key pieces have helped shape these experiences. Each piece interacts with the other, and the pieces shape and define each other; the pieces have also been shaped by interactions with society and cultural experiences throughout my life. I have basically always lived in large cities—Kansas City, Missouri; Los Angeles and Sacramento, California; with a shorter time in the small town of Bozeman, Montana. My father, as I was growing up, was in the media—a disk jockey and sports announcer. And my family is in the middle socioeconomic level. The combination of these pieces of my background has led me to expect certain things out of life—many options of events and activities, sports and media, travel, and multicultural sets of people and experiences. Then when I moved to Los Angeles to go to graduate school at UCLA, I lived in an international graduate dormitory and had friends from many parts of the country and of the world. In short, all of my experiences allowed me to fit well in U.S. society, gave me unquestioned access to these experiences, and gave me the knowledge that I would be able to continue doing so in the future.

This background, without my realizing it, also allowed me to become firmly entrenched in the dominant culture of society. It intentionally and unintentionally shielded me from the lives and cultures of people who are not part of that culture. It also stifled my need to incorporate multiculturalism as part of my identity. Along with many who can be similarly described, I never realized that easily fitting into society—sharing the beliefs, attitudes, patterns, and traditions of the dominant culture—is a privilege, and it is not experienced by everyone.

As it did so many people who study identity issues and teach with a focus on the development of identities, it took my feeling uncomfortable in a new setting to cause me to examine the society that helped form me and the factors that helped shape who I am. For a number of people of color, this examination of socially constructed identities begins as youngsters. As a White, middle-class person, my study of identity began later in life. Upon my moving to a rural, isolated setting in Montana, nothing was familiar at all. I was uncomfortable. I could not find any events or components of lifestyle with which I was familiar. I was an outsider. While I still had my California license plates on my car, my car windows were smashed twice. Everything that I thought was just "regular" was, I was discovering, a life that was informed by a comfortable placement within the dominant cultural views of the United States. I had always been able to take part in many activities and events, yet I did not know that my life consisted of a view of the world that had as yet been unchallenged and unrecognized.

Being in such a setting for the first time, new questions arose that brought up a sense of confusion in me. The active constructing of my identity had come in the attempt to understand questions such as: If I have always flowed easily within society, why can't I now? What is it that makes me feel so different from others in this community? Why is my perspective so seemingly different from those around me? Why am I resisting so strongly the efforts of others to shape my identity in a way that would fit more easily within the community? In my case, it is not race or language differences, since Bozeman, Montana, is approximately 95 percent White and English speaking. I am not seen by others as an "other," so I can, in fact, by the nature of my physical appearance and language patterns, choose whether to become part of the community's flow. My realization that I have this choice, that others do not, and that I, and probably others, do not want to give up what we have constructed as our identities, has focused my attention on the importance of recognizing and retaining one's lifelong developing sense of self.

The next part of my identity story comes with my move to California State University, Sacramento. Seeking a greater opportunity to work within diversity, and to return to a larger city where I felt more comfortable, I moved to Sac State and became a Faculty Liaison for the Equity Network (Wong & Glass, In Press). In this role, I served as the connection between the university and a Professional Development School, one of 12 schools in a network of urban, low-income, culturally and linguistically responsive schools. Moving further into the practice of teacher education in diverse settings, I embarked on another new endeavor, cocreating and coordinating the Urban Teacher Education Center (Noel, 2006). Strengthened by the research literature that stresses the importance of connecting urban teacher education more strongly with the community (CREDE, 2004; Howey, 2001; Moll et al., 1992; Murrell, 2001), we moved the center into the field, and made it a community-oriented center. Our center is located at Jedediah Smith Elementary School, a 100-percent free-and-reduced-price-lunch school, whose student body is 99 percent students of color, including 55 percent African American, which serves only students from two public housing projects. With this move into the school came the opportunity to get to know more about the neigh-borhood and some of the families. And this move solidified my burgeoning awareness that my students and I need to become more integrated with the school's community.

Thus, I applied for and received a sabbatical and spent the Fall of 2006 serving as an unofficial "community liaison" between the elementary school, the university, the Urban Teacher Education Center, and the community. I was fortunate to be able to connect with two men, Tony and Malcolm, who grew up in the projects, left to get their college degrees, and now give back to the community by running an after-school tutoring and mentoring program. My students now serve as tutors within this center within the neighborhood. I have been able to get to know two women who serve as matriarchs for the neighborhoods, Pam and Tata. I got to take part in community events, attend meetings of the local social service agencies, meet with the public housing agency, and volunteer at back-to-school day within the neighborhood. My students and I helped open a Family Resource Center, help run an after-school math and science club, helped open the library when there was no funding for a librarian, and help lead a tour of our Sac State campus.

As should be clear, my focus has shifted from an individual approach to multicultural education located on a university campus to a school- and com-munity-based approach that involves community organizing at a basic level (Oakes, Rogers, & Lipton, 2006) and school reform efforts. But the consistent thread throughout the beginnings of my study of the social construction of identities while in Montana, through to my increased involvement in multi-cultural communities in California, has been the idea that I must continue to study my own identity, especially in relation to the local context within which I work. I have privilege due to my race and my economic and educational level. But I am an outsider to communities of color, be it in predominantly African American urban public housing complexes or on Native American reservations. I need to continuously reflect on what I bring to the social con-text, my racial and economic background, and how that is perceived as "other" by those who share their community with me. I must always listen, learn, and reflect.

It is my hope that readers of this text, both the instructors and the stu-dents, will engage in similarly serious reflections on the social constructions of their identities and on their connections to multicultural society and schools.

Conclusion

This text, then, asks readers to do the difficult work of examining how society has shaped our identities, and how our identities will shape our interac-tions with the world. This approach to multicultural education can be psycho-logically risky because it asks us to put our long-developing belief system under examination. Our preconceived notions, our knowledge, our understanding, and our very ways of knowing are under question. We are asked to confront our attitudes regarding other people. Additionally, we may begin to have doubts about our own competency. We engage in struggles with multicultural issues and feel uncertain because of the complexity of those issues. But even though this work on actively constructing our identity may be emotional, it is important because, as Nieto (1996) describes, "Without this transformation of ourselves, any attempts at developing a multicultural perspective will be shallow and superficial" (p. 353).

Chapter 1

Culture

Identity Development Related to Culture

We live in a world and a society that has been forming itself for hundreds and thousands of years, being made into what it is today through countless sets of interactions between individuals, groups, and institutions. Our identities reflect and are shaped out of these numerous sets of historical and current interactions. In order to more clearly understand who we are as individuals, we need to better understand who we are as a society and as a culture. In large part, understanding our culture will help us understand ourselves and others.

A helpful way to begin this discussion is to look at some of the social and cultural factors that help shape our identities. Researchers used the term "social construction" to indicate that our identities are formed within a complex mix of social and cultural influences, or, as Taylor and Spencer describe, "human identity is socially, historically and culturally constructed" (2004, p. 2). The influences that help shape who we are include our immediate family, our community, the media, and the schools. Aspects of our cultural background that can affect our identities include family size and family structures, geographic location, size of community, socioeconomic status (SES), religion, and pieces of literature that have formed our beliefs about values and relations with others. Each of these factors of our cultural background, along with countless others, is a source that helps us define who we are. Some of these sources give us views about ourselves. Some give us views about others. Some require us to fit into a particular model. Some give us many options from which to choose. From this complex mix, we construct our identities and determine our relation to those around us. An understanding of what our culture tells us about ourselves, and the ways that our families, communities, and schools pass along cultural patterns from generation to generation, is the goal of this chapter.

Preliminary Activities

Individual Activity

Think of who you are today. Why do you think certain people or things are important? What made you believe the things that you believe? What is it about your background that makes you who you are today?

For an initial individual activity, examine Figure 1.1. Each piece of the background pie represents an important part of our identity. For each of us, some of these pieces of our background may be very important to us. For others, these same pieces may not be anything that we have even thought about as important.

As the examples in Figure 1.2 illustrate, two people who appear to be very similar in their identities in actuality can be very different in terms of what they feel is most important in their personalities. Will these two women have the same views about the world? Will their beliefs about education be the same? Or will their perspectives be different?

Think about your own characteristics, and draw your own background pie to illustrate what parts of your background have affected who you are today.

Small Group Discussion

As a college student living on or near campus, what has been most different about living in this town, compared to your hometown? Or, if you are already from this town, what has been most different about living in this *part* of town? What has been most different about coming to college? What different perspectives about your new setting have you heard from others in your class or your community?

Figure 1.1   Cultural Background Pie

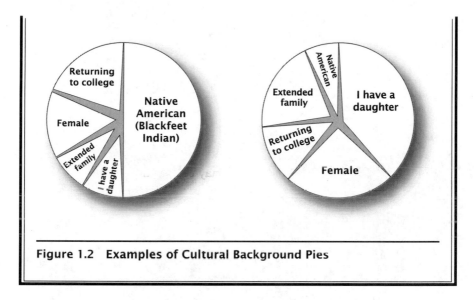

Figure 1.2   Examples of Cultural Background Pies

The Concept of Culture

Definitions of Culture

Culture is a way of seeing, perceiving, and believing. Although earlier definitions focused more on artifacts and customs, items and activities that can be physically observed, current conceptions of culture look at the underlying beliefs and perspectives that give rise to those manifestations of culture. This way of looking at culture moves the focus away from the surface, outward aspects of culture and points our attention to the deep structure of culture, to people's beliefs and understandings of the world. In a definition that helped explain the field of culture in 1871, Tylor listed the individual components of culture: "that complex whole which includes knowledge, belief, art, morals, law, custom, and any other capabilities and habits acquired by man as a member of society" (p. 1). Some of these components can be visualized as the branches of a tree, as the outward and observable customs of a culture. It is the roots, however, that provide the deeper, shared values and beliefs out of which the branches grow (see Figure 1.3). Current definitions of culture focus on the roots of the tree, emphasizing the idea that a culture's values and beliefs will shape the customs and traditions of that culture.

The relationship between the roots and the branches of a tree serves an important illustration to help us understand how the visible characteristics of a culture arise from and are framed within the root beliefs and perspectives of that culture. As an example, note that language is one of the roots of a culture, and linguistic patterns are one of the visible branches of the cultural tree. Let us look at the visible component first, the linguistic patterns of a group. The visible signs of language are the actual words spoken and the speaker's

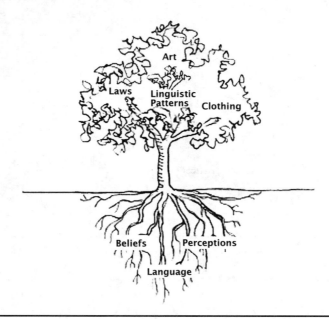

Figure 1.3   Root and Surface Conceptions of Culture

dialect and accent, which are all influenced by regional language patterns within the country and the world. Although we are constantly exposed to these surface aspects of language, they are relatively basic features of a culture. We tend to ignore or be oblivious to the deeper patterning effect of language. When we consider language as one of the roots of culture, however, we see that language helps organize lives, patterns the way people think, and defines social relationships. These roots of language within a culture, the deeper sense of language, help give rise to the visible (or audible) linguistic patterns of a culture. Similarly, the beliefs, attitudes, assumptions, and perspectives that have historically developed within a culture give rise to the visible, outward components of that culture.

Functions of Culture

What role does culture play in the organization and functioning of human life? Anthropologists, psychologists, sociologists, and philosophers have made this a central question in much of their work. To put it simply, culture is a historically developed and developing way for a group of people to deal with the natural and social world. Culture evolves from a specific history of a specific group that has a shared set of social and political behaviors. Culture includes practices within families, communities, and societies that have been developed and agreed upon over time. As Taylor and Spencer describe, "the individual has been steeped in the specific traditions of a group, embodying all its social codes" (2004, p. 2). In other words, culture operates in a *sociohistorical* context.

The functions of culture can be seen in terms of why cultures are developed. Maslow (1943), especially, has structured the discussion of the needs of people that are met by culture. These are needs that must be met in order for the person to develop completely as a person.

1. At the basic level, culture provides a means by which the most basic human survival needs can be met. This is the lowest level of Maslow's hierarchy of needs: the physiological needs and safety needs of the person. For an individual or a culture to continue in its development, these basic needs must be met. Culture plays a crucial role in life by creating ways to meet these needs, ways that have developed within a specific social and historically developing context. For example, think about the foods that the people in your culture eat. To what extent are those foods selected based on availability? On economic factors? On geographic region? On religious beliefs? On storage and preparation beliefs and techniques? On genetic intolerances? Cultural factors to a large extent determine how we will satisfy our needs for food, as well as other basic survival needs like shelter.

2. Culture also plays an important role in giving us a sense of belonging. Maslow lists these needs as love and belonging needs and esteem needs. Being part of a culture helps us realize that there are others who will share our beliefs, views, and perspectives. One's cultural group can provide such esteem-strengthening supports as group cohesion, mutual support, and maintenance of group boundaries. By sharing a sense of identity with others, the sense of self can be turned into a sense of we.

3. Additionally, culture sets for us what would be regarded as important in becoming the best person each of us can be. Each of the previous needs must be met before a person can reach this final goal. At the top or upper level of Maslow's hierarchy of needs is the need for self-actualization. A culture that has been shaped by its members provides our sense of what is important in society, of what we can aim for in our lives to make us feel complete. In this sense, culture defines what we do and what we value in situations. We develop a sense for what is acceptable and unacceptable, appropriate and inappropriate, in different situations. For instance, in your culture, are there equal expectations of men and women in the household, or are there roles that are unacceptable for men and others that are deemed appropriate only for men? Culture helps determine such patterns of appropriateness in social settings. Culture also defines for us what is important and unimportant, attractive and unattractive, and even what is interesting and uninteresting. What is an important bonding activity between a parent and a child in your culture? Father and son hunting trips? Going to the child's school play? Teaching the child the parents' original language?

Culture has many functions in our lives. It is created by groups of people in response to the world around them. It helps us survive, feel a sense of belonging, and patterns our behaviors and beliefs so that we can locate our roles and meet certain expectations within society.

Cautions about Culture

Although an important role of culture is providing a sense of belonging for its members, there is a danger of creating an "us" and "them" dichotomy. Young (1990) describes this concern:

> Identification as a member of such a community often occurs as an oppositional differentiation from other groups, who are feared or at best devalued. Persons identify only with some other persons, feel in community only with those, and fear the difference others confront them with because they identify with a different culture, history, and point of view of the world. (p. 311)

An example of this "oppositional differentiation" can be seen in an exchange that occurred on a radio call-in show in Bozeman, Montana. On this particular occasion, the disc jockey asked a caller, "Where are you from?" The caller responded, "I'm not from California. That's all that matters." This caller's words implied that she devalued one culture by setting herself as clearly distinct from it.

Another caution about culture is one that is often overlooked. As described earlier, culture provides ways for our basic needs to be met. However, it can also actually create new needs for people of that culture, needs that may be harmful. For example, through the media (films, TV shows, magazines, and the Internet) fashion models and trends are highly visible, and the desire by many young women to be thin like these models and wear trendy clothes has resulted in an increase in eating disorders—bulimia and anorexia. These culturally created disorders have developed in conjunction with the perceived need in a particular culture.

Finally, culture is not static. A group of people does not have *a* culture, an unchanging and unalterable view of the world. An increase in geographic mobility, access to worldwide media, and the influx of new information contribute to a dynamic conception of culture and cultural change. Norms of acceptability, morality, beauty, and so on change. Since perspectives are formed on the basis of cultural and social aspects of life, when these aspects change, the perceptual lens through which we view life also changes.

Summary of the Concept of Culture

In summary, then, culture shapes how we perceive the world. Our perspectives on life are shaped by our experiences within our particular society and communities. Culture is a useful concept in that it helps provide a comfortable and understandable set of ways to meet our basic human needs, it defines for us what is appropriate and what is valued in everyday situations, and it gives us a sense of belonging. Even though it is important for us to understand the culture that helped shape our identities, it is equally important to recognize that a culture is not perfect and it is not static. Thus, an understanding our own cultural perspective and the value of other cultural perspectives is important in our world.

Components of Culture

The way people understand their world is shaped by their culture's history, traditions, and ways of thinking. In addition, each culture provides its own particular styles of communication, patterns of interaction, and ways of knowing. It is the complex interaction of these patterns of living that shape how people act and how they expect others to act. This section will focus on three main components of culture, with descriptions of many of the variations of how those components are seen, enacted, and interpreted by different cultures. Table 1.1 lays out these components of culture.

Communication Style

Communication, at its basic level, is the sending and receiving of messages. But within the system of communication, there are many subtle variations in how different cultures communicate, differences in what is expected

Table 1.1 Components of Culture

Communication Style	Organizational Style	Intellectual Style
Structure • Vocabulary (words used) • Semantics (meanings of words) • Grammar (sentence structures) **Expressiveness** • Phonology (level, pitch, rhythm, tempo) **Participation patterns** • Reading, discussing, understanding • Listening, imitating, recalling • Creating and telling stories, taking the lead in verbal communications • Listening prior to speaking, telling stories	**Space** **Time** • Monochronic • Polychronic **Interpersonal relations** • Community related • Individual and functional	**Social relations** • Written • Oral **Decision making** • Analytic, logical, detailed • Intuitive, global

and accepted by different cultures. Structurally, the meanings given to words and how the words are organized (in a sentence) to communicate an idea are shaped by a culture's traditions, beliefs, and patterns. A set of vocabulary is transmitted through cultural groups, as is the grammatical form of sentences.

But it is not only the structure of our communication; it is also the expressiveness of our communication style that is shaped by our culture. Our expressiveness is made up in part by the phonology of our communication: its level, pitch, rhythm, and tempo. Think about your conversations with other people. Is there a certain voice level (loud or soft) that you prefer? Do you like to hear high- or low-pitched voices? Do you sometimes feel that people are speaking too fast, or too slow? Does your own voice level, pitch, rhythm, or tempo change depending on the situation? Or how you feel about the topic? These are all aspects of how we express ourselves through communication, and it is likely that other people within our own culture and community will share many of these styles of expressiveness.

Another key component of communication style is the participation patterns in which members of a culture engage. The following paragraphs discuss a few patterns of participation that differ from culture to culture. It is very important to note that not everyone from a culture will have the same communication characteristics. Think about your own culture. Does every person from your particular culture have the exact same communication style? No, they will not. Within specific cultures, there are differences in socioeconomic levels as well as age groups and generations. People of any particular race or nationality live in a broad spectrum of geographic regions and towns, resulting in additional differences within cultures. Thus, there is much diversity not only across different cultures, but also between individuals within each culture. To further understand this, talk to others in your classes and your school. The best way to learn about individuals is to hear their own stories rather than applying one style to every member of a particular culture.

1. Speakers may communicate in a manner that shows high emotion and high energy; they may be highly animated and very actively involved in the whole speaking–listening process of communication. For a person with this style, communication may not be complete unless there is an emotional or physical involvement with the ideas being communicated. The act of conveying a message is highly interactive, verbal, physical, and emotional. Research by Shade (1997) and Hale (2001), among others, have indicated that African American cultures and speakers commonly demonstrate these types of communication styles and participation patterns.

2. Another type of participation style is quite different from that previously described. In the participation patterns most commonly associated with White Americans, emotions are kept separate from the message, and the physical expression of one's ideas is kept to a minimum (Shade, 1997; Bennett, 2006; Pai and Adler, 2006). In this style

of communicating, the speaker is more passive. Speakers of this style are "more oriented toward a passive style, which gives the impression that the communicator is somewhat detached, literal, and legalistic in use of language" (Shade and New, 1993, p. 320). This style has also been termed the "linear expository style," in which speakers relay a series of events, with a clearly focused topic (Lee & Slaughter-Defoe, 2004, p. 473), with an emphasis on sequence more than on emotions.

3. A look at the communication and participation patterns that have been seen in the interactions of Native Americans illustrates a third type of communication style. In this participation pattern, observation and reflection play the key role in communicating with others (Pewewardy, 2002). This style of communication could be called private learning (Swisher and Deyhle, 1989; Pai and Adler, 2006). In this participation pattern, it is more important to listen than to speak. Many people who share this pattern will avoid public expression of their feelings. Other characteristics of this communication style and participation pattern include patience in communicating, appearances of being at ease in interactions, and the avoidance of direct eye contact.

What does culture and cultural background have to do with all this? Cultural background strongly shapes communication style because we learn to participate with others through family and community traditions of communication. Heath (1982) has studied patterns of interaction within different communities, relating a child's cultural traditions directly to communication and interaction patterns. In her studies, she examined the bedtime book-reading and storytelling practices of three different cultural communities: a middle-class White community, a working-class White community, and a working-class Black community. She found that, "The three communities differ strikingly in their patterns of language use and in the paths of language socialization of their children" (p. 49). Specifically, her findings were as follows: The middle-class White parents used bedtime as a time to read stories from books with their children. They taught their children, through this tradition, "not only how to make meaning from books, but also how to talk about it. . . . They have learned to listen, waiting for the appropriate cue which signals it is their turn to show off this knowledge" (Heath, p. 56). For the working-class White families, the parents also used the time before bed to read books with their children. However, their "book-reading time focuses on letters of the alphabet, numbers, names of basic items pictured in books, and simplified retellings of stories in the words of the adult" (Heath, 1982, p. 59). But for the working-class Black children, on the other hand, the bedtime sharing was not the sharing of a written book. Instead, it was oral storytelling time. "For the Black children, storytelling was a part of daily life, with the children encouraged to participate in story creating and telling; however, the children had little or no experience with reading" (Educational Research Service, 1991, p. 6, from Heath, 1982, pp. 64–70).

The lessons learned by children through these participation patterns are clear. In those families who shared the reading of the bedtime book, the subtle lessons that children learn are that communication and participation patterns involve *reading, discussing,* and *understanding.* The families in which the adults read the story to the children but focused on individual pieces of the book like names and numbers, gave the message that communication and participation for children involves *listening, imitating,* and *recalling.* And for the children who were encouraged to actively create and tell stories, the children learned that communication and participation means that children actively *create and tell stories,* thereby *taking the lead in verbal communication.*

In making connections between the cultural and family background of Native Americans and communication style and participation pattern, Philips (1983) describes how adults in one Native American community interact with their children: "Warm Springs adults taught children to pay attention, to observe, to practice on their own, and only then to undertake public performance or demonstration of a new skill or knowledge" (Lomawaima, 1995, p. 339). In another example from another Native American reservation, "Navajo children seemed more comfortable when the teacher read a story straight through before beginning discussion" (O'Hair and Odell, 1993, p. 215). To illustrate the importance of listening in Native American communities, a group of young Native Americans called the "Young Native Scholars" (www.native-scholars.org) describes a "talking circle," in which each speaker can speak uninterruptedly for as long as is needed to tell the story. The lessons learned by children here are that *listening is prior to speaking,* and that communication is in the form of *telling a story* rather than making a direct and factual point.

To summarize the discussion of communication style, it refers to the language structure, expressiveness, and participation patterns used by people to communicate. Communication style is influenced by the cultural background, family, and community traditions of communication. Studies have found that several clearly distinguishable communication patterns are shaped by culture. In one style of communication, children learn that participation in reading, for instance, involves engaging in reading and discussing ideas. A second communication pattern involves listening rather than reading, with the encouragement to imitate, repeat, and recall information. A third pattern focuses much more on storytelling, with children encouraged to create and tell stories, thereby taking the lead in verbal communication. Finally, a fourth cultural style of communication also involves telling a story but emphasizes listening and reflecting prior to speaking. All these communication patterns may be exemplified by students in a single classroom or school. Thus, the idea that there is a single preferred communication pattern in the school denies the culturally influenced patterns of many students.

Organizational Style

In addition to those components of communication already discussed, an additional aspect of communication is demonstrated by different people.

Think again about your conversations with other people. How close to the other person do you stand? An arm's length away? Closer? Farther away? Do you feel uncomfortable if someone stands "too close"? Do you think someone is being rude or uncaring if he or she stands "too far away"? Are you more at ease if there is a physical object, say, a table or a desk, between you and the person with whom you are speaking? Or do you like to be in physical contact with others when you speak—a hand on the shoulder or arm? All this has to do with what is called personal space.

In the United States, people tend to require a layer of personal space that keeps people and objects at a distance. Our feelings about personal space go beyond communication to how we act in virtually all public aspects of our lives, from how we arrange our household furniture, to where we walk on a crowded sidewalk, to how we set up our work area in a library, to how we hold our bodies when we are standing near others on an elevator. Thus, elevators and libraries are good places to observe people's expressions of personal space. Edward T. Hall (1966) describes a common organizational style on an elevator: "In crowded elevators the hands are kept at the side or used to steady the body by grasping a railing. The eyes are fixed on infinity and are not brought to bear on anyone for more than a passing glance" (p. 118). And in libraries, we can commonly see territorial practices, such as clearly demarcating one's study space with the arrangement of papers, books, and pencils. These examples clearly illustrate the importance of personal space in many people's lives.

In addition to how we organize our lives in relation to the physical space surrounding ourselves, we also organize our lives into certain time orientations. Hall focuses on two types of time orientations: monochronic and polychronic. For people and cultures that see time as monochronic, there is a compartmentalization of time. Specific activities are done at specific times. Events are scheduled and accomplished one at a time, according to a schedule, with one event following another. Monochronic time is seen very clearly in the ways schools and universities schedule their courses. To meet the schedule, classes must start and end at specified times, even when a particular class may be engaged in an exciting activity that would lose significance if cut off at a predetermined time.

Think about your daily life. What events do you have tightly scheduled throughout the day? Examples from my life include specific times when I must be teaching a scheduled class. Because of that schedule, I must hurriedly fit in time to eat lunch. And since I often take a bus to work, I must leave my home at a specific time in order to get to the bus that will in turn get me to my classes on time. What events can you list that are specifically designated at specific times during the day?

In contrast, people and cultures who live by polychronic time keep several activities going at the same time. Time periods are not structured into specific times for specific activities; rather, there are loose schedules. Events like powwows, for example, may begin when people arrive and may continue for an unspecified period. Business meetings in some cultures may not be scheduled within a particular block of time, but rather at a leisurely pace over several days.

Differences in how people view personal space and time contribute to different patterns of interpersonal relations. For instance, a polychronic time orientation puts the concerns of people ahead of the structure of a schedule. Schedules and individual concerns are less important than those of the group. In a very community-oriented culture, people interact with a desire to continue the traditions and relationships within that culture. This organizational style stresses personal relationships, involves storytelling, and makes group or community involvement a priority in every aspect of life. To people with a polychronic time orientation, a society based on rigid time schedules and large personal distances between people when speaking can feel unfriendly and antisocial. For people in monochronic cultures interpersonal relationships focus more on individual, rather than group, efforts. In a monochronic time orientation, interactions are often brief and used to make a specific point. Thus, the persons engaged in interpersonal relationships are often expected to provide specific components for the interactions. In other words, interactions are intended to fulfill specific functions.

To summarize, organizational style refers to how we organize our lives in relation to the physical space surrounding ourselves as well as in relation to our orientation toward time and toward other people. The physical space surrounding us is often referred to as personal space—whether we prefer to be close to or far away from other people and other objects. Time orientation refers to how tightly our culture structures its activities in relation to time, as well as whether we generally have multiple events occurring simultaneously or if events have to be linearly and chronologically organized. Depending on the organizational style of the culture, interpersonal relationships can be very group oriented or they can be oriented to the individual. In thinking about organization style, we see that some cultures and communities have organizational styles that are similar to the schools', whereas others have organizational styles that are different from the schools'. Are you able to determine which organizational style is most prevalent both within schools and within U.S. society today?

Intellectual Style

Intellectual style, in this discussion, refers to a *community's* style of thinking and decision making, what knowledge is most valued in a culture and the way that learning takes place most prominently for people within that culture. A key distinction drawn between is between written and oral cultures. Some communities are based more clearly on the written style and others emphasize the oral style, but many endorse and use both ways of thinking.

The phrase "seeing is believing" illustrates the written intellectual style in which people believe and trust information more or only if it is in written form. This style develops from and leads to a legalistic culture. When persons from a culture with this type of intellectual style see words written on a page, they take the intent of those words more seriously than if they merely hear them. For example, rules that structure our society and institutions in are written into laws and regulations; in schools, textbooks and written materials make up the curriculum; university faculty are often required to publish scholarly work in written form such as journal articles and books.

As an example of this intellectual style put into practice, reflect on the policies at your college, university, or school. How do you learn about the schedule of courses? How do you register for courses? What permissions must you get for any variations in scheduling? In short, how many forms must be filled out in the average school year?

Furthermore, the use of written words encourages an intellectual style of analytic thinking, in which the formal principles of reasoning are used to evaluate information. Details of a topic are presented as the beginning point for the study of the topic. We process information in a sequential fashion in order to better understand the possible consequences of a problem or situation before making a final decision about how to handle it. Words and logic are key factors in decision making.

In other cultures, however, societies gain knowledge, pass information to others, and come to agreements through an oral tradition. Agreements are made binding by "giving one's word" or with a handshake. This oral intellectual style lends itself to using intuition and feelings in decision making. The person in this culture will be interested in knowing the global implications of a topic, including cognitive, physical, and emotional aspects involved. A discussion or study of a topic will not look at the details, but rather at the overall picture. So when a student asks, "What does this have to do with the real world?" the student may not be asking that question in order to try to provoke the teacher. Rather, it is quite likely that the student wants to know the real-world implications, wants to relate the information to his or her own life outside the school setting.

In examining the culture of the school, we may be able to determine that the schools encourage a particular intellectual style over all others. Can you determine which intellectual style is more often used and required in the schools and universities of the United States?

Styles That Are Privileged in Schools

When reflecting on these different components of culture, it becomes clear that some styles are more often accepted and expected within schools. Teachers and other staff members treat students who display these styles with high esteem. One way to describe this practice is to say that certain styles are "privileged" within the schools. These styles are considered more appropriate, respectful, and important in school interactions. Table 1.2 lays out some of these privileged styles, with examples of each of these privileged styles within the classroom. Kim and Markus (2005) discuss the nature of these privileged styles within school in their analysis of the "cultural practice of talking" (p. 181). In their analysis, they detail the expectations regarding talk-

Table 1.2 Styles That Are Privileged in Society and in Schools

Style	Privileged Patterns of Behavior	Examples in the Classroom
Communication Style	• Direct expression • Serial exchanges (taking turns) • Assertiveness and competitiveness	• Give direct answers • No tangents • Speak one at a time • Volunteer an answer quickly • Make sure an answer is "right"
Organizational Style	• Individual achievement • Self-motivation • Personal competence	• Do your own work • Be the best you can be • Don't share answers • Strive for good grades
Intellectual Style	• Objective, analytic, and detail-oriented • Separate the cognitive and the affective • Trust in written word forms	• Explain answers in further detail • Tested over facts, not feelings • Use of written permission forms • Use of written texts and materials almost exclusively

ing that are expected within Western and European American traditions. They point out that these expectations proceed by "assuming that the speaker has the responsibility to speak directly and to convey what is on one's mind" (p. 185), and that "speech, verbal expression, and debate" (p. 181) are most valued in American schools. In delineating the concept of "talking" valued within European American schools, "talking is powerfully associated with notions of individuality, freedom, equality, democracy, reason, intelligence, and honesty" (p. 182), all values that are emphasized within schools. As Kim and Markus (2005) describe, these are not the same cultural meanings of talking held by other cultures, including East Asian cultural contexts. Have you noticed these expectations within your own schooling? Can you point to similar examples as those in Table 1.2 within your own schooling? Think about how those students who have these styles as part of their daily lives and as part of their cultures have a more smoothly functioning school experience. Then consider how those students who do not have these styles as part of their culture struggle within the school environment. The section "Characterizations of Culture" discusses various combinations of these styles and characteristics of thinking and behaving.

Summary of the Components of Culture

In studying culture, it can be seen that there are multiple ways of communicating, organizing, and thinking. Patterns and styles within families, communities, and societies help shape each individual's communication, organizational, and intellectual styles. Some communication styles involve highly expressive communication and the telling of stories, whereas others have rigid language structures and focus on reading and discussing what is read. In addition, some cultures encourage listening before speaking or reading. With regard to how cultures organize themselves, one type of organizational pattern is very community oriented, with interpersonal relations being more important than strict adherence to time schedules. Other organizational patterns emphasize individual effort, personal space, and strict time schedules. Additionally, cultures can be seen as having different types of intellectual styles. Some prefer written, analytic, logical thinking in all decisions and interactions. Others encourage oral transmission of ideas based on intuition and feelings.

In thinking about how schools are structured, some cultures and communities have similar styles to the schools', whereas others have styles that function in ways different from the schools'. The outcome of these culturally influenced styles is that some students may have a different set of patterns of participation in school from what is expected by the school.

Characterizations of Culture

A number of researchers have interpreted the actions of different cultures by providing characterizations of cultures, pointing out and combining communication, organizational, and intellectual styles. Some distinguish cultures based on race, others distinguish them based on culture alone, and yet others make distinctions based on whether they are rural or urban. As discussed earlier, it would be foolish to assume that all people from a particular race, from a high or low context culture (see the section below), or from a rural or an urban setting will communicate, organize, and think in the exact, same ways. Perhaps the way that the following characterizations of cultures can be most helpful is to help us recognize that people are different. Although we may think that the way we act is "normal," clearly a wide variety of cultural differences result in a variety of ways of acting.

High Context and Low Context Characterizations of Culture

Edward T. Hall, having analyzed cultures from across the world, believes cultures can be described using two distinct sets of characteristics: high context and low context (see Table 1.3). The key distinction here is how different cultures view and interact with their context—their environment, their social surroundings, and their organizational networks within their setting.

Table 1.3 High and Low Context Characterizations of Culture

	High Context	Low Context
Time:	*Polychronic*	*Monochronic*
	Loose schedules, flux, multiple simultaneous activities. Last-minute changes of important plans. Time is less tangible.	Tight schedules, one event at a time, linear. Importance of being on time. Time is more tangible (e.g., is spent, wasted, is "money").
Space and tempo:	*High-Sync*	*Low-Sync*
	Synchrony, moving in harmony with others and with nature, is consciously valued. Social rhythm has meaning.	Synchrony is less noticeable. Social rhythm is underdeveloped.
Reasoning:	*Comprehensive Logic*	*Linear Logic*
	Knowledge is gained through intuition, spiral logic, and contemplation. Importance of feelings.	Knowledge is gained through analytical reasoning (e.g., the Socratic method). Importance of words.
Verbal messages:	*Restricted Codes*	*Elaborate Codes*
	"Shorthand speech," reliance on nonverbal and contextual cues. Overall emotional quality more important than meaning of particular words. Economical, fast, efficient communication that is satisfying, slow to change; fosters interpersonal cohesiveness and provides for human need for social stability. Stress on social integration and harmony; being polite.	Verbal amplification through extended talk or writing. Little reliance on nonverbal or contextual cues. Doesn't foster cohesiveness but can change rapidly. Provides for human need to adapt and change. Stress on argument and persuasion; being direct.

(continued)

24

Table 1.3   High and Low Context Characterizations of Culture, *continued*

	High Context	Low Context
Social roles:	*Tight Social Structure*	*Loose Social Structure*
	Individual's behavior is predictable; conformity to role expectations.	Behavior is unpredictable; role behavior expectations are less clear.
Interpersonal relations:	*Group Is Paramount*	*Individual Is Paramount*
	Clear status distinctions (e.g., age, rank, position), strong distinctions between insiders and outsiders.	Status is more subtle, distinctions between insiders and outsiders less important.
	Human interactions are emotionally based, person oriented.	Human interactions are functionally based, approach is specialized.
	Stronger personal bonds, bending of individual interests for sake of relationships.	Fragmented, short-term human relationships, broken action chains when relationship is not satisfying.
	Cohesive, highly interrelated human relationships, completed action chains.	Individuals are first, groups come second.
	Members of group are first and foremost.	Fragile interpersonal bonds due to geographic mobility.
Social organization:	*Personalized Law and Authority*	*Procedural Law and Authority*
	Customary procedures and whom one knows are important. Oral agreements are binding.	Procedures, laws and policies are more important than whom one knows.
	In face of unresponsive bureaucracies, must be an insider or have a "friend" to make things happen (e.g., going through the "back door").	Written contracts are binding.
		Policy rules, unresponsive bureaucracy.
	People in authority are personally and truly responsible for actions of every subordinate.	People in authority try to pass the buck.
		Impersonal
		Legal procedures

Source: From Christine I. Bennett, *Comprehensive Multicultural Education: Theory and Practice, 3rd ed.* © 1995 by Allyn & Bacon. Reprinted by permission.

As you read Table 1.3, you may recognize some of the characteristics described earlier in this chapter. For instance, considering again communication style, Hall places some of the descriptions discussed above into the categories of high and low context cultures. In the communication style of low context cultures, for example, the message itself is more important than the speaker, and the message is intended to persuade or convince. In high context cultures, on the other hand, the meaning comes only when the context of the communication is understood since the setting, the people involved, and the emotions are all important parts of the message. Regarding organizational style, the emphasis on a rigid time schedule is important to low context cultures, whereas high context cultures place more value on keeping life in harmony with the natural rhythms of time, such as weather patterns and seasons. To continue, high context cultures tend to organize themselves around group activities and needs, whereas low context cultures place the organizational focus on individual achievements. Finally, tying intellectual style to Hall's characterizations, high context cultures reason and make decisions by relying on intuition and feelings, whereas low context cultures use analytic and word-oriented reasoning.

As you review Table 1.3, reflect on your personal and your community's characteristics. Do you fall in one column fairly consistently? Or do you share the characteristics of both groups? Think about these cultural characteristics further. Does one column of characteristics portray the way of life while you are at home or with your family? Do you fall into one category more when you are at school or at work? When you are on vacation? And finally, which set of characteristics most clearly describes the organization, expectations, and practices within the K–12 schools that you attended, or where you now work, or within your university's teacher-education setting?

Rural/Gemeinschaft and Urban/Gesellschaft Characterizations of Culture

People who live in rural places live in geographic, economic, and social contexts that are often very different from people living in urban locations. Thus, each group's lived experiences of the world will differ. Accordingly, each may see, perceive, and believe differently. There have been numerous studies that describe the cultural characteristics of rural and urban cultures. As in the previous characterizations of culture, however, a caution must be offered here. There are many variations within any supposedly homogeneous culture, and this is important to rural–urban discussions as well. "Rural," entails a variety of settings and people; they might be agricultural communities (farming, ranching), natural resource extraction communities (mining, logging), small business owners, and social service providers, to mention only a few. In urban cultures, different ethnic groups, economic levels, jobs, family backgrounds, and so forth, illustrate the diversity within these areas.

Any analysis of rural and urban cultural characteristics must include a historical and sociological examination of the lived experiences of groups and individuals. Logan and O'Hearn (1982) have provided such a historical and sociological understanding of why many rural and urban people may have developed specific cultural characteristics. The key features of life that lay the foundation for these characteristics are, for rural cultures, the emphasis on family or group-oriented work and traditions that are necessary for the continued survival of the community. In a rural, especially agricultural, community, children are informally socialized into this way of life on a daily basis. This is seen today in states like South Dakota and Idaho, where some schools dismiss classes during the peak harvest season. Children are needed for the work that will ensure their family's and community's survival and success. Much of what children "needed to know was acquired almost incidentally as they participated in the work experience, acquired knowledge and skills from their elders, and learned also by observing and imitating the adults with whom they worked" (p. 518). This also helps ensure the child's identity within the group and within the historical life cycle of that group. Because children's participation in work, has been a practice handed down through many generations, "their sense of place within the historical continuity of their people was also reinforced" (p. 518).

With the move away from rural areas into the cities, both historically and today, there is a move toward the necessity for individuality as the new means of survival. In urban settings, there are new and diverse types of jobs and occupations. Identity is based on the individual effort to find or create new jobs. Identity is based on responsibility, but in this setting, it is individual responsibility for oneself rather than responsibility for the group to continue. In this type of culture, learning does not proceed through observing and imitating adults who work in the job, because unlike children in rural settings, the urban child most likely won't take over the job from the adult and instead will forge a new path based on his or her own interests and abilities. Urban education, therefore, has evolved to become future oriented. "Education in the future-oriented, achievement-oriented era . . . tended to instill a systematic, convergent, goal-directed, future-directed style of thought, with a problem-solving emphasis" (Logan and O'Hearn, 1982, p. 522).

One additional way to identify the differences in rural and urban cultural characteristics is through the German concepts of *gemeinschaft* and *gesellschaft*. Defined by Tönnies (1887), a culture based on gemeinschaft is one that is personal and sharing oriented. It is a community that expects members to look out for one another, and it exists for the purpose of supporting its members. People who live in a gemeinschaft culture may not have chosen that way of life; rather, they are more likely to have been born into a family or community that shares the same values. Tönnies describes that a gemeinschaft must have a commonality of wills and purposes among its members. Three ways to instill this sense of commonality are through tradition, patriotism, and religion. Some of the characteristics shared to varying extents by people in a gemeinschaft include self-reliance, group orientation, importance of work, value of traditional wisdom, and the desire for similarity (Gougeon, 2000). This gemeinschaft type of culture is most often identified as rural.

A gesellschaft culture is one that is based on deliberately chosen association rather than natural birth into a community. Tönnies (1887) characterizes gesellschaft relationships to be rationalistic (deliberately choosing actions rather than actions being based on tradition), negotiated (contracts, rules and regulations), and individualistic. The gesellschaft type of association is typically identified as existing in urban societies. This type of association is most often contractual, with relationships developed for the purposes of providing opportunities for individuals to achieve. Characteristics that may be shared by individuals in gesellschaft association with one another include individual achievement, material gain, leisure and recreation, individualism, and personal freedom (Christenson, 1984, p. 164).

Many people have taken the discussion of the difference in orientations between rural and urban to mean that there is a dichotomy between the two—a view that the two groups are exact opposites. Reflect on this idea. Do you believe that different communities are completely distinct? Think about your personal and your community's characteristics. Do you or your community seem to share the values of gemeinschaft or gesellschaft consistently? Does one set of characteristics portray the ways of acting, believing, and thinking within your home? Within your community? And finally, which set of characteristics most clearly describes the organization, expectations, and practices within the K–12 schools that you attended? Were your schools more like the rural—gemeinschaft—community and tradition-oriented culture? Or were they more like the urban—gesellschaft—individualistic and regulation-oriented culture? Can you distinguish between the characteristics of the social interactions within your school and with the policies of your school based on this rural/gemeinschaft and urban/gesellschaft characterization of culture?

Summary of Characterizations of Culture

There is always a concern with assuming that a culture can be distinguished by a few characteristics. The danger is that stereotypes about entire groups of people will be formed. Perhaps the most helpful reason to study the sets and types of characterizations of different cultures is to realize that there are multiple ways of being. In reality, cultures have developed ways of life that may share some characteristics with other cultures but may also have a number of specific differences.

One way to characterize cultures, as presented here, is to look at distinct sets and patterns of characteristics that may be shared by a number of cultures. In Hall's concepts of high and low context, cultures can be described based on how they interact with their context—their environment, their social surroundings, and the organizational networks within their settings. In these characterizations, cultures have developed specific ways of dealing with life in response to the context and setting, including different ways of seeing time, relationships, communication, and other aspects of life. The study of characterizations of rural and urban cultures, when examined historically and sociologically, shows how cultures can develop over time. The concept of gemeinschaft illustrates the development of a group-sharing orientation within a culture, while gesellschaft is a term that encompasses an individual orientation. These characteristics, along with others, have developed over long histories of cultures.

All these types of characterizations of cultures presented here show the numerous ways of life of different peoples. Each cultural way of life has developed within a culturally influenced set of histories, traditions, and patterns that have helped shape the identities of people today.

Social Foundations of Education

Throughout the history of American education, one of the main functions of education has been the socialization of students into the dominant culture. Both directly and indirectly, schools and teachers help instill within their students the values, beliefs, routines, and expectations of the dominant society in which they live. Education can be a lifelong endeavor, and can occur in and out of school, but it is schools that most clearly perform this socialization. So, although schools have the important purpose of teaching "reading, writing, and arithmetic," they also serve the role of reproducing and perpetuating the established social, cultural, political, and economic structures and norms of society.

As you read the information on the social foundations of education that follows, reflect on the statement, "Schools serve the purpose of socializing students into the dominant culture." In what ways do schools socialize students into society? For what reasons do schools practice this socialization? There are a number of philosophical underpinnings for the schools' practices of socialization. In particular, these philosophical perspectives address *why* society would want schools to practice socialization, *who* controls the beliefs and values that are transmitted by the schools, and the *goals* of this socialization. The answers to each of these questions reveal why some students feel comfortable and confident, whereas others are discouraged from feeling confident in schools.

Cultural Discontinuities between Home and School Cultures

In reflecting on the different components and characterizations of culture (see especially, Table 1.2), it should be clear that there are certain patterns of thinking, believing, and valuing that our schools encourage in students and that other patterns are discouraged by schools. One of the main conflicts that results from these socialization practices is the concept called *cultural discontinuities*. The main idea of discontinuities between home and school cultures is that for many children, the culture of their home and their community is very different from the culture of the school system. Children are socialized to believe, think, and act in specific ways by their families and their communities. As such, their styles of communicating, organizing, and thinking at home are considered natural and are encouraged and accepted. However, for many children, these same behaviors are improper and unacceptable at school. The cultural socialization of students in school involves the encouragement or outright requirement of patterns and beliefs that are specific to the school and to certain cultures but that are foreign to other cultures. Sometimes the school's culture contradicts the home culture. Often, the culture and language of children are disregarded and devalued. The result may be such harmful effects as misinterpretations of students' actions, inconsistencies in expectations and treatments of students, and possible failure in the schools.

Community "Funds of Knowledge": Strengths and Resources within Communities

With the recognition of the cultural discontinuities between home and school, many educators are now taking steps to learn more about the neighborhood community of the school, to learn about the resources that are offered to families and that come from families and other community members, and to learn about the students' and families' cultural backgrounds. Moll, Amanti, Neff, and González (1992) have created the term "funds of knowledge" to describe the social history, daily functioning, and household maintenance strategies of families that have resulted in types of knowledge beneficial to the families and communities. As they define it, "We use the term *funds of knowledge* to refer to these historically accumulated and culturally developed bodies of knowledge and skills essential for household or individual functioning and well-being" (p. 72). This may include knowledge in such areas as economics, household management, and material knowledge, including knowledge of renting or selling, getting loans, consumer knowledge, childcare, repair skills, among many others. Murrell (2001) describes the importance of "community teachers." "A community teacher is one who possesses contextualized knowledge of the culture, community, and identity of the children and families he or she serves and draws on this knowledge to create the core teaching practices necessary for effectiveness in diverse settings" (p. 52).

How are teachers able to engage in learning about community if they are not from the actual physical neighborhood of the school? Teachers, or preservice teachers, can engage in "community studies" in an effort to understand the sets of knowledge that children bring with them into the classrooms and that provide levels of both external and internal support for families (Noel, 2006). Community studies get teachers out into the community to get to know families, events in the communities, social service agencies serving the communities, churches, locally-owned businesses, and types of activities that families and children do together. A caution about community studies is that it is difficult to enter a community and expect to fully understand the dynamics of its members. We each bring the lenses of our own backgrounds with us as we enter communities, and we may not recognize the meanings behind much of what we see in a new setting. This can lead to misinterpretation of events and interactions. To counter this problem, it is a good idea to do a community study with someone who lives within the community, maybe a parent of a student, or a local business owner, or a community organizer. In this way, teachers and pre-service teachers can learn from the local point of view what matters to the community. In the long-run, there are several important outcomes of such a community-based approach. One is that teachers can implement curricular ideas that draw upon the strengths and resources of the local community, making lessons meaningful both locally and culturally to the students. Another beneficial long-term outcome is the strengthening of relationships between teachers, students, and their families. Teachers can be invited to take part in neighborhood events; teachers and families can engage in planning together; in short, trust can be built.

Functionalist Perspective on Cultural Socialization

The functionalist perspective on cultural socialization explains these cultural discontinuities by emphasizing as its key educational concern the continuation and perpetuation of the existing society. This perspective is driven by the desire for a society in which citizens share a common bond, common beliefs, and common goals, in order to enable society to function smoothly. Sadnovik, Cookson, and Semel (2001) layout the essentials of the functionalist perspective:

> [T]he values, beliefs, and norms of society are internalized within children so that they come to think and act like other members of society. In this sense, schools socially and culturally reproduce the existing society through the systematic socialization of its youngest members. (p. 22)

How do schools serve to perpetuate the existing culture? They must work to transmit the cultural values of the existing culture to students. "In the traditional functionalist view of social transmission, each elder generation passes on to each succeeding generation the rules, customs, and appropriate behaviors for operating in the society" (DeMarrais and LeCompte, 1995, p. 6). Schools work to ensure that students will be able to fit into the existing culture, thereby allowing that existing culture to retain its viability from generation to generation. In a society in which people are asked to continue with the mainstream version of society, a main part of their lives will necessarily be the jobs that they hold. In a smoothly functioning society, each person's job will be a necessary piece of the functioning of society. We need school teachers, political leaders, parents, custodial and janitorial workers, fast-food servers, and bankers, among thousands of other jobs, for our society to function the way that it does. Therefore, a crucial part of the continuation of society is the development of people who will be able to fill each of these types of jobs. Spring (1976) introduced the term "sorting machine" to describe this function of schools: it decides which individuals will be prepared to do which jobs, and then sorts them accordingly. The schools determine who will fit into which role within society, set up requirements for students who will fit into those positions, and then create reward systems that encourage students to "fit in their proper place" within society.

Important to the philosophical basis for the functionalist perspective on cultural socialization is that the purposes and goals included in this view are not written or listed in the curriculum of the schools. They are not found within textbooks or teachers' manuals. Rather, these ideas are part of what is termed the "hidden curriculum." The concept of a hidden curriculum refers to the schools' indirect and unstated ways of socializing students into the norms and standards of the dominant culture. The hidden curriculum can refer to the points of view of the textbooks, the expectations of participation patterns in the classroom, the types of courses that are offered, and the hierarchy of authority within the school. Even the physical structure of the school building transmits messages to students about how they are expected to believe and behave to fit into the dominant society.

As part of this functionalist cultural socialization process, students must believe in the value of such socialization. In order to have students who are able and willing to fit into this existing society, according to this perspective, it will be crucial to produce students who will want to and be able to share in and continue the standard beliefs and practices of the dominant society. Students must share the views of the functionalist perspective that there is a consensus on the values and beliefs to be held within society. They must see themselves as willing participants in their cultural socialization into the existing cultural, economic, and class structures in society. They will need to share the perspective that cultural socialization is neutral, that it does not benefit or harm any particular groups or individuals. They will need to accept the perspective of functionalist cultural socialization, as described by DeMarrais and LeCompte (1995): "Functionalism unquestioningly views the social system as benign and accepts existing class structures as appropriate" (p. 7). Thus, students are both taught and expected to believe in the importance of workplace-oriented values of punctuality, conformity to rules and authority, and task orientation.

Critical Perspective on Cultural Socialization

The critical perspective on cultural socialization also recognizes the role that schools play in the socialization of students into the existing society. A crucial distinction between the functionalist and critical perspectives, however, is in the societal purposes for that socialization. Whereas the functionalist educator socializes students to enable the existing society to function smoothly, from the critical perspective, "the school functions to serve the interest of the dominant, the powerful, and the wealthy by perpetuating socioeconomic inequities" (Pai and Adler, 2006, p. 134). As Hytten (1999) describes, "schools currently function to reproduce the status quo (so that those groups with power retain power, and those that are marginalized or powerless remain so)" (p. 528). Thus, whereas the functionalist educator believes that schools help produce bankers, teachers, and manual laborers because each of these jobs is needed in our society, the critical perspective illustrates that those who have power in society use the schools to keep their power. In this way, the differential socioeconomic status system remains in place. In this view, it is not society as a whole that sets the standards, norms, values, and behaviors that are expected and socialized within the schools. Rather, it is the dominant group in society that sets these standards, and sets them in a way so that they will remain the dominant group. Larson and Ovando (2001) call schools one of the "institutionally sanctioned systems of inequity" (p. 107). As they describe further, "Because social, racial, and gender inequities have penetrated our institutions throughout history, not all people have had sufficient power, position, or opportunity to influence the social agreements that have been institutionalized in our society and its institutions" (p. 107).

The issue of power—who has it, who controls it, how is it used to dominate the system—is key to the critical perspective on education and is a key issue for the field of cultural studies. Cultural studies draw from fields such as philosophy, history, sociology, and anthropology to focus a critical lens on the way that our institutions such as schools and the popular media contribute to inequities among people. One particular focus is on the relation between culture and power. Hytten (1999) explains that "cultural studies practitioners explore the links between culture, knowledge, and power, and they aim to uncover disempowering educational and social practices" (p. 528).

How is this set of power relations enacted in the school systems of the United States? There are a number of ways. Examples from the schools revolve around issues of who holds the power to control the types and pieces of knowledge given in the schools; to determine the patterns of distribution of the knowledge among different students; to establish both the academic and cultural standards and expectations of the school; and to give differential rewards or to withhold those rewards based on perceived competence in those standards. Here are some of the aspects of schooling that are controlled by those in power, according to the critical perspective on cultural socialization: educational objectives, student evaluation, school finance, values, norms, norms of thinking, what counts as knowledge, gender roles, lifestyles, language patterns, communication styles, learning styles, and political principles (Provenzo, 2002). Delpit (1995) has proposed five aspects of power, called "the culture of power," that summarize the relationship of power to the domination over some cultures by the group that holds the power in the classroom. In each of these five aspects, all of the components of schooling discussed above end up being issues of power. Students must fit into the patterns of those who have the power to set the norms in schools and in society.

1. Issues of power are enacted in classrooms.

2. There are codes or rules for participating in power.

3. The rules of the culture of power are a reflection of the rules of the culture of those who have power.

4. If you are not already a participant in the culture of power, being told explicitly the rules of that culture makes acquiring power easier.

5. Those with power are frequently least aware of—or least willing to acknowledge—its existence. Those with less power are often most aware of its existence. (pp. 23–26)

What are the results of these cultural socialization practices, according to critical theorists? Once again, the concern is about power relations, about some groups of people using their "authority" as policy setters to keep their own group in control while keeping others out of any opportunity to join the group in power. McLaren (1997) describes this view when he writes that "the schools serve the interests of the wealthy and powerful, while simultaneously disconfirming the values and abilities of those students who are most disempowered in our society already: minorities, the poor, and the female" (p. 163).

Bowles (1975) describes the ways that these cultural socialization practices help continue differences by answering to the needs of the dominant class. He writes that schools have developed as a way "to meet the needs of capitalist employers for a disciplined and skilled labor force, and to provide a mechanism for social control in the interests of political stability" (p. 38). The long-term outcome, as Pai and Adler (2006) describe, is that "schooling is used to identify and help 'insiders' to stay in their status culture and discourage 'outsiders' from entering a more prestigious status group" (p. 136). Thus, the more prestigious and higher paying jobs will be available only to certain people. Sadovnik, Cookson, and Semel describe how schools enable such results.

> Schools, through such practices as tracking, academically stratify students by curricular placement, which, in turn, influences the long-term social, economic, and cultural destinies of children. In effect, schools play a major role in determining who will get ahead in society and who will not. (2001, p. 122)

The result: schools serve the role of reproducing the dominant culture.

Cultural Socialization Practices in the Schools

How are cultural socialization practices carried out in schools? Philosophers of education who study this question discuss socialization in terms of the arrangement of the classroom, the materials used, and the methods of teachers interacting with students.

Philip Jackson (1998), Robert Boostrom, and David Hansen, in their book *The Moral Life of Schools*, identify virtually every aspect of schools and the classrooms as being designed to lead students to believe and act in specific ways—in other words, to socialize students into the expectations of society. They have listed eight categories of school life that deal with socialization. Can you think of examples from your own schooling that apply to each or some of these eight categories?

1. *Moral Instruction as a Formal Part of the Curriculum.* This is most often seen in private schools but is sometimes used in regular public schools. In this category, the school has written moral lessons and courses as part of the school's curriculum, lessons such as values clarification that directly address moral values and the clarification of those values.

2. *Moral Instruction within the Regular Curriculum.* In this category, moral instruction is not written into school policy, but it is used regularly by teachers within their individual classrooms. Commonly addressed lessons in this category revolve around issues of morality in society: slavery, economic inequities, and so on. This may be direct instruction, or it may be seen through indirect means, such as when a teacher extols the virtues of public characters like Rev. Dr. Martin Luther King, Jr.

3. *Rituals and Ceremonies.* The list of rituals and ceremonies within schools can be quite lengthy. Here are some examples: pep rallies, the DARE (Drug Abuse Resistance Education) program, the U.S. Pledge of Allegiance. Ceremonies such as these socialize students to hold certain "approved" beliefs, such as patriotism to school and country.

4. *Visual Displays with Moral Content.* This category refers to posters, visual displays of rules, student work that reflects hard work and excellence, and slogans. In all the cases in this category, the slogans, images, and words displayed give students a recommended pattern for living and acting. In schools, we commonly see slogans on posters such as, "If at first you don't succeed, try, try again," or "Be kind to others," which encourage specific "socially acceptable" behaviors in students.

5. *Spontaneous Interjection of Moral Commentary into Ongoing Activity.* Examples from this category are seen when a teacher makes comments to students throughout the class day. For instance, a teacher may say to a student, "Thank you, John, for raising your hand," or "I like how Roberto and Susan are working together quietly." Like the examples in the previous categories, these words are designed to encourage specifically "approved" behaviors.

6. *Classroom Rules and Regulations.* Often displayed on posters on the walls of classrooms, these rules require specific behaviors that are designed to socialize students into orderly, adult life. Some examples of rules include "Do not run in the hallways," and "Raise your hand before speaking."

7. ***Morality of the Curricular Substructure.*** This category refers to the organization of the curriculum. For instance, how many days per week is Art offered, compared to how many days Math is taught? How many years of Music are required for graduation, and how many are required in English? What this tells students is that the schools place more emphasis on certain subjects than others. Students are taught, indirectly, what subjects "count" in life. Similarly, the term *elective* lets students know that those courses are less important than the "core" or "required" courses.

8. ***Expressive Morality within the Classroom.*** Earlier in this chapter, the expressiveness of different communication styles was discussed. This expressiveness may be seen as "expressive morality" when the teacher, for instance, frowns at a student who speaks without raising a hand first, or when the teacher raises an eyebrow at what he or she considers to be an "inappropriate" remark by a student.

Summary of the Social Foundations of Education

As the setting in which children will spend countless days and hours of their lives, schools have a key role in shaping children. In effect, schools are one of the key sources of the development of each next generation of society. As such, schools—the teachers, administrators, curriculum, physical structure—tend to socialize students into the dominant view of society that largely determines the structure of society. Both directly and indirectly, schools and teachers help instill within their students the values, beliefs, routines, and expectations of the dominant society in which they live. Schools not only teach subject areas, they also serve the role of reproducing and perpetuating the established social, cultural, political, and economic structures and norms of society.

There are two perspectives on this practice of cultural socialization within schools. The functionalist perspective proposes that schools serve this function of keeping society together, of ensuring a continued set of shared beliefs and traditions that will enable the country to function effectively. The critical perspective, on the other hand, proposes that there is an intentional effort on the part of the organization of schools to continue the social inequities that currently exist within society. Those who study the moral structure of the schools propose that through its practices the schools intentionally and unintentionally instill a specific set of moral beliefs within students. The result is that schools help reproduce the dominant society by socializing students into the values, beliefs, and perspectives of that dominant society. The differences in the perspectives are in the focus on why society would want schools to practice socialization, who controls the beliefs and values that are transmitted by the schools, and the goals of this socialization.

Summary

Our cultural background helps shape our identities. Our perspectives on life are shaped by our experiences within our particular society and communities. Our culture helps give us a way of seeing and perceiving the world. In studying culture, we see that there are multiple ways of communicating, organizing, and thinking. Patterns and styles within families, communities, and societies help shape each individual's communication, organizational, and intellectual styles. Cultures can be studied by looking at the way their members interact with their physical and social surroundings. Variations in cultural styles include a group or individual focus, analytic or intuitive types of thinking, and rigid or loose orientations toward time. Looking at culture historically and sociologically, these cultural characteristics have developed over long periods of time. Each cultural way of life has developed within a culturally influenced set of histories, traditions, and patterns that help shape the identities of people today. The result is a multitude of different ways of life experienced by different peoples.

The schools in U.S. society also have a large role in the cultural shaping of identities. Virtually all aspects of the schools—teachers, administrators, curriculum, physical structure—help shape students' identities. Specifically, the schools tend to socialize students into the dominant culture, both directly and indirectly, schools and teachers help instill within their students the values, beliefs, expectations, and perspectives of the dominant society in which they live. There are several perspectives on why cultural socialization is practiced within the schools and on who benefits from these practices. One way to look at it is that if students gain the knowledge, values, and beliefs of the dominant culture, then as they become adults, society will function more smoothly. Another way to view cultural socialization in the schools is to see it as a way to keep the dominant groups powerful and to ensure that those who have little position or power remain less powerful. A major role for schools, including the teachers who work in them, is to recognize the cultural socialization of students, to understand the effects on students' identities, and to determine the steps to take to provide an educational and social experience for students that does not harm students' socially constructed identities.

Reflective Writings

1. *Cultural Identity Development.* How does your background, as represented by your pie, affect your views about your community? For instance, how has your socially constructed identity shaped your perspectives on the size of your community? The population makeup? The opportunities available in your community? The services offered to families? Speculate on how your perspectives might be different from those of someone who has a different socially constructed identity.

2. *Defining the U.S. Macroculture.* A number of books and articles have attempted to lay out the characteristics of what is called the "macro-culture" of the United States. The macroculture is the set of cultural characteristics that virtually everyone who lives in the United States shares. Examine again Tables 1.1, 1.2, 1.3, and think about the char-acteristics of your K–12 schools and of the general U.S. culture over-all. Identify and list the characteristics that you believe define U.S. schools and society.

3. *Cultural Discontinuities.* This reflective writing has two parts. (A) Read the three case studies at the end of the chapter—"A Blackfeet Son," "Sarah Stein," and "Ililani and Luka"—and describe the cultural dis-continuities that these students felt between their home and their school cultures. (B) Think about your own background in K–12 schools. Did you feel any conflict between the expectations and pat-terns of your home and of your school? Write about any cultural dis-continuities that you felt between home and school. If you did not feel any conflict, reflect on how that may have affected your progress in school as well.

4. *Outward Manifestations of a Culture.* What might be some reasons why members of a culture would not want to be defined solely by the out-ward manifestations—artifacts, products—of their culture? On the other hand, why might some members of a culture see their artifacts as a way to strengthen their sense of culture?

5. *Meaning of Culture.* If your understanding of culture has changed since reading this chapter, what are your new understandings of the concept?

6. *Effects of Cultural Membership on Perspective.* How does being a mem-ber of the dominant group affect someone's perspective as compared to being a member of a minority group? Which parts of a person's per-spective would be most strongly impacted by a person's group mem-bership? Which parts of a person's perspective would lead to the most differential treatment within society?

7. *Two Perspectives on Cultural Socialization.* Compare and contrast the functionalist perspective and the critical perspective on cultural social-ization in the schools. Specifically, address the following questions:

   — From each perspective, why do the schools want to practice cul-tural socialization?

   — Who controls the beliefs and values that are transmitted in the schools?

   — What are the intended goals or outcomes of those practices, according to the two perspectives?

   — What are some examples from your own experiences as a K–12 student of when the schools practice cultural socialization?

8. *Hidden Curriculum.* Describe who benefits and how they benefit by the hidden curriculum remaining hidden.

9. *Addressing the Concerns of the Critical Perspective.* What are some practices that a teacher or an administrator could take to address the critical theorist's concern that schools continue the social inequities of society?

10. *Empowering and Disillusioning.* Which students in your schools are empowered to be leaders? Which students are discouraged from succeeding? Which practices in your schools contribute to this differentiation of students?

11. *Examples of Cultural Socialization in Schools.* In 15 minutes, write down as many examples as you can of how schools socialize students to fit into the dominant culture. Then indicate which examples could be seen, and why, by the critical perspective as practices that serve to continue social inequities.

12. *Moral Life in Schools.* Think of examples from each of the eight categories in The Moral Life of Schools either from your own K–12 schooling experiences or from a classroom in which you are currently working. When you have examples from each category, you will get a sense for the pattern of socialization that your school is encouraging.

13. *Determining Your School's Pattern of Cultural Socialization.* See if you can determine and lay out the pattern of cultural socialization found within the schools that you attended or that you work in now.

14. *Effects of Characterizations of Culture.* Several characterizations of different cultures were presented in this chapter. Some were based on race, some on cultural patterns, and some on geographic locations. Discuss the positives and negatives of studying and following characterizations such as these in the classroom. What are the benefits for students when teachers learn about these different characterizations and cultural perspectives? How are characterizations such as these harmful to the development of students of groups different from that of the teacher, the administrator, the school, and the community of those students?

15. *Is Equal Treatment of Students Possible?* Some teachers claim to treat all students equally in their classrooms. Others claim that it is not possible to treat students equally within a school system that has in place formal and informal measures to differentiate between students. Take the role of each of these teachers, and explain each of their views.

16. *Conduct a Community Study.* At the school where you are either teaching or student teaching, find out if there is a community liaison, or a parent, who will take you on a community study of the school's neighborhood. Note the activities and events in the community, the

social service agencies serving the community, the locally-owned businesses, the churches, the activities undertaken by families and their children, etc. A nice end-of-the semester idea is to present your community study to a gathering of families, either on the school grounds or in a neighborhood center.

Case Studies

A Blackfeet Son

A member of the Blackfeet tribe, a mother is raising her son on the reservation. This is her story. Long dark hair, brown eyes, and an olive complexion, her son is shy and quiet in the classroom. He is just a kindergartener, but he has already been labeled a "slow learner." He is constantly "staring out the window" and he does not seem to understand how to do math problems.

As he was growing up, he was closely bonded to his mother. He went everywhere with her. They were up at daybreak, saying their prayers, and gathering wood and food. He has been with his mother and grandmother as they gathered roots and healing herbs and prepared the traditional foods. He has watched his father, uncles, and ceremonial leaders prepare the colorful feathers and sing the different kinds of songs while getting ready for the sacred dances and rituals. He has danced with his mother for seven days straight in the hot sun, fasting and praying at the Sacred Sun Dance. He has watched and listened to the elders as they told stories and animal legends and sang songs. He has attended sacred ceremonies and is well acquainted with the cultures and languages of other tribes. He has been in more than 20 different sacred sweat lodge rituals used by tribes to purify mind, body, and soul.

He listened to his mother count out every bead and watched as she numerically sorted out the different colors for the belts and necklaces. He learned his basic numbers by helping his father count and sort the rocks for the sweat lodge. He was taught to learn mathematics by counting the sticks we use in our traditional native handgame. His aunts and grandmothers taught him to count and know his numbers while they sorted out the complex materials, beads, and abstract designs. He could probably tell you of 40 different kinds of birds, where they live, the seasons in which they appear, and the sacred ceremonies to which they belong.

His mother writes: "It takes a long time to absorb and reflect on these kinds of experiences, so maybe that is why you think my child is a slow learner."

Sarah Stein

Sarah Stein grew up in New York City, where she was close to her maternal grandmother, an Orthodox Jew. Although some members of Sarah's extended family consider themselves to be Reform Jews, her parents are Conservative. They observe the Jewish Sabbath and holidays, and Sarah has attended Hebrew schools twice a week throughout her school years. The family also follows many of the traditional dietary rules.

Sarah has moved to the Midwest, where her parents took new jobs at a large university in a city that has retained its small-town flavor. Sarah attends one of the two high schools in the community where she excels in all of her classes. Nevertheless, Sarah is experiencing pressures in school and at home.

A bright and eager student who is accustomed to a learning environment where students are continually encouraged to ask questions and discuss while new learning is going on, Sarah has begun to turn off many of her new teachers and classmates. She frequently interrupts lecturers with questions of clarification, violating school expectations that students should be quietly attentive until the teacher's presentation is over. She is often perceived as rude, obnoxious, and pushy.

For the first time, Sarah feels embarrassment over missing school during special holidays. She worries about missing important schoolwork during her absences, and this year she missed two days of the Iowa Tests because they were scheduled during Rosh Hashanah.

In her desire to make new friends, Sarah wants to participate in Friday evening activities, such as school parties and football games. However, this conflicts with her parents' demands that she share the Sabbath meal before going to the synagogue.

Other conflicts have caused her to drop out of the school band, although she still continues private clarinet lessons.

Sarah is becoming aware of being an exception to, if not in conflict with, the way of life in her new school and community. She feels set apart when she wants to feel accepted.

Story from Christine I. Bennett, *Comprehensive Multicultural Education: Theory and* Practice, 3rd ed. © 1995 by Allyn & Bacon. Reprinted by permission.

Ililani and Luka

Ililani and Luka are two children from Hawaii, now in 4th grade in a school in Portland, Oregon, where there are very few Hawaiian children and no Hawaiian teachers. In their Hawaiian culture children often tell stories collaboratively, feeding off of and building on each other's routines. While this may look like interrupting to those not familiar with this style, they see it as helping each other and working together. When they do this in school, their teacher tells them that they need to develop more independent skills and learn to tell stories on their own. They aren't interested in this as they think that the best stories are ones told together as a partnership.

During Meeting Time in their classroom Ililani and Luka often choose to tell stories together. Their teacher discourages this, telling them that Meeting Time is a time for individual sharing. She wants them to develop skills in telling a story straight through, on their own, from beginning to end. Both girls think this is silly. They imagine they could do that if they wanted to, but they see no need for it. They know their classmates love their collaboratively told stories. Whenever they are telling these the classroom is silent and everyone is paying attention to them.

The school is planning their spring performance for parents and the community. One section of it will be storytelling. Ililani and Luka want to enter together to tell a story in their informal and collaborative style. The teacher says that the forum only has a space for one child to tell at a time and that is the way the performance is designed. She says they may not enter their names unless they plan to tell separately.

Reprinted with permission from *Open Minds to Equality: A Sourcebook of Learning Activities to Affirm Diversity and Promote Equality, 3/E* by Nancy Schniedewind and Ellen Davidson, 2006. Published by Rethinking Schools. www.rethinkingshcools.org

Chapter 2

Stereotyping, Prejudice, and Racism

Identity Development Related to Stereotyping, Prejudice, and Racism

Many people react to discussions of stereotyping, prejudice, and racism by denying that they hold any stereotypes or have any prejudices. Some claim that they are not affected by racism; others believe that if such issues are not discussed, then stereotyping, prejudice, and racism will cease to exist. An example from one of my students displays these types of beliefs:

> I did not like talking about racism, prejudice, and stereotypes. When people talk about it and point it out, it only gets worse. I know it is there, even if people deny it, but pointing it out only makes it worse. When it is shown and talked about, people think about it and it happens more often.

Beliefs such as these deny the presence of stereotyping, prejudice, and racism within society and within ourselves and indicate a lack of understanding about the role prejudice and the other concepts play in our daily lives, beliefs, values, attitudes, and practices. The prejudice and racism that are embedded within society, that are in part constitutive of society, have framed the society in which we live. In coming to understand our own identity, we must recognize the indelible impact that stereotyping, prejudice, and racism have played in our identity development. The existence of prejudice within societies has had such a profound influence on us that Gadamer (1993) claims "that is why the prejudices of the individual . . . constitute the historical reality of his [or her] being" (pp. 266–267).

However, it is not easy, perhaps it is not even possible, to recognize that our identity is framed in part by such concepts as stereotyping, prejudice, and racism. For we are all raised in, and have as part of our personalities, communities and societies that are historically informed by prejudice. As part of the prejudice-informed situation itself, we are an integral and structural part of that situation and cannot understand objectively everything in that situation. As Kimball and Garrison (1996) describe, "In fact, while under the influence of a prejudice, it is impossible for us to fully recognize it as one" (p. 53). In discussing Gadamer's writings on the idea of the hermeneutical situation, Dunne (1992) writes, "What can never be available to us [Gadamer insists], is a technique which would make our prejudices transparent to us (p. 115).

If it is so difficult to recognize the prejudices that are constitutive of our identity, then how are we to understand prejudice and its role as part of our identity? To begin the process, we can adopt what is called a *hermeneutical consciousness*. When thinking within this perspective, we can recognize that prejudices exist without trying to deny them. Thus, the task is to bring those prejudices to the front of consciousness and then to recognize that they will necessarily affect all future understandings (Noel, 1996). Kimball and Garrison (1996) describe hermeneutical consciousness by writing that the point is "to examine our historically inherited and unreflectively held prejudice" (p. 53). Our efforts, in this view, need to be aimed at recognizing these personal and societal prejudices and coming to understand how they affect our views of and interactions with others.

Since we do not easily recognize our prejudices, the first step in developing a hermeneutical consciousness is for our prejudices or for the issues surrounding them to enter into our consciousness—to "disturb" our identities. We must be confronted with the nature of prejudice within our identities. The concept and surrounding issues of prejudice, using Gadamer's terms, must "address" us. They must enter into our horizon. Gadamer describes horizon as our range of vision, as a vantage point from which we see the world. In hermeneutical consciousness, that range of vision must include our prejudices. Once it does, our horizon will begin to be informed by an understanding of what prejudice is, how it is formed, and how we address or ignore prejudice within us.

Developing a hermeneutical consciousness of prejudice, then, means to recognize that context—society, its traditions, its prejudices—is not isolated from our identity. But rather, our identities have been forged with and fused with that of society, including the stereotypes, prejudices, and racism within that society.

Stereotyping

Stereotyping is the creation of mental categories in order to group people, items, or events. When a stereotype is formed, it is assumed that all peo-

Preliminary Activities

Individual Activity

Draw a scientist.

Individual Activity

Use three words or phrases to describe someone from New Jersey. Use three words or phrases to describe someone from Mississippi. From Los Angeles. From Idaho. From your city or state.

Small Group Discussion

Share your scientist drawing with others in your class. What characteristics do all of your scientists share? Gender? Race? Hairstyle? Clothing? Can you identify or pinpoint the direct source of these ideas? Do you know a scientist? Or have you seen depictions of scientists in textbooks or in movies?

Regarding your descriptions of the people from different locations—have you lived in one of the places listed? Or do the words or phrases that you used come from the media? Or has the media provided similar descriptions? How much experience have you had with each of these different people?

ple in that category share a single trait or a set of shared characteristics. For example, your drawing of a scientist most likely includes stereotypes and displays the assumption that all (or most) scientists share the same characteristics. Stereotyping is a cognitive, as opposed to an emotional or behavioral, component of our perceptions of other people.

Forming Stereotypes

Why Stereotypes Are Formed

Why do human beings engage in stereotyping? Why do we feel the need to put people, items, or events into preconstructed categories? The fields of social psychology and cognitive psychology direct much of their attention to the study of these questions. The basic answer to the question of why we stereotype is that we encounter so much information and so many experiences every day that we are not able to assimilate all of it. Put simply, we are overloaded by the world. In order to keep from being cognitively overwhelmed, our brain has developed the mechanism of stereotyping, of creating categories to sort large amounts of information. The categories are created to help simplify the multitude of information that we experience in our lives. Categories can then be used to relate phenomena to each other, to organize our perceptions, and to make sense of phenomena. If we place our own terms and labels onto phenomena, we then feel as though we have a better chance to interpret them with regard to our own experiences. Stereotypes, then, give us a way to organize and simplify the world, to conveniently group objects and people without taking the time to really get to know people.

How Stereotypes Are Formed

The next question, now that we have examined *why* we have an intellectual need to stereotype, is the question of *how* a stereotype gets formed. To answer this question, we need to study how the mind perceives the world. Basically, our minds tend to notice certain characteristics and to assume that all people in a particular group will share that characteristic. The attributes that we are most likely to notice are those that stand out to us. Jones (2002) calls this a "tendency to focus on distinctive stimuli" (p. 88).

This concept is also called *salience*. Think back to your drawing of a scientist. Each characteristic you included in your drawing would be called a salient feature of a scientist. These salient features might be gender, hairstyle, and clothing. In everyday life, these features, along with race, are salient; they draw our attention more frequently because they are easy to see.

Another term used to describe this concept of salience is *vividness*. When a characteristic is vivid, it is more likely to be salient—noticeable and important—to us. Nisbett and Ross (1980) describe three components of an event or characteristic that make it more vivid and salient. The first component lays out a hierarchy of "emotional interest." The highest level of emotional interest occurs for events that happen to us; the next level of emotional interest occurs for events that happen to those whom we care strongly about; and the least level of interest is when events happen to people whom we do not know personally. The second component is called *concreteness*. Concreteness is a term that entails a "degree of detail and specificity about actors, actions, and situational context" (p. 47). The more detail associated with an event or characteristic when it is presented to us, the more likely it is that that characteristic will be vivid, salient, and memorable. The third component that Nisbett and Ross describe entails "temporal, spatial, and sensory proximity of information" (p. 50). In other words, if something happens that is recent, close, and seen or felt through our senses, it will be memorable to us for a longer time.

Such salience and vividness are a natural part of human thinking, of what is called *heuristic* thinking. As defined by Aronson, Wilson, and Akert (2002), *heuristics* are "the mental shortcuts people use to make judgments quickly and efficiently" (p. 74). That is why we so often base our stereotypes on visible features: because it is easy. As Aaronson, Wilson, and Akert (2002) add, we make judgments based on "the ease with which you can bring something to mind" (p. 74). We tend to notice salient and vivid events more frequently, and we remember those events for a longer time. Fiske and Taylor (1991) use the term *cognitive miser* to describe this desire for ease and comfort in dealing with perceptions of other people. Individuals look for only enough characteristics to give a basic categorization, to avoid having to do the hard work of really getting to know another individual.

Many aspects of a situation are involved in the forming of stereotypes. Stereotypes are as much a result of the stereotyper's characteristics as they are the perceived characteristics of the people about whom the stereotypical assumptions are being formed. Look again at the words that different people used to describe the people from each of the locations listed in the opening exercise. How different are the descriptions of each person? In thinking about your descriptions in particular, how much are your own history, culture, interests, motives, and beliefs involved in the formation of your stereotypes? In addition, what were the settings during which your stereotypes were formed?

Social Foundations of Stereotyping

The discussion so far in this section on stereotyping has treated it as though it is unaffected by social, group, or power relations. However, stereotyping has a strong impact on social, cultural, and racial relationships. The problem of stereotyping is that, most often the stereotypes that are formed about people assume a set of stable and unchanging emotional or behavioral characteristics. Take a comparative look at both of the previous exercises in this chapter. It is likely that your descriptions of people from different locations will be substantively different from your drawing of a scientist. Did you move your descriptions into the arena of emotional or behavioral characteristics? Do these words or phrases describe a way of acting? A way of thinking (for example, a person who is from _____ acts this way or believes that way)?

Attributions of Dispositional and Nondispositional Characteristics

Several patterns of stereotyping have been indicated by researchers. One pattern developed from social identity theory (Tajfel and Turner, 1979). In this theory, individuals gain their sense of self-worth in part from the groups that they are part of or identity with. This group is called the in-group. In order to receive a positive self-esteem from one's group, the individual will attribute positive characteristics to that in-group and, correspondingly, will assign negative characteristics to out-groups.

This assigning of positive or negative characteristics has been the focus of attributional theory (Weiner, 1985). Two general types of attributions are dispositional and nondispositional characteristics. Defining a characteristic as dispositional indicates that it is consistently displayed, is stable over time, and is under the control of the individual. Examples can be found in the area of "effort" (see Figure 2.1). Effort is often seen as dispositional, because if we attribute to someone the characteristic of being "hard working," or having a "good work ethic," we consider that this characteristic will be evident in all actions of that person—across all tasks, across all times. Similarly, when we attribute to someone the characteristic of "lazy," we expect that laziness will be evident in all situations and at all times. Neither context nor background is considered in dispositional attributions. Nondispositional characteristics, however, are seen as being out of the individual's control. A nondispositional character-

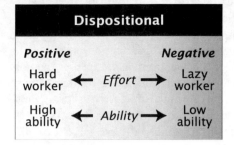
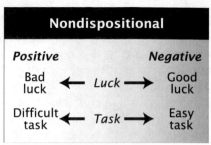

Figure 2.1   Attributions of Dispositional and Nondispositional Characteristics

istic or behavior is not the individual's "fault"; rather, it is viewed as the result of outside circumstances. Think about how people explain their poor performance on a test: "It was bad luck"; "The teacher asked the wrong questions on the test." These attribute poor performance to nondispositional factors.

In what Pettigrew (1979) calls the ultimate attribution error, people make attributions of characteristics of groups of people based on their tendency to present the in-group more positively than the out-group. Aaronson, Wilson, and Akert (2002) discuss this further, pointing out that we tend to assume that one person's behavior in an out-group applies to all people from that group. In other words, "if you know something about one out-group member, you are more likely to feel you know something about all of them" (p. 470). On the other hand, when an individual within what we have defined to be our in-group behaves in a particular way, we are more likely to attribute that only to that individual. This ultimate attribution error is displayed in Figure 2.2. The statements in each of the cells are reasons that are often given to explain how someone scores on a test. Notice the positive dispositional statements for the in-group, whereas the out-group is assumed to have negative dispositional characteristics. What reasons do you give for your own performance on a test? Do your reasons fall within one or more of these cells?

Overlapping Categories in Stereotyping

As you can see by the examples given throughout this section, stereotyping can occur on the basis of many different categories: race, gender, location, job, or position. But it is important to recognize that these are overlapping categories. Think again about the very first activity in this book—making your cultural background pie. You probably had a number of different pieces in that pie, and these pieces together represent overlapping categories. Each of us is not simply our race, our gender, or our socioeconomic status. But owing to salience factors, each of us may pay more attention to different categories. To reflect on this idea, write a two- or three-word description or ste-

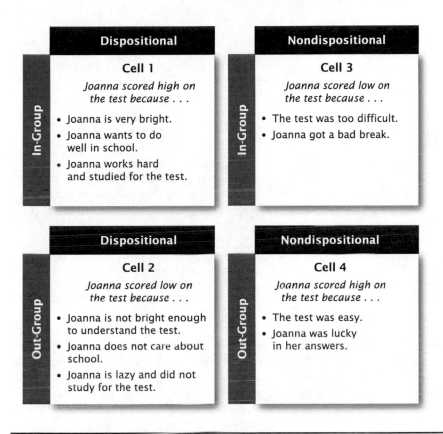

Figure 2.2   **Application of Attributions to In-Group and Out-Group Test Scores**

reotype of each of the categories in Table 2.1. After completing this exercise, would you say that you were surprised at any of the descriptions you chose? When additional categories were added to the description, were you surprised by the more fully developed description of the person? Would your stereotypes of this person have led you to imagine a different person than the one described? Which further description surprised you most: Race? Language? Any other category? How would your stereotypes change if this hypothetical person were, for instance, a man? A Caucasian? Which of the overlapping categories involved in this example are more salient for you? Were any of your stereotypes more positive if you shared a particular category, such as gender or race? Did you assume dispositional characteristics when certain categories were involved and not when others were involved? As this exercise indicates, sometimes the addition of multiple categories of social identity can lead to the creation or alteration of our set of stereotypes, and thus the way that we view groups of people and individuals.

Table 2.1 Overlapping Categories Within Stereotyping

Category	Stereotype	Person
Gender	_____	A woman
Gender and race	_____	A woman who is Hispanic
Gender, race, and language	_____	A woman who is Hispanic and who speaks both Spanish and English
Gender, race, language, and family status	_____	A woman who is Hispanic and who speaks both Spanish and English and who is a grandmother with two grand-children
Gender, race, language, family status, and SES	_____	A woman who is Hispanic and who speaks both Spanish and English and who is a grandmother with two grand-children and who works as an admissions officer in a hospital

Summary of Stereotyping

Stereotyping is a mechanism we use to create categories into which we can place large amounts of information. When we notice events or objects, we tend to notice the features that are vivid, or salient, and that can be used to put things into categories. Some commonly constructed categories include sizes, colors, functions, or sounds. In transferring these salient features to our mental representations of people, we form stereotypes based on skin color, hair color, body size, language patterns, and gender, to mention a few.

When studying the process of stereotyping people, some additional factors determine what our stereotypes will be. These are factors based on boundaries that separate people—some as "us" and others as "them," as part of our in-group and as part of the out-group. In basic terms, we decide who is like us and who is unlike us. Once these distinctions are drawn, we feel it is appropriate to use what is called attributional theory to develop further stereotypes of people. Through this process, we feel that we can attribute certain characteristics to be part of the personalities, or dispositions, of some people, while attributing the characteristics of other people to external circumstances, to nondispositional forces. Dispositional attributions allow us to make stereotypes about others' moral characters, by allowing us to assume that there is something permanent about those characteristics. This type of stereotyping is perhaps the most dangerous for relationships among people and societal structures since it provides justifications for treating people differently based on stereotypes.

Prejudice

Preliminary Activity

Individual Activity

Think about a group of people that you are prejudiced against. (Although many people do not like to think about the possibility that they might hold a prejudice, for this exercise and this section it is very important to be able to name a group of people that you hold negative opinions about.) How did your prejudice or your negative opinions form?

As was described in the previous section, stereotyping is the cognitive, or mental, component of our perceptions of other people. Prejudice is also a concept that describes our perceptions of other people, but prejudice is the attitudinal component of our perceptions. Whereas stereotyping deals with how we describe people, prejudice deals with how we feel about people. Whereas stereotyping is our way of trying to understand the world, prejudice is our way of judging the world in a positive or negative way. Definitionally, prejudice is a judgment about a certain person or object or event prior to understanding that person, object, or event. Grammatically, the word *prejudice* comes from the root prejudge. When we form a prejudice, we judge someone—we make a value judgment as positive or negative—before we meet or get to know that person.

Forming Prejudices

Think again about how your own prejudices may have formed. Can you identify specific reasons or events that played a part in the forming of your prejudices? Or is it a feeling that is indefinable, with no clear causes that you can identify? For the past 40 years, researchers have studied the possible reasons why people form prejudices. Some researchers have posited the idea that people's experiences can lead to prejudice formation. Others have pointed to the prejudice found within society as a general foundation from which people draw and form their prejudices. And still other researchers have proposed that people with certain personality types will be most likely to develop prejudices. Following are five theories of prejudice formation, synthesized from the research literature on prejudice. As you read these theories, reflect on whether any or all of them help explain why your prejudice was formed.

Racial and Cultural Difference Theory

People have an instinctive fear and dislike of individuals who are physically and culturally different from themselves. Going back again to social identity theory, we are reminded that people form in-groups from which they gain their self-esteem. Those who are not within that comfortable in-group then are disliked or feared. It may also be that we are uncertain about the beliefs and behaviors of people whom we do not know; thus there is discomfort when asked to talk about or interact with those people.

Does this theory help explain any of your prejudices? Do you feel this instinctive concern about a group of people different from you? This theory may help explain the prejudice formed by some individuals; however, it will not fully explain all prejudice. In studies of the social interactions of young children, for instance, it has been found that while children do see differences among people, they do not make judgments based on those differences. For example, a fairly common response of young White children who have never seen a person of color is to ask a parent: "Why is that man Black?" upon seeing an African American for the first time. These young children recognize color but do not understand the concept of race. They recognize male and female distinctions, but do not understand the concept of gender. Young children only begin to display signs of judging people when they have learned many of society's judgments of groups of people, when they hear the social and political meanings of race and gender.

Economic Competition Theory

Prejudice results from antagonism caused by competition among various groups for jobs and other economic rewards (housing, services, and so on). This theory sheds light on many historical and current examples of prejudice, at each of the national, local community, and individual levels. A 1994 instantiation of this theory at the state level is California's passage of Proposition 187, which states that individuals who are living illegally in the United States (who are not yet citizens or do not have work visas) can no longer receive social services, education, or health care. This means that approximately 400,000 school-aged children would not be allowed to go to school and would not be allowed to receive the free inoculations against disease that all other children are allowed to receive. It further means that their parents would get no assistance such as Medicare to help pay for such things as dental care and basic medical checkups. The economic competition-based prejudice that gave origins to this proposition is stated very clearly in the actual text of the bill. The text begins: "The People of California find and declare as follows: That they have suffered and are suffering economic hardship caused by the presence of illegal aliens in this state." It is clear in this legislation that those people who voted for Proposition 187 feel "antagonism caused by competition among various groups for jobs and other economic rewards (such as housing, services, etc.)," which is the definition of the economic-based theory of prejudice.

At a more local level, members of a community who have for generations shared a sense of similar values and traditions may develop prejudice against newer members of the community or against other members of the community who don't share the same values and designate them as an out-group.

This designation is based on real or perceived feelings that the out-group is threatening that sense of tradition and security—a threat to the in-group's economic stability.

As can be seen by these examples, it may be more likely that the prejudice resulting from economic competition will arise and develop especially in times of national, political, or personal turmoil. This prejudice can arise mainly as a response to the feeling of a loss of control, with a corresponding need to figure out why these hardships are occurring. Allport (1958), a leading scholar on the origins of prejudice, has described this phenomenon as scapegoating. Relating to the concept of dispositional factors in attributions of people's reasons for their behaviors, scapegoating would fall in the cell of a nondispositional characteristic of an in-group (Figure 2.2, cell 3). In other words: someone or something outside my control is causing my struggles and misfortunes.

Does this theory help explain any of your prejudices? Are your prejudices based to any extent on this sense of loss of economic stability? This theory does seem to explain a number of prejudices. But similar to the objection to the first theory described here, this theory will not be able to explain all examples or types of prejudice. In particular, economic competition theory fails to explain why an individual or a group continues to hold certain prejudices even when it no longer profits economically from doing so.

Traumatic Experience Theory

Prejudice emerges in an individual following a traumatic experience involving a member of another group. Does this theory help explain any of your prejudices? This theory may operate on two different levels. If you actually have had a direct traumatic experience with one or more members of a particular group, you may have developed a prejudice against the group based on that primary experience. Many of these primary experiences are related to violent acts. For instance, a woman who has been raped may develop a prejudice against men. This prejudice may be against all men or only against the particular race of the man who raped her, or his income level, body shape, nationality, or language spoken. At whatever level of prejudice, the prejudice is the result of an actual, physical experience. The theory may also operate on a second level. This level does not involve actual physical trauma of the individual. Rather, we may take on the prejudices of others, especially those close to us, who have themselves had a traumatic experience and then pass on their views to us. This secondary sense could be called experience with a traumatized individual. This secondary sense of prejudice can help explain why children will most likely take on the prejudices of their parents or community, rather than the prejudices of an unrelated group of people. Which of these levels of traumatic experience theory—the primary or secondary sense—is closest to a possible reason that you may have formed your prejudice?

Once again, the traumatic experience theory will not explain every instance of prejudice, for the theory does not help explain why only some people who have traumatic experiences will develop prejudice as a result, whereas others will never form that prejudice. An additional component needs to be examined to further understand the formation of prejudice: the conditions under which that prejudice was formed; the formation of prejudice occurs not in a vacuum but within a complex web of personal beliefs, desires, and perceptions of a situation.

Frustration–Aggression Theory

Prejudice results when individuals become frustrated because they are unable to satisfy real or perceived needs; this leads to aggression directed at other groups. This highly psychological theory, called a personality theory of prejudice, basically says that a certain type of personality is more prone to being prejudiced. This theory was promoted early by Adorno (1950) in what he called the authoritarian personality. In reviewing multiple studies, Adorno summarized what he believed to be the characteristics of the prejudiced person. The proposed characteristics are laid out in Table 2.2.

Allport (1958) echoes the idea that there can be a prejudiced personality. In his review of the research on prejudice, he lays out the characteristics of authoritarianism in combination with a need for concrete and definiteness in all situations. Because the prejudiced personality needs such definiteness, this type of person will see rules, actions, and behaviors in strict "right or wrong" determinations. This personality "grows overconcerned with sin in others" (Allport, 1958, p. 375) because he or she sees anyone who is different as breaking the rules. Allport continues: "When he sees any lapses from the conventional code in others he grows anxious. He wishes to punish the transgressor" (p. 375). The personality thus becomes prejudiced through this combination of needs for authoritarian and definite standards of right and wrong.

There are two key criticisms of this personality-based theory of prejudice. The first criticism is that the studies that created the base for this theory have, themselves, been criticized over time. Questions have been raised such as how the "prejudiced" people were selected for the studies, who judged them to be prejudiced, and how their characteristics were ascertained. Since the original studies have been questioned, the accuracy of their results must also raise some concerns. Questions have arisen that ask whether this identification of a supposed set type of personality is a form of stereotyping.

The second criticism is that this theory proposes a sort of free-floating feeling of prejudice, with the resulting aggression not really aimed at or focused on any specific target group. The idea behind this theory is that the prejudiced individual has such a feeling of frustration that he or she will lash out at any nearby or highly visible groups. But once again, this theory cannot on its own explain prejudice entirely, for there is still the question of why one group becomes a target rather than another group. If the frustration and aggression were to be truly randomly distributed, then all people would be equally violated. In reality, however, certain groups of people are more commonly targeted for violence than others. Each year, the FBI keeps track of

Table 2.2 Proposed Characteristics of the Authoritarian Personality

Characteristic	Description
Conventionalism	Rigid adherence to conventional middle-class values
Authoritarian submission	Submissive uncritical attitude toward idealized moral authorities of the in-group
Authoritarian aggression	Tendency to be on the lookout for, and to condemn, reject, and punish, people who violate conventional values
Anti-intraception	Opposition to the subjective, the imaginative, the tender-minded
Superstition and stereotypy	The belief in mystical determinants of the individual fate; the disposition to think in rigid categories
Power and "toughness"	Preoccupation with the dominance–submission, strong–weak, leader–follower dimension; identification with power figures; overemphasis on the conventionalized attributes of the ego; exaggerated assertion of strength and toughness
Destructiveness and cynicism	Generalized hostility, vilification of the human
Productivity	The disposition to believe that wild and dangerous things go on in the world; the outward projection of unconscious emotional impulses
Sex	Exaggerated concern with sexual "goings-on" [including homosexuality]

Source: Adapted from *The Authoritarian Personality* by T. V. Adorno, E. Frenkel-Brunswik, D. Levinson and N. Sanford. Copyright © 1950 by the American Jewish Committee.

reported hate crimes—crimes in which an offender targets a member of a specific group and makes that target status clear through verbal or written attacks on that person's group membership.

According to the FBI statistics for hate crimes reported by law enforcement agencies in 2005, certain individuals are clearly targeted more frequently, based on their group membership. The statistics show that among the single-bias hate crime incidents in 2005 there were 4,895 victims of racially motivated hate crime; 67.9 percent were victims of an anti-Black bias. The clear distinction based on race is evident when we see that 19.9 percent were victims of an anti-White bias. Hate crime incidents also involve sexual orientation; of the 1,213 victims targeted due to a sex-orientation bias, 61.3 percent were victims of anti-male homosexual bias. And finally, another highly targeted group for hate crimes is comprised of people who practice the Jewish religion; of the 1,405 victims of an anti-religion hate crime, 69.5 percent were victims of an anti-Jewish bias (http://www.fbi.gov/ucr/hc2005/victims.htm).

Social Control Theory

Because individuals are forced to conform to society's traditions and norms, they are taught and socialized to hold prejudices. This theory takes the emphasis off the personality of the individual and recognizes instead the crucial impact of society on the individual. The theory points out the critical interactions of person, family, community, and social institutions such as schools, government, and the media.

The City Kids Foundation, a multicultural youth group founded in 1985 by Laurie Meadoff, specifically addresses these issues of society and individual interaction. In their book *City Kids Speak on Prejudice* (1994, p. 4), they write about their experiences and views on the development and effects of prejudice. The following is a poem by 15–year-old Brigitte:

Meet Kim	*Kim is not black*	*Kim is not white*	*Kim does not see color*
Meet Kim	*Kim is not Christian*	*Kim is not Muslim*	*Kim knows no religion*
Meet Kim	*Kim is not rich*	*Kim is not poor*	*Kim does not understand the meaning of money*
Meet Kim	*Kim is not a Crip*	*Kim is not a Blood*	*Kim belongs to no gang*
Meet Kim	*Kim hates no one*	*All this will change when Kim grows up*	

Can you identify the societal factors that will likely affect Kim's beliefs about others as she grows up? The questions to reflect on here are similar to those asked in the previous section on stereotyping. Might she hear negative opinions about targeted groups from her friends? Could her parents hold the same prejudice while unintentionally passing it on to her? Will her prejudice also be the one that is negatively emphasized by the media? What would be your answers to all these questions regarding your own prejudices?

Social Foundations of Prejudice

Research has indicated that a positive and well-developed understanding of identity enables people to more readily accept those who are culturally different, while being less likely to develop and continue prejudices. Hoare (1991) lays out this view: "In the Western world, a well-grounded, mature psychosocial identity is necessary for the acceptance of persons who are culturally different and who may have different cultural realities" (p. 45). A number of researchers writing in the psychological vein have described both the importance of identity development and the stages that individuals go through in developing a clear understanding of their identities, how those identities developed, the relationship of self to society, and the recognition that identities are not static but rather are constantly open to change and are in flux. Erikson (1959, 1963) is perhaps the most famous scholar of identity development. He describes the active examination of identity as coming approximately during the time of adolescence and early adulthood. For our purposes in this text, it is most helpful to understand the process of coming to understand identity at any point in adult life. In what he calls the identity versus role confusion stage, Erikson posits that individuals begin asking "Who am I?" and "What do I believe?" Marcia (1980) has expanded this stage to include identity diffusion, when people make no attempt to establish or understand their identity. An additional stage from Marcia is identity foreclosure, when people believe they have a strong sense of who they are but in reality have not thought much about it. And finally, Erikson describes the identity achievement stage, when people have clearly thought about their identity and are secure in who they are. This identity achievement stage is similar to Banks's (1994) stage of ethnic identity development that he calls ethnic identity clarification. In Banks's words, this is the stage in which "the individual is able to clarify personal attitudes and ethnic identity. . . . The individual learns self-acceptance, thus developing the characteristics needed to accept and respond more positively to outside ethnic groups" (p. 225).

An important twist in linking discussions of prejudice with the ideas of identity development is the idea that we do not "achieve" an identity and remain there permanently. Rather, identity is contingent on a number of factors within society. So although we may feel confident about our sense of self, certain experiences, contacts, images, overheard words, or discussions with people we consider "others" can cause our confidence to be shaken. On the other hand, if an individual has a low or negative sense of identity based on ethnicity, the same factors within society can cause a movement toward a more positive sense of self, toward a more clarified identity. Luckily, as Gadamer (1993) writes, "The self-awareness of the individual is only a flickering in the closed circuits of historical life" (p. 276). In a Vygotskian sense, we are constantly undergoing alterations and new understandings of ourselves due to the sociohistorical society in which we live. In Vygotsky's (1962) view and as presented in this text, most of the things around us—items, events, people—help shape who we are, what we believe. Thus, in looking at the concept of prejudice through the lens of social foundations, the active reflection on personally, ethnically, and sociohistorically developing identity is very important to understanding the concept. The moratorium stage described by Marcia (1980) explains this stage of active reflection: "Moratorium describes the status of an individual currently undergoing an identity crisis, actively exploring and questioning the options and choices that confront her" (p. 88). This active and movement-oriented sense of identity is crucial to any discussions of how prejudice affects us and society.

Summary of Prejudice

Some of the five theories about how prejudice may form within us focus on the psychological variables involved in prejudice formation, while others focus on the role that society plays in this process, and still others draw out the ways that individuals react to events within society. The five theories presented here explain possible reasons for the development of prejudice: racial and cultural difference, economic competition, traumatic experience, frustration-aggression, and social control. As discussed here, none of these theories is adequate on its own to fully explain prejudice. Some problems with each of the theories are also described, making clear that prejudice formation is not a simple matter. It is more likely that there is going to be a complex interaction between the society, the person who is the target of a prejudice, and the person who holds the prejudice.

In keeping with this book's goal of identity development, prejudice is discussed in this chapter in terms of its effects on identity. Research by Erikson, later expanded by Marcia, has identified a sequence of stages that individuals will go through as they come to understand their identity. In their terms, individuals pass through a sequence of not thinking about who they are, to questioning themselves in order to gain a sense of self, to feeling comfortable with their identities. Important to the study of prejudice, though, is that individuals be constantly open to changes in their world that may affect their identities so that the reflection on, and social construction of, identity continues throughout one's lifetime.

Racism

Preliminary Activities

Individual Activity

Read each of the statements in the checklist below. Put a check before each event that you think is an example of racism (as applied to race, gender, religion, nationality, social class, or sexual orientation).

Checklist of Possibly Racist Events

1. ____ A man said, "A Black family moved into our neighborhood this week."
2. ____ A female police officer in Philadelphia was suspended from duty in 2003 for wearing a hijab to work. (A hijab is headscarf worn by some Muslim women that sometimes includes a veil that covers the face except for the eyes.)
3. ____ The United States Declaration of Independence includes the following statement: "He [the King] has excited domestic insurrections amongst us, and has endeavored to bring on the inhabitants of our frontiers, the merciless Indian Savages, whose known rule of warfare, is an undistinguished destruction of all ages, sexes and conditions."
4. ____ As of 2007, 70% of hazardous waste facilities in the United States are located in communities with "disproportionately high" percentages of people of color.

5. ____ An English professor at a university in a small town wrote in an editorial stating that "Black students are safer in [this town] than they would be among people of their own color in [large cities]."

6. ____ According to a national survey in 2004, approximately 8% of the population of the United States reported that they did not know if the Holocaust actually happened.

7. ____ George Wallace, former governor of Alabama, reacted to a new law requiring desegregation by proclaiming, "Segregation today, segregation tomorrow, segregation forever."

8. ____ A famous African American entertainer stated that Black parents have begun to raise their children "like pimps."

9. ____ A male student stated that women should be studied in history classes because they supported the men who made the history.

10. ____ The Confederate battle flag, a sign of Confederate strength for the South during the Civil War, flies atop the state capitol of South Carolina.

11. ____ On 9/13/2001, a man was arrested in West Sacramento for blocking the entrance to a Sikh temple and draining a pool of sacred water.

12. ____ At one point, California proposed a bill that barred employees from speaking any language other than English during their breaks.

13. ____ A prosecutor was allowed to remove a juror because she was "overweight and poorly groomed, indicating that she might not have been in the mainstream of people's thinking."

14. ____ A White male elected representative, guest speaking in a university course, turned to a Crow Native American student in the class and asked, "Aren't your people better off since we came to this country?"

15. ____ During the early 1900s, Chinese women and children were barred from entering the United States with their husbands.

16. ____ In doing an Internet search for articles for a famous African American author, an advertisement popped up touting a company that helps Black singles meet.

17. ____ The chairman of the Joint Chiefs of Staff, America's highest-ranking military officer, proclaimed that homosexuality is "immoral."

18. ____ A 1996 presidential candidate, speaking to a reporter, argued that "the U.S. annex English-speaking Canadian provinces as a way to counter the flood tide of blacks and browns" (*Newsweek*, March 4, 1996).

19. ____ The president of the United States stated that America should allow immigrants to come into the country as temporary guest workers, because they "do the jobs Americans won't do."

20. ____ The city manager of a town in Florida was fired after he revealed that he was going to have a surgery to be able to live as a transgender person.

21. ____ A security guard for a Los Angeles store routinely follows around Latinos as they shop in the store.

22. ____ A sign in a motel window in the 1980s stated, "No dogs or Indians allowed."
23. ____ After an African American community in the Bronx was featured in a book about "the poor," a church in a small town in Montana moved a family from that community to its town.
24. ____ As of 2007, women were paid $0.77 for every $1.00 that men were paid for their jobs.
25. ____ A group of people in Idaho have declared the five U.S. northwestern states Washington, Oregon, Idaho, Montana, Wyoming—as the "White Homeland."
26. ____ In 1997, a federal court ruled that a New York state university employee acted properly when he gave the police a list of all Black male students at the university. The police asked for the list after a 77–year-old woman claimed that she had been attacked by a Black man. They questioned 80 of the 125 Black men on the list.
27. ____ A Florida school district passed a new requirement that its schools teach students that "American culture is superior to any other."

Small Group Discussion

Share your checklist with others in a small group. Which statements does your group agree exemplify racism? Which statements does your group agree are not racist? Which statements led to the most discussion of disagreement within your group?

What was it about some of the statements in the checklist that made you feel that the statement was racist? Was it related to the belief implied in the statement? Was it related to whether an unfair action was taken against a particular person or group? Was it your feeling that it was either a stereotype or a prejudice taken to an extreme? How can it be possible that people disagree about what constitutes racism?

One possible reason why there is so much controversy and disagreement over the concept of racism is that the concept of race involves more than just skin color. There are actually at least two main components of the concept of race. The most common approach has been to classify people based on their biological skin color. However, scientists have shown that there is actually more biological difference among members of the same race than there would be across the different races. Think of what makes up the physical appearance of an individual: hair color, hair texture, facial features, height, length of limbs, bone structure, size, and so on. Asians (Japanese, Korean, Chinese, and others), for instance, have physical characteristics that are different from those of Caucasians. And within those nationalities and ethnicities are multiple variations of biological characteristics. And more and more commonly, people have multiple races in their biological background. Thus, although we use the race of the individual as a defining characteristic of that person, race itself is only a minor characteristic related to the rest of one's physical, cultural, and emotional characteristics.

When we move into the issue of racism, we move into the second component of the concept of race: the social and emotional implications of skin color. With a history of differential treatment of people based on their skin color, the concept of race has also become a socially constructed definition rather than strictly a biological one. This has been called a race-consciousness that encourages a society to define people based on race, which is not really a clear-cut biological distinction. An example of how history, science, and society have moved the definition of race into the realm beyond skin color comes from Linnacus, a nineteenth-century biologist who provided what was supposedly a scientific definition of the different races. As can be seen in Linnaeus's characterizations, people have included in these depictions not only physical characteristics but also emotions and mannerisms, clothing style, and societal ways of thinking:

1. American (Native American): Copper-coloured, choleric, erect. Hair black, straight, thick; nostrils wide, face harsh; beard scanty; obstinate, content, free. Paints himself with fine red lines. Regulated by customs.

2. European (White, Caucasian, European): Fair, sanguine, brawny. Hair yellow, brown, flowing; eyes blue, gentle, acute; inventive. Covered with close vestments. Governed by law.

3. Asiatic (Asian): Sooty, melancholy, rigid. Hair black, eyes dark; severe, haughty, covetous. Covered with loose garments. Governed by opinion.

4. African (African, Black): Black, phlegmatic, relaxed. Hair black, frizzled; skin silky; nose flat, lips tumid; crafty; indolent, negligent. Anoints himself with grease. Governed by caprice (from Bennett, 1998, p. 80).

Clearly, these characterizations of people go far beyond skin color. This is called the *social construction* of race. Can you guess which race Linnaeus is a part of? Which race does he give the most positive characterization of? It is clear how this social component of race can turn into stereotyping, prejudice, and racism.

Forming Racism

Racism is the belief that one's race is superior to another's and, conversely, that another's race is inferior. Racism includes beliefs in the behavioral, moral, and intellectual superiority of one's particular race. A connected development is the hatred of other races. How does an individual develop his or her beliefs in a way that involves such feelings of superiority? The factors that contribute to the development of racism are similar to those seen in the development of stereotyping or prejudice. In addition, however, the connection to hatred of other races makes the causes of racism similar to the causes of what makes people open to joining hate groups. Kronenwetter (1992) in his *United They Hate*, describes the individual and social conditions that contribute to the development of racism and the joining of hate groups. Kronen-wetter lists six such characteristics. While reading this list, compare it to the previous discussions in this chapter on the development of stereotyping and prejudice. Are there differences between the development of each of the concepts or belief systems? Are they similar in their development?

1. *Social upheaval.* Racism and membership in hate groups seems to grow in times of social and economic turmoil.

2. *Idealism.* Many people who are on their way to becoming involved in racism find a strong appeal in the ideals espoused by racists. For some, Kronenwetter writes, racial beliefs can even take the place of religious beliefs.

3. *The need to belong.* Individuals on the verge of racism or of joining hate groups most often feel the need to be accepted, to feel as though they are surrounded by others who share their beliefs.

4. *Ambition.*

5. *The "power" thing.* Some individuals see in racism the chance to become important. They espouse beliefs of a superior race as a way to give themselves a greater sense of control and power over society.

6. *Self-hatred.* People who are drawn to racism are often those who have low self-esteem and insecurities.

Social Foundations of Racism

Institutional Racism

Racism does not develop only within individuals; it cannot exist in a vacuum. The way that society has developed over time has both allowed and solidified racism in its policies. Racism exists not only within individuals but also within the society at large. From actual laws that did not allow Blacks to attend some public schools, to unwritten customs that do not allow Jews on certain public golf courses, to science textbooks that mention fewer than five women out of the whole history of science, to banks that will not loan money to people who live within prescribed "red-line" districts because of a belief that the people within those districts will not pay back their loans, racism (as applied to race, gender, religion, or sexual orientation) exists and thrives within the institutions within society. In what is called institutional racism, there is an existence of "a pattern of racism embodied in the policies and practices of social institutions—the educational system, the legal system, the economic system, family, state, and religion—that has a negative impact upon certain groups" (Jones, 2002, p. 32).

The key component that allows institutional racism is the settlement of power within one particular race. In fact, racism remains at the individual level until a level of power is introduced. Institutional racism can be defined by the formula:

Individual racism + Power = Institutional racism.

Jones (2002) explains that institutional racism "may be intentional or unintentional, overt or covert, but it functions to dominate, exploit, and systematically control members of the oppressed group" (p. 32). Institutional racism is the greatest cause of concern for society since it penetrates virtually all aspects of life. Think about how often you are exposed to a world that is controlled by Whites: television, newspapers, politicians, textbooks, and so on. Table 2.3 gives examples of how our daily lives are influenced by institutional racism.

Table 2.3   Influences of Race, Gender, and Socioeconomic Levels on Daily Life

Event	Who Influences Event
Read morning newspaper	Newspaper owner is a White male Reporters are White males and females
Get breakfast at fast-food restaurant	Owner of restaurant chain is White male Workers are of many races, both male and female, and are making minimum wage
Go to class	President of college is a White male Professors are generally White males and females; 5% are not White Textbook companies owned by White males 80–90% of material in texts is about Whites Cafeteria workers are of many races, both male and female, and are making minimum wage
Watch news on television	News anchor is a White male 80% of stories about non-White individuals or groups are negative

Yamato (1992) discusses racism further by describing four types of racism that she, as a Black woman, has noticed in society today. These four types of racism can be seen in the interactions of individuals with each other and individuals with society.

1. *Aware/blatant racism.* This is when someone who is acting in a racist manner fully knows that it is a racist action and even says that the action is based on hatred of a certain race. A number of states now have harsher penalties for criminals who engage in crime against a person while calling out racist slogans.

2. *Aware/covert racism.* This is more difficult to recognize because the actions are not so obviously based on race. However, since the person

engaging in racist acts is aware that the actions are based on race, he or she keeps the reasons hidden or covert. Examples of this are when a taxi driver picks up a White passenger but refuses to pick up that White person's Black friend. It is also seen when an apartment that was for rent is suddenly not available when the applicant is a person of color.

3. *Unaware/unintentional racism.* People engaging in this type of racism are unaware that they are doing so. Many Whites are unaware of their racism, and when they are told that their actions are offensive they claim that they did not know it. Examples include telling a Native American that he is "such a good person for an Indian," or asking a Black man "does he know someone in jail" (both are examples from courses at Montana State University).

4. *Unaware/self-righteous racism.* Yamato describes this type of racism as when a person from one race is indignant if someone from another race is not actively involved in fighting racism, or if that other person does not speak an original language, or does not engage in traditional customs and rites.

Semiotics

An important part of society that portrays and continues institutional racism is society's symbols, slogans, and signs. Signs and symbols are strong identifiers for individuals and members of a society. They may serve as group strengtheners or binders, they may indicate to us what a group or an idea stands for or signifies; they may trigger emotional responses within us; and they may socialize us into unknowing racism. Sports team logos are examples of symbols that trigger loyalty in some fans. Flags trigger patriotism in some citizens. But both of these examples can also socialize us into racism. The Washington Redskins, the Atlanta Braves—these names let people feel that the mainstream society has ignored and can continue to ignore the beliefs of Native American culture and can use their beliefs without understanding them to incur further gains within a capitalistic system. The NCAA (National Collegiate Athletic Association) made an effort to reduce the co-opting of Native American symbols for the uses of college athletic teams; in 2006 it banned any college that has as its mascot a Native American symbol from participating in post-season events such as tournaments or playoffs. Another symbol, the U.S. flag, intended as a symbol of unity among the American people, is seen by many historically mistreated people of color as a symbol of a society that legally and immorally mistreats them. Even music can be viewed as a symbol: country music is a binding force for many who relate to the songs' words that speak of a world that is rapidly changing and leaving the common person behind. Jazz and blues music, originating in the United States among African American musicians, is seen by many as a proud recognition of African American strength in the United States.

A series of events in Jena, Louisiana, in 2006–2007 pointed out painfully the effects of semiotics, of interpretation of symbols, on our lives. A series of events in the Fall of 2006 involved Black and White students in the town of Jena. Two of these events were episodes of White violence and threats of violence toward Black students, with police taking no action against the White students. After several months, an additional series of events occurred that directly involve semiotics. The main incident revolved around a tree and three nooses, which, in their own ways, served as symbols of oppression, marginalization, fear, and death. There was apparently a tree on the Jena High School grounds that students had reserved for Whites to sit under. It was known as the "White tree." After asking and receiving permission from the vice principal to sit under that exact tree, a Black student sat under it. Later, three nooses were hung from the tree. The next event in the series was the beating of a White student who received a concussion and bruises. Six Black students were charged with attempted murder for this event, and one of the Black students was sentenced as an adult and received a sentence of up to 22 years in prison. The perceived inequities in the charges in this case led to a march of approximately 10,000 people from across the United States in the town of Jena. Of interest in this section on semiotics is the interpretation of the nooses. In the many post-event interviews with multiple news organizations, a number of White residents of the town expressed that the nooses were a "prank," and that no racial implications should be drawn. However, a number Black residents interviewed expressed that the nooses hanging from a tree could only mean implied or outright threats of violence, given the history of lynchings of Blacks by Whites in the deep South of the United States in the late 1880s and early 1900s. Since the case became public, there have been at least 10 additional cases of nooses being hung on the buildings and doors of African Americans throughout the country, indicating to many that the nooses are indeed a symbol of racial threats.

Floyd Cochran, a former recruiter for the White supremacy group Aryan Nation who now tries to help educators understand hate and racism, writes about how such symbols are used to recruit young people into racial groups. He writes:

> Many tactics come into play in racist recruiting. . . . Flags, symbols, and uniforms are strong social binders. This is reflected in the regalia of armies, sports teams, and even fast-food restaurants. Symbols identify a person as one who belongs, who has a place in a group. Symbolism can have a powerful effect on a person's identity and can be used to motivate the individual to relinquish personal identity into the power of a group. (1992, pp. 10–11)

The study of such symbols, signs, and slogans is the purpose of the field of semiotics. Studies within semiotics have shown that even the interpretation of symbols and signs may differ based on race. In an interesting study by Golombek (1993), Black and White children were interviewed about their interpretations of several pictures. In one example, for instance, there is a clear difference between how the children of different races interpreted the picture of a police officer looking at a Black man and girl on a bus. The results showed that "Black children were almost three times as likely to describe the policeman in negative terms as white children" (p. 99). Some of the descriptions of this scene by Black children depict their impressions of policemen as unfair and unjust: "He's telling a Black man to go sit in the back or get off the bus." "It looks like with Martin Luther King when they told the lady to go to a back seat and give it to someone else." The White children, on the other hand, saw the policeman as engaging in helpful actions. Some examples of these interpretations include: "He is searching for criminals." "He is watching so there's no trouble." "He is checking that everybody paid. The man stole." In these descriptions from White children, we can see that they have an implicit belief that the Black persons on the bus are doing something wrong and that the policeman is there to keep them in line. What would be your interpretation of a picture like this? Would it be similar to any of these here? Or would you derive a different meaning?

Sandra Cisneros (1989) describes how these interpretations of people as symbols of power, or of support, affect relations within and across neighborhoods.

> Those who don't know any better come into our neighborhood scared. They think we're dangerous. They think we will attack them with shiny knives. They are stupid people who are lost and got here by mistake.
>
> But we aren't afraid. We know the guy with the crooked eye is Davey, the Baby's brother, and the tall one next to him in the straw brim, that's Rosa's Eddie V., and the big one that looks like a dumb grown man, he's Fat Boy, though he's not fat anymore nor a boy.
>
> All brown all around, we are safe. But watch us drive into a neighborhood of another color and our knees go shakity-shake and our car windows get rolled up tight and our eyes look straight. Yeah. That is how it goes and goes. (p. 28)

Summary of Racism

Racism, along with its accompanied forms such as sexism, classism, or regionalism, carries with it the belief that one race is superior to others. Racism has been carried out throughout society both by individuals and by institutions of the society at large. For individuals who proclaim or display racism, racism often is triggered by certain needs of the individual, such as need for approval or need for power. Their needs and beliefs, in addition, can be fueled by certain conditions in society, such as economic turmoil.

When racist ideas are translated into powerful policies that can affect the lives of others, racism has become institutionalized. Through countless formal and informal regulations, certain races have been denied or kept away from being able to take part in some of the most basic parts of everyday life. Some would argue that since we live in a society that is race conscious, and we have a history of practicing policies designed to keep many races away from basic tenets of life, that even if it is not intentional, we are each tacitly supporting institutional racism by not working to overturn the practices and the beliefs that lead to it. Semiotics, or the study of signs and symbols, shows us several ways that institutional racism is enabled within society. Through such emblems as logos, songs, or mottos, our society perpetuates models of racism, without encouraging us to examine what those words and symbols mean to different people. Racism, then, especially when institutionalized, becomes firmly entrenched and continues to affect the lives of all by remaining unexamined.

Effects of Stereotyping, Prejudice, and Racism

Effects on Personal and Ethnic Identity

When an individual is commonly and consistently told, either in direct words or through subtle images and ideas, that his or her ethnic group is less worthy, the person's reaction can be seen as an effort to protect his or her identity. The reaction can fall into two categories: rejection of one's ethnic identity group, or a total and unreflective embracing of one's ethnic group. In either case, the result is a lack of discourse with and understanding of others.

Minority Groups and Marginalization

The types of reactions mentioned above have been described as ego defense mechanisms by Smith (1991, p. 185) and as ego self-defense by All-port (1958, p. 141). As Phinney (1990) describes, "If the dominant group in a society holds the traits or characteristics of an ethnic group in low esteem, then ethnic group members are potentially faced with a negative social identity" (p. 501). Banks (1994) describes one of the possible results for the individual in his first stage of ethnic identity development. (Banks's theory, along with the identity development theories of several other researchers, is presented in more detail in chapter 5.)

> *Stage 1: Ethnic Psychological Captivity.* During this stage the individual absorbs the negative ideologies and beliefs about his or her ethnic group that are institutionalized within the society. Consequently, he or she exemplifies ethnic self-rejection and low self-esteem. The individual may respond in a number of ways, including avoiding situations that bring contact with other ethnic groups or striving aggressively to become highly culturally assimilated. . . . The more that an ethnic group is stigmatized and rejected by the mainstream society, the more likely are its members to experience some form of ethnic psychological captivity. (p. 224)

A number of possible behaviors may result from the prejudice felt by individuals who are in this stage of internalization of prejudices. Individuals may deny their membership in their own ethnic group, trying instead to "act White," for instance. Ogbu (2004) calls this desire to distance oneself from one's racial group the development of an oppositional identity. As he writes, some Blacks in today's society

> choose to abandon Black cultural and dialect frames of reference to behave and talk primarily according to White frames of reference. . . . they believe that their choice is more likely to help them succeed in education, upward social mobility in the wider society and acceptance by White people. Some other Blacks think that the assimilating Blacks not only reject Black dialect but also appear to have a kind of linguistic self-hatred. (p. 21)

These individuals may attempt to rid themselves of all vestiges of their own ethnicity or race: clothing styles, hairstyles, places of living, language and dialect, friends, and even choice of family partners. Because of conflict between outward recognition of who one is and one's internal feeling of who one is, the individual may withdraw from most social situations and feel passive in discussions of race and prejudice.

Allport (1958) describes what the overall feeling can be for individuals who have been affected by prejudice in this way: "Storm and stress result, tension and strain, and occasional irrational outbreaks. . . . Many minority group members are never permitted to belong fully, to participate normally, or to feel at home . . . they belong neither here nor there. They are marginal beings" (p. 155). The words of one person who is a self-identified members of such a marginalized group illustrates the effects of both marginalization and internalized negative identities. The words come from Mark Miller, a homosexual male who speaks about the effects of marginalization on the developing young adult:

> Because of a very realistic fear of prejudice and rejection, homosexual teens are often denied a support group. They are desperate for role models. They often can't receive support at home. Because of this they perceive themselves as inferior because they have internalized homophobia from our society. Believe me you needn't criticize a teenager for being gay. I guarantee you they crucify themselves everyday. Praying and wishing with all their will to be something they're not. Then comes the self-hatred.

Understandably, many people tire of hearing and incorporating the negative ideology that they hear about themselves. In desiring to overcome the years of marginalization that they have felt, they instead attempt to make their identity stronger, undertaking actions such as strengthening in-group ties, reversing the feeling of prejudice and turning it toward other out-groups, and engaging in aggression or rebellion. Banks (1994) describes this second stage in his theory of ethnic development:

> *Stage 2: Ethnic Encapsulation:* Individuals who have experienced ethnic psychological captivity and who have newly discovered their ethnic consciousness tend to have highly ambivalent feelings toward their own eth-

nic group and try to confirm, for themselves, that they are proud of their ethnic heritage and culture. Consequently, strong and verbal rejection of outgroups usually takes place. Outgroups are regarded as enemies and racists and, in extreme manifestations of this stage, are viewed as planning genocidal efforts to destroy their ethnic group. The individual's sense of ethnic peoplehood is escalated and highly exaggerated. (p. 225)

Smith (1991) continues the discussion of these reactions to continued prejudice: "The individual may redraw his or her boundary line even more narrowly, so that members of the outer boundary ethnic group are excluded more thoroughly than ever" (p. 185).

Caucasians: The Dominant Group

Caucasians, however, who are part of the politically, economically, and culturally dominant group within society, go through a somewhat different set of stages in their development and awareness of their ethnic identity. Students who are White and who have never felt any direct encouragement to think about another race are in what Helms (1990) describes as the "contact" level of awareness. They do not think of themselves as "White," but simply as "normal" (Tatum, 1992). Tatum (1992) describes individuals at this stage of life as living within the contact stage. At this point, individuals are unaware of their own racial identity. They will typically not recognize or acknowledge "White privilege." They may have a naive curiosity or fear of people of color, often based on stereotypes. Often they will perceive themselves as completely free of prejudice, unaware of their own assumptions about other racial groups. Individuals at this stage will often see their views as normal in society, perhaps as proper.

A common follow-up to this stage is what Tatum (1992, 2003) calls the disintegration stage. In this stage, awareness of racism and White privilege increases as Caucasians begin to see how much their lives and the lives of people of color have been affected by racism in our society. Some responses from people in this stage of identity and prejudice awareness are to feel guilty about the historical and current racial injustices in society. They may try to persuade others to quit telling racist jokes, for instance. But their understanding is still new and confusing because they are still attempting to understand their role in prejudice. Therefore, they may exhibit the similar outward patterns of behavior as those described earlier who have internalized negative prejudices, by withdrawing from discussions of prejudice and by remaining passive during those discussions.

However, a third stage may follow, resulting from not wanting to think about issues of prejudice. Tatum calls this the reintegration stage, in which the individual may feel pressured by others to "not notice" racism. The common response is to blame the victim. Whites may turn to explanations for racism that put the burden of change on those who are the targets of racism. The individual will usually choose to avoid the issue of racism, if possible, rather than struggle to define a nonracist identity. Levinson (1997) describes this stage in additional terms as the "attempt to escape the 'fatefulness' of social positioning by attempting to ignore it, downplay it, erase it or refuse it." The result is a lack of awareness of how one's own actions and prejudices can affect others.

McIntosh (1996) provides some examples from her reflections on her own life as a White heterosexual woman of how institutional racism benefits someone of her identity while it denigrates others. She lists 56 advantages that a White heterosexual has merely by being White and a heterosexual. These include:

- I can be reasonably sure that if I talk to "the person in charge," I will be facing a person of my race.

- I can turn on the television or open to the front page of the paper and see people of my race widely and positively represented.

- I can remain oblivious to the language and customs of persons of color who constitute the world's majority without feeling in my culture any penalty for such oblivion.

- Our children are given texts and classes that implicitly support our kind of family unit and do not turn them against my choice of domestic partnership.

McIntosh (2000) then offers a description of how institutional racism affects both Whites and minority groups.

> I see a pattern running through the matrix of white privilege, a pattern of assumptions which were passed on to me as a white person. . . . I could think of myself as belonging in major ways, and making social systems work for me. . . . In proportion as my racial group was being made confident, comfortable, and oblivious, other groups were likely being made inconfident, uncomfortable, and alienated. Whiteness protected me from many kinds of hostility, distress, and violence, which I was being subtly trained to visit in turn upon people of color. (p. 118)

Charles Taylor (1994) summarizes the importance of studying and understanding identity. In what he describes as the politics of recognition, he points out the effects of prejudice on identities, the devastating effect of the attempt to deny or withdraw recognition of people's identities. He writes:

> The thesis is that . . . nonrecognition or misrecognition can inflict harm, can be a form of oppression, imprisoning someone in false, distorted, and reduced mode of being. . . . Within this perspective, misrecognition shows not just a lack of due respect. It can inflict a grievous wound, saddling its victims with a crippling self-hatred. Due recognition is not just a courtesy we owe people. It is a vital human need. (p. 75)

Effects in School

Self-Fulfilling Prophecy

What are some of the results of stereotyping, prejudice, and racism within schools? Numerous studies have been conducted on the effects of teachers' known or unintentional stereotypical assumptions on students in the classroom. A number of these studies have found evidence of the self-fulfilling prophecy (term coined by Merton, 1948). In one of the more classic studies, which described the Pygmalion Effect, the self-fulfilling prophecy is a key result of stereotyping. In the 1968 study by Rosenthal and Jacobson, the researchers invented IQ scores for students in several classes, randomly assigning students to different scores. The teachers were told that certain students were likely to show great gains in their IQ scores as the year went on, and that they would be "academic spurters." The study examined how the teachers treated students, how students reacted, and the year-long effects of the treatment on IQ scores. Because of what is called the self-fulfilling prophecy, the teachers treated students differently depending on the students' supposed IQ scores. As a result, students acted according to how they were treated. And finally, guess what happened? Those students who were targeted as being likely to gain in IQ did indeed improve their scores more than those who were not targeted.

Three steps are required for the self-fulfilling prophecy to be evident: "(1) Perceivers develop erroneous expectations. (2) Perceivers' expectations influence how they treat targets. (3) Targets react to this treatment with behavior that confirms the expectation" (Jussim and Fleming, 1996, p. 164). These three steps can be seen in the Rosenthal and Jacobson (1968) study. In the chain of events in that study, teachers believed that some students were going to improve; the teachers then treated those particular students differently; and the students fulfilled those beliefs by indeed improving their IQ scores.

Another example of the steps of self-fulfilling prophecy in the schools is seen in the overassignment of boys to special classes for "behavioral problems." (1) Boys have long been perceived as more aggressive and active than girls. As a result, a teacher may expect boys to act that way in the classroom. (2) The teacher is consciously aware of and notices in particular when boys are aggressive or active. Girls may also be aggressive or active, but since the teacher is not expecting it, he or she does not notice it. (3) A boy is active, the teacher notices it, and the boy is placed into a class for behavioral problems (after a lengthy legal process in which the teacher documents the student's overactivity). Thus, stereotyping is a vicious cycle that leads to differential treatment and achievement within schools.

Achievement and Quality Gaps

A concept receiving a lot of attention at the beginning of the twenty-first century is the "achievement gap." This refers to the fact that poor students of color, especially African Americans and Hispanics/Latinos statistically score lower on standardized tests and have a higher high school drop out rate than White students.

> In every subject tested and at every grade level, low-income students perform at a lower level than more economically advantaged students, and Latino and African American students do worse than White and Asian students. Students with limited English score less well than those who are proficient. This is what has been commonly known as the "achievement" gap. (Oakes and Lipton, 2007, p. 23)

Much of this achievement gap has been tied directly to the inequalities in schooling received by students based on low-income status. According to Barton (2003), there are different levels of quality each of the following in low-income vs. high-income schools: teacher preparation, teacher experience, technology-assisted instruction, and school safety. Correspondingly, there are also differential amounts of lead poisoning and hunger in low- and high-income schools.

Another important set of educational items that has been found to be provided unequally in low- and high-income schools is instructional materials and decent and safe school buildings. In the Williams court case in California (2004), a group of students and their parents filed a lawsuit against the state claiming inequality in the educational system.

> They provided compelling evidence that schools across the state lacked 'trained teachers, necessary educational supplies, classrooms, even seats in classrooms, and facilities that meet basic health and safety standards.' They also showed that these schooling basics were systematically less available to low-income students of color. . . . The Williams students argued that, by permitting such schools, California's educational system failed to meet its constitutional obligation to educate all students and to educate them equally. (Oakes and Lipton, 2007, pp. 18–19)

As a result of these successful efforts in court, the state of California now requires equality in all of the items listed in the lawsuit.

Attempting to bring equity to inequitable school systems was similarly at the heart of the origination of the No Child Left Behind Act (NCLB), enacted by President George W. Bush in 2002. Two important goals within this Act were improved test scores for all children and improved training for all teachers, especially children and teachers in low-income schools. Focusing on improved test scores, NCLB requires that all children reach a level of reading, math, and science proficiency by 2014. Accompanying this requirement is a set of consequences for schools that do not meet their test score targets each year, with consequences beginning at providing additional professional development for teachers and extends through a series of consequences with the final one being the firing of all school teachers and administrators and being taken over by an outside agency. The reports of countless educators and researchers working in low-income urban and rural schools illustrate the entire restructuring of schools for the sole purpose of meeting test scores. Wood (2004) explains:

Simply put, with a focus on testing the curriculum is narrowed, leading to the most ineffective teaching practices becoming the norm. As non-test areas (art, music, social studies) and "frills" (field trips, naps, even recess) are eliminated, the school experience becomes limited, and everyone— children parents, and communities – reports less satisfaction with the school. To make matters worse, these effects of the reliance on one test are disproportionately felt in schools that serve the poor. (xii)

As low-income schools struggle to achieve target test scores set by the government, while not having complete sets of textbooks, chairs and desks, or highly qualified teachers, they are being pushed further and further toward teaching only the basics. If social studies or art is not tested, offering these subject matters won't help the school remain open. As can be seen, inequities still remain.

Tracking

Another example of differential treatment in schools based on race and socioeconomic class is in tracking. Some school districts enforce rigid tracking policies, while even more schools engage unknowingly and unreflectively in tracking. The general concept of tracking is that students who are determined to be potentially academically successful are placed into "high tracks," where they are offered college preparatory courses and learn the higher-level skills. Students who are assumed to be of lower ability are placed in "low tracks," where they are taught only the basic materials and skills. Although many school district officials claim that they do not base tracking decisions on race or income level, in reality the facts show that the enrollments in high and low tracks do differ based on race and socioeconomic status. Jeannie Oakes has studied tracking in schools for over 20 years and has found clear and obvious connections between race and track. She summarizes the findings: "In virtually every study that has considered this question, poor and minority students have been found in disproportionately large percentages in the bottom groups" (2005, p. 64).

What happens within the classroom in each of these high and low tracks? Are there differences in instruction in addition to different types of courses offered? Oakes (2005) details these differences in high and low tracks through the words of students who have gone through schooling in the high tracks and of those who have experienced schooling in the low tracks.

"What is the most important thing you have learned or done so far in this class?"

—Interviewer (p. 67)

"I've learned how to get a better job and how to act when at an interview filling out forms."

—Low-track English, junior high (p. 70)

"I have learned things that will get me ready for college entrance examinations. Also, many things on how to write compositions that will help me in college."

—High-track English, junior high (p. 69)

"How to sew with a machine and how to fix a machine."
—Low-track Vocational Education, junior high (p. 71)

"About businesses—corporations, monopolies, oligopolies, etc., and how to star, how they work, how much control they have in the economy—prices, demand, supply, advertising."
—High-track Vocational Education, junior high (p. 68)

When the ideas of self-fulfilling prophecy and tracking are linked, we can see that students who are placed in lower tracks (1) are perceived as low achievers, (2) are treated as low achievers, and (3) will likely react to this treatment by fulfilling those lowered expectations. A teacher interviewed by Larson and Ovando (2001) tells a story of how obvious it is to students when they have been treated as if they have lower levels of capability.

> I was substituting in a high school English class. I brought in a very interesting article on Ebonics for the students. I thought that a lot of these kids would relate to this issue. So I passed out the article and asked them to read it and write their reaction to it. One kid, who was apparently the leader of the class, looked around the room and then finally raised his hand. I said "Yes?" And he said, "You buggin', Mista. That stuff's for the smart kids. We can't do that. We're a C class. (p. 79)

With such low expectations, from teachers and from within students themselves, another impact on student identity is the internalized feeling that they do not deserve to be in gifted and talented or honors classes. Yonezawa and Wells (2005) include the words of an African American student in an honors class in their description of the impact of being part of the tracking system. They describe this effect as "Not wanting to be with people who don't respect you" (p. 55).

> [student] I was swearing because I was like, "Oh man, I don't even belong in here," because it was like 30 Caucasian kids and one African student. I felt like I had to prove myself and prove that blacks aren't stupid. [I felt like] if I were to get a problem wrong and raise my hand, they would look at me and say, "Ah, that black." I was always under pressure. (p. 56)

Yonezawa and Wells explain that "These formerly low-track students of color carried into honors classes the double burden of having to defend both their capability and the capability of their race . . . [they] entered high-track classrooms knowing that their appearance and accents often caused teachers and classmates to question their presence" (p. 56).

Students know when teachers think they are less capable, less intelligent, and less able to succeed in school and in life. The self-fulfilling prophecy means that students start to believe these ideas themselves, and have a resulting lowered sense of self-worth.

Subtractive Schooling

A third type of practice in schools that has resulted from differential treatment based on race, nationality, and native language is termed "subtractive schooling" by Angela Valenzuela (1999). In her work with Mexican and Mexican American students, Valenzuela notes that the U.S. school system works to "subtract" the Mexican culture and language from students in two ways. The first subtractive strategy can be found in efforts of schools to deny the language of students. This refers not only to the requirement that all students learn English but also to a deeper practice—that of denying that one's native language is important or meaningful in any way to students. Cummins et al. (2005) explain that teachers need to "affirm the identities of English language learners, thereby increasing the confidence with which these students engage in language and literacy activities" (p. 38). By subtracting language as a key feature of identity, teachers take away students' abilities to draw on their own strengths in their learning situations.

Valenzuela goes on to describe how subtractive schooling in the U.S. specifically impacts students from Mexican culture as she explains the concept of *educación*. "*Ser bien educado/a* (to be well educated) is to not only possess book knowledge but to also live responsibly in the world as a caring human being, respectful of the individuality and dignity of others" (2005, p. 91).

How does this translate into subtractive schooling for Mexican American children? Schools deny this cultural understanding of what education should be about when teachers do not develop relationships with students that show genuine and authentic caring. As Valenzuela describes, the concept of *educación* held by the Mexican culture is that "learning should be premised on relation with teachers and other school adults having as their chief concern their students' entire well-being" (2005, p. 91). As discussed in the section on tracking, students recognize when their cultures or when they as individuals are devalued.

Summary of the Effects of Stereotyping, Prejudice, and Racism

The effects of stereotyping, prejudice, and racism can be seen in schools, in society, and especially in an individual's sense of identity. At any of these levels, the effects are long-term and are extremely difficult to overturn or erase. For some individuals, the ever-present consistency of these concepts turns their sense of self into a negative feeling, lowering their self-esteem. Not only are these beliefs about self imposed from the society at-large, but the schools can also serve to heighten this developing lowered sense of self-esteem. Through regulated and undocumented practices of tracking, students, especially ethnic minorities, women, and the poor, are designated as low achievers and are treated as such through offerings of classes, treatment by teachers, and post-K–12 expectations. Through the steps of the self-fulfilling prophecy, students receive treatment that is based on stereotyping, prejudice, and racism. Through this treatment, they internalize these "constructed" attitudes and start to believe them. And this cycle often leads to failure in school and society. Contributing to this lowered self-esteem are the attitudes and actions of those from groups who do not experience institutional racism. By overlooking the struggles with identity that society forces upon students, schools and teachers often unwittingly continue to encourage positive self-esteem in some students and negative self-esteem in others.

Summary

That there are even the concepts of stereotyping, prejudice, and racism tells us a lot about our historical and contemporary society. These ideas are part of our psychology, philosophy, and sociology as an individual, community, nation, and world. Stereotyping, which is often described in a neutral way—as just a way to help us organize our world—has the result, when used with human interactions, of seemingly allowing us to treat people differently based on those stereotypes. Most stereotypes are based on physical, observable features; thus stereotyping usually ends up occurring as a way to distinguish race, gender, language, and socioeconomic status. Stereotyping is one of the bases for developing in-groups and out-groups, clearly indicating who we want to consider a part of our community versus who we do not want to have identified with us in any way.

Often, a stereotype that begins as a categorization turns into a prejudice. Prejudice can be formed in a number of different ways, mainly involving an interaction between our personal experiences and our interpretation of what society tells us about different groups of people. Similarly, racism can be seen as an interaction between the psychology of an individual and the sociology of a community. Racism in its most harmful form comes in what is called institutional racism. We all are part of a society that has been formed in part by institutional racism, through the laws, policies, practices, and regulations of our society and the institutions within society.

The practices of stereotyping, prejudice, and racism have great effects on an individual's sense of identity. When they are practiced so often and become regulated by people in power, they become firmly entrenched in society and continue to affect the lives of all. Practices based on these concepts can lead to lowered sense of self-esteem, affecting students' capabilities and attitudes toward school, society, and life itself. Key to the study of these concepts is that individuals be constantly open to the idea that each of our identities has been formed from and within a society that is undergirded by stereotyping, prejudice, and racism, and therefore that we will have to struggle with these issues constantly in understanding who we are.

Reflective Writings

1. *Identity Development.* Reflect carefully on your understanding of your own identity, and comment on each of the following questions.

   —Do you believe that you are in the identity versus role confusion stage, in which you are just beginning to ask, "What do I believe?"

—Have you been operating at the identity diffusion stage, which means that you have not begun to make an attempt to understand your identity?

—Do you feel that you are in the stage of ethnic identity clarification, in which you understand who you are and what that identity means in relation to other people in the world?

—Are you in the contingency stage, during which you are constantly and consistently attempting to further clarify your understanding of who you are and what you believe?

—Do you recognize yourself as being located within one of the particular ethnic identity stages for your ethnic group?

2. *Attributions of Characteristics within Stereotyping.* Select five stereotypes that you either hold personally, have heard throughout class discussion, have read within this or another text, or have noticed within the media. Do the stereotypes rely on attributions of dispositional characteristics? In other words, is the group of people being described being "blamed" for the characteristics being stereotyped? How does this attachment of dispositional and nondispositional characteristics affect the treatment of and policies toward different groups?

3. *Recognizing Institutional Racism.* Keep a log of one day in your life. Record what you do and who has the biggest influence over those daily events. Determine who owns businesses, who controls what is produced, how much money the average worker makes, and so on. Table 2.3 may help you begin your log.

4. *Effects of Institutional Racism.* Much of the discussion about institutional racism is concerned with its harmful effects on minorities. In what ways has institutional racism been harmful to Whites as well?

5. *Racism, Sexism, and Socioeconomic Status.* Compare racism and sexism. How are they similar? How are they different? How does socioeconomic status affect each? What are the long-term effects of each of these practices?

6. *Connecting Stereotyping, Prejudice, and Racism.* Look again at the checklist of statements on pages 58–60. Select at least five statements that you marked as displaying racism and examine them further to uncover the roles of stereotyping, prejudice, and racism in developing those statements. Specifically, try to determine the following:

—Are there any stereotypes involved in the statement or in society that might have led the person to make the statement or take part in the action described?

—Can you determine which of the five theories of prejudice formation listed in this chapter may have led the person to make the statement or take the action?

—Is the statement influenced by individual or by institutional racism?

—Which views and practices in society make up the institutional racism within the statement or action?

7. ***Theories of the Formation of Prejudice.*** Reflect on the long-term impact of each of the theories of prejudice formation presented in this chapter. Does the prejudice that is formed as a result of one of the theories last longer than the others? Do the prejudices that form on the individual level eventually become instilled at the societal level? Or vice versa? Which of the theories of prejudice formation do you believe has the longest negative impact on society and the groups within society, and why?

8. ***Meaning and Effects of Claims to Be Color-Blind.*** Some teachers claim to be "color-blind" in the classroom. Describe what this statement means. How can this belief by the teacher result in the further disenfranchising of students of color?

9. ***Impacts of Stereotyping, Prejudice, and Racism on Your Own Life.*** Reflect on and describe the effects of stereotyping, prejudice, and racism on your own life. Focus especially on how the active presence of these concepts has affected your perspectives on the world. How has the practice of these concepts on your own part affected the way you live, and how has the practice of these concepts on the parts of other people and society affected the way you perceive the world?

10. ***Examples of Subtractive Schooling.*** Either think back to your own K–12 education as a student, or observe in your current school, and document examples of how the school and teachers are engaging in subtractive schooling. You may want to examine teacher–student interactions, the curriculum, after-school groups or clubs, involvement of family and community members from the cultures of the students in the school, or anything else that you might find.

11. ***Revisiting the Concept of Culture.*** Look back at your reflective writings from chapter 1 that describe cultural socialization in the schools. After having completed the exercises and readings from chapter 2, how would you now undergird your discussions of cultural socialization with your knowledge of institutional racism?

Chapter Three

Immigration
and Imposition

Identity Development Related
to Immigration and Imposition

The United States has been forged out of countless interactions between different cultures. The quality and tenor of these interactions and the relationship of power to these interactions have different social, political, and economic impacts on individuals and groups. All these factors affect the construction of identities. Examples of these societal practices include war, economic strife as well as upswings, legalized segregation, among many others. One general type of interaction comes when a group of people immigrate voluntarily to the United States, purposefully intending to interact with the people living there. Since the country was founded, there has been an ebb and flow of people immigrating to what is now the United States, along with an inconsistent series of policies regarding immigration. A second general type of contact between cultures comes when one group imposes its culture onto another group, giving the latter group no choice or say in the matter. Many of the practices of cultural imposition can be seen as an attempt to establish, solidify, and strengthen the dominant culture.

The histories of immigration and culture imposition are inexorably intertwined. The complexity of the interactions among cultures and people can be seen in numerous levels of interactions. Take the following examples as illustrations of the complexity of immigration and imposition both between groups and within groups: European Americans immigrated to the land that is now the United States and imposed a culture on Native Americans, but some European Americans had cultures imposed on them. Mexicans residing in what was then Mexico but is now the United States had a culture imposed on them literally overnight with the signing of the Guadalupe Hidalgo treaty; now Mexicans are immigrating to the United States. Asian Americans have long immigrated to the United States, and at various times also have had cultures imposed on them. African Americans were imposed on by slavery, whereas Blacks have also immigrated to the United States voluntarily.

John Ogbu (1992, 1988, 2004) has been a leading scholar on the effects of minority status on the identities of individuals and groups. His work will be included here in reference to the United States, but his ideas are also reflected in the interactions of peoples worldwide. It is his use of the terms *voluntary minorities* and *involuntary minorities* that gives the impetus for the distinction used in this chapter between immigration and imposition. Voluntary minority is used to describe an immigrant to the United States. Involuntary minority refers to those people who had the dominant culture of the United States imposed on them. Ogbu (1992) distinguishes between these groups based on "the initial terms of their incorporation" and describes the groups in this way:

> *Immigrant or voluntary minorities* are people who have moved more or less voluntarily to the United States because they believe that this would result in more economic well-being, better overall opportunities, and/or greater political freedom. Even though they experience subordination here, the positive expectations they bring with them influence their perceptions of the U.S. society and schools controlled by Whites.
>
> *Involuntary minorities.* Involuntary minorities are those groups that are part of the United States society because of slavery, conquest, or colonization rather than by choice because of expectations of a better future. They usually have no other "homeland" to which to return if their experiences in the United States become unbearable. (pp. 290–291)

These two categorizations of groups of people will be the focus of this chapter, but Ogbu (1992) uses two additional categories in his description of minorities within the United States. One group is *refugees,* which will be discussed later in this chapter, and another major group Ogbu terms *autonomous minorities.* These are groups that "may be culturally or linguistically distinct but are not politically, socially, or economically subordinated to major degrees" (p. 290). Ogbu gives the example of Mormons as autonomous minorities, and he states that there are no non-White groups in this category.

In any of these categorizations laid out by Ogbu, the ways that a group of people have been treated in relation to the dominant culture will affect their identity. If a group has voluntarily chosen to immigrate to a country and to become a part of society, and especially if that group has characteristics that place it within the dominant culture, then their identity will be constructed in certain ways. In particular, the expectations held by many immigrants are that the way of life in the United States is better than that "back home." They have come to the United States expecting better opportunities and more freedom; they are more likely to see the United States as a land of opportunities for themselves and their children. If, on the other hand, a group has become part of society through the imposition of the will of the dominant culture, while seeing their cultural heritage destroyed, they are less likely to hold positive expectations for or reactions to U.S. society. It is these responses to differential treatment by the dominant U.S. culture that create for individuals and groups a different way of constructing their identities.

Preliminary Activities

Individual Activity

Think of the United States as a combination of many groups of people coming together to form communities. How does society organize itself to deal with all these different groups? How can the relationships among these groups, and between groups and society, be depicted?

Following are four formulas depicting possible societal organizations. These were first proposed by Newman (1973) in his description of American society. In each of these different formulas, the A, B, and C represent a different group of people, with group membership defined based on such characteristics as race, nationality, income level, or some other self-defined combination of characteristics. The number of groups is virtually endless, but each formula will present only three alphabet letters for simplicity.

$$A + B + C = A$$

This formula represents the concept of assimilation, in which all people are expected to accept the values, beliefs, and patterns of the dominant culture, the A group. People are expected to take on the characteristics of the A group as their own. Often, this means that people will have to give up or replace their own cultural selves in the process. In the United States, the A group is usually considered to be White and middle class.

$$A + B + C = D$$

This formula represents the melting pot society. It depicts the society resulting from the combination of many groups into the development of a unique new cultural group. In theory, a new culture and society will be formed as characteristics of many groups blend together, while any characteristics that are too ethnically distinct will melt away. Historically, this can be seen as the process of Americanization, where any new immigrants would be expected to blend into and contribute to the new American society.

$$A + B + C = A_1 + B_1 + C_1$$

In the representation here of modified cultural pluralism, when different groups come together they each remain who they are—a member of group B is still a B at heart, at the core. But the subscript 1s indicate that people have also picked up some beliefs, traditions, linguistic styles, and so on from various other groups. In this type of society, there is a high level of interaction among groups without an expectation of giving up what makes up one's core identity.

$$A + B + C = A + B + C$$

In the classical cultural pluralism represented with this formula, different groups live within the same society but without interaction with each other. A member of group C, for example, remains wholly a C. No one and no group becomes altered by any other group. Theoretically, groups would coexist peacefully while maintaining their cultural identities.

For each formula, list two positives and two negatives if society were to be structured that way. What would be two positive results? What would be two negative results? This can be considered in terms of results for society, for education, or for the individual.

Small Group Discussion

Discuss your list of positive and negative results with others in a small group. Do some of the formulas have more positives attached, whereas others make it easier to think of negatives? For each formula, were the positives more often attached to society or to individuals? What about the negatives in relation to society and to individuals? And finally, do any of these formulas more clearly describe the United States historically? Currently?

Small Group Discussion

With your small group, can you think of any additional formulas or other ways to present how society organizes itself? Following are two sample formulas that some of my students have created in my courses:

$$A + B + C = A^6 + B^3 + C^1$$

$$A + B + C = A^A + B^A + C^A$$

Each of these formulas depicts the power relationships between the different groups. In the first one, many characteristics of the dominant A group have been adopted by society in general, whereas very few of the beliefs and traditions of group B and even fewer of group C have been adopted. Thus the superscript numbers represent how much of themselves people of each group will see within the daily life of society. In the second formula, A is the dominant group and is in a superordinate position over all groups. A member of group B or C constantly feels the presence of the A society in their lives. Can you create a new formula representing the possible arrangement of groups within society?

Immigration

Throughout the history of the United States, the rate of immigration has varied from decade to decade, with some periods seeing a great deal of immigration and others seeing a very limited rate of immigration. In the 1980s, fewer than one million people per year immigrated to the United States. In the 1990s, the percentage of foreign-born people in the United States was approximately 8.5 percent of the total population (Simon, 1995), and the percentage in 2000 was 9.5% (http://www.rapidimmigration.com). Simon compares these recent immigration statistics with those at the turn of the twentieth century. The statistics show that the rate of U.S. immigration in the 1990s was about one-third of the rate of immigration at the beginning of the century, during which time more that 15 percent of the U.S. population was foreign born. Figure 3.1 displays the ebb and flow of immigration from the 1820s to the 2000s. As will be discussed further in this chapter, the great distinctions from decade to decade are a direct result of U.S. restrictions on immigration.

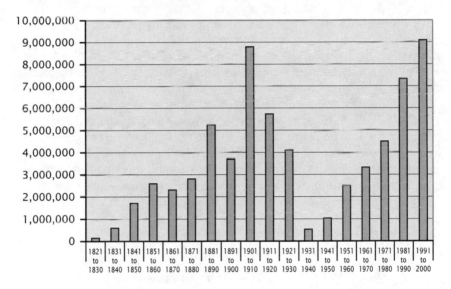

Figure 3.1   Patterns of Immigration by Decade

Immigration involves a complex mix of personal, family, community, regional, and national factors in both the immigrant's home country and the new country. Many people immigrate in the hope of having a better life for their families. Others immigrate to escape persecution or economic hardship in other countries. Still other immigrants have established themselves economically in other countries but want to develop professionally in a new country. This commonly held view of immigration is described by Portes and

Rumbaut (1996) as the push–pull model. According to this model, people are pushed out of their home countries while being pulled by seemingly better conditions in other countries. As Portes and Rumbaut (1996) describe, the push–pull model "is constructed around 'factors of expulsion' (economic, social, and political hardships in the sending countries) and 'factors of attraction' (comparative economic and political advantages in the receiving countries)" (p. 271).

As will be seen in further discussions of immigration in this chapter, though, immigration is not always initiated solely by individuals and their families. For many immigrant groups, the policies of the receiving country originally encouraged immigration from certain designated countries for several purposes, such as to serve labor and workforce needs. According to Portes and Rumbaut (1996), "Immigrant flows are not initiated solely by the desires and dreams of people in other lands, but by the designs and interests of well-organized groups in the receiving countries, primarily employers" (p. 270). After a cycle has been developed, immigration factors become mixed and entangled between personal and national concerns. Once people from one country have been purposely recruited by and arrive in another country, many citizens from the country of origin join the immigration pattern. It is common for friends and relatives to join immigrants who have already become established in their new country. So the factors underlying immigration involve a complex interaction of historical and economic policies as well as personally felt economic and social needs.

The following discussion is not intended to be a complete history of immigration in the United States. Rather, selected examples of immigrant groups are presented in order to lay the groundwork for discussions of how immigration affects the identities of immigrants. The themes presented here, including patterns of immigration and policies of the United States regarding immigration, are intended to give an overall idea of how immigration affects identity.

Patterns of Immigration and Immigration Restriction Policies to the 1920s

Western and Northern European Immigration

The earliest immigrants to come to the land that is now the United States in large numbers were overwhelmingly from the countries of western and northern Europe. During the 1700s through 1870, more than five million people moved to the United States, with 98 percent of all U.S. immigrants by 1870 coming from western and northern Europe. The heavy influx of this population gave the numbers and concentration of people needed to establish a soon-to-become dominant set of cultural beliefs and values. Chu (1997) argues, in fact, that the development of a dominant culture was actually the intent of the framers of the Constitution of the United States. Chu writes that "their concern was to build and maintain one dominant culture from the political and economic factions represented in the original 13 states" (p. 182).

This dominant culture was imposed on Native Americans, and all future immigration has been shaped and controlled by the now-dominant western and northern European culture. The values, traditions, and language of Western Europe were the standards by which schools functioned.

The ideal image of this time of heavy immigration can be illustrated by the term *melting pot*. The beliefs of many were that when all these people from different countries, different languages, different traditions, and different beliefs came together in their new country of the United States, they would all blend together and form a new type of person: an American. The formula from the initial reflective activity for this chapter that best illustrates this version of immigration is A + B + C = D, with D representing the new American that was created by all the people joining, melting, and blending together. In reality, though, rather than a neutral blending of cultures, the melting pot theory in practice resulted in the attempt to form all new immigrants into the image of an American. American, at that time, meant the large and dominant culture of the western and northern European immigrant to the United States.

Chinese Immigration

In the late 1800s, the nativist movement began to include anti-Chinese sentiments because of concerns by Americans over losing jobs to Chinese immigrants. The first Asians to enter the United States in large numbers were from China. Passing through the West Coast's version of Ellis Island—Angel Island in the San Francisco Bay—male Chinese entered the United States originally as workers who intended to return to their families in China. Chinese immigrants were males of working age, and they found work mainly in the gold mines, in mining communities, and later as workers on the railroads. In numerous western U.S. states, where many Chinese lived and worked in manual laborer positions such as mining and railroads, racial riots began to erupt. In 1871, a group of Whites killed 19 Chinese in Los Angeles. In 1885, 28 Chinese were killed, and Chinese-owned property was destroyed in Rock Springs, Wyoming. Additionally, Chinese were often barred from owning property, running businesses, and in Montana, from owning mining claims. When attempts to correct these inequities were undertaken, the claims were not allowed in court. Part of the reason such anti-Chinese sentiment could be enacted and continued was because Chinese were not allowed to testify in court against Whites.

After several decades of this racial tension and rioting, the U.S. Congress passed the Chinese Exclusion Act in 1882. This anti-immigration act was the first to deny immigration rights to a specific race. With the Chinese Exclusion Act of 1882, no Chinese were allowed to enter the United States. Since Chinese immigrants to that point had been primarily males involved in laborer positions, the Chinese Exclusion Act created a "bachelor society" in which no women or children could enter the country. In the 1880 census, more than 105,000 Chinese were documented in the United States. But following the 1882 act, the number of immigrants from China had decreased to

472. In 1892, the Chinese Exclusion Act was renewed for another ten years, and when that ten years was up, the act was renewed indefinitely. It was not until 1943, following World War II, that the United States "rewarded" China for its work as an ally by allowing a mere 100 immigrants per year to enter the United States.

Japanese Immigration

Japanese immigrants also felt the sting of nativist-driven anti-immigration acts. Japanese immigrants to the United States, known as issei, came to Hawaii and California in the late 1800s, mainly to work in agriculture, in homes as domestic helpers, and in small businesses. Beginning as tenant farmers, Japanese immigrants worked very successfully in Hawaii's and California's agriculture, buying land and setting up plantations and farms in these states. By 1920, Japanese farmers owned and worked on more than 50 percent of California's vegetable-growing acreage. In the early 1900s, a series of increasingly restrictive bills were passed, designed to limit the number of immigrants from Japan. First, in 1907, President Theodore Roosevelt signed the Gentlemen's Agreement between the United States and Japan. Under the terms of the agreement, if Japan would stop issuing exit visas to Japanese laborers, then those Japanese already in the United States would be allowed to bring their families to the United States. Following this informal agreement, which greatly reduced the numbers of Japanese immigrants to the United States, states such as California passed additional restriction acts that made it illegal for the issei to own land. In what was called the California Alien Land Bill of 1913, the Japanese immigrants were barred from owning or leasing land because of their noncitizen standing. By 1920, 13 additional states had passed such legislation. To avoid being restricted by such laws, many Japanese purchased and leased lands in their children's names. Their children, who were born in the United States and were thus citizens, should have been legally allowed to own and work on the land. However, the 1920 passage of the Alien Land Bill denied the Japanese Americans even that right.

Southern and Eastern European Immigration

With the end of the 1800s and beginning of the 1900s, the countries of origin of the newest influx of immigrants were in Southern and Eastern Europe. The tide turned so clearly that by 1910, 21 percent of all immigrants to the United States were now from southern and eastern European countries. In the 24 years between 1890 and 1914, more than 15 million new immigrants entered the United States. The largest numbers of people to immigrate during this time were from southern and eastern European countries. By 1909, 58 percent of the students in the school systems in the 37 largest cities in the United States had foreign-born parents (Tyack, 1993, p. 14).

Based on the dominant culture's attempt to keep America dominated by its now-established culture, in 1907 the Dillingham Commission was formed to study the idea of a fundamental, provable, and unmistakable difference between older (western and northern European) and newer (southern and eastern European) immigrants. On the basis of their study, they concluded that there is such a fundamental difference. With ideas such as these put out by governmental commissions, the common citizen felt empowered to make such statements as if they were truths. Some took this feeling to the point of claiming contamination of the old by the new. One prominent journalist of the time wrote that:

> The American nation was founded and developed by the Nordic race, but if a few more million members of the Alpine, Mediterranean and Semitic races are poured among us, the result must inevitably be a hybrid race of people as worthless and futile as the good-for-nothing mongrels of Central America and Southeast Europe. (Roberts, 1922/1972)

Mexican Immigration

Mexicans, many of whom already lived on the land that became the United States, also came to the southwest region of the country as immigrants beginning in the late 1800s. Similar to the immigration movements of other groups, much of the immigration of Mexicans was for purposes of labor. Some intended to work in the United States and then return home. Others planned to come to the United States for labor and then to remain in the new country. Additionally, laborers from Mexico were encouraged to come to the United States by many different types of land-based economic sectors within the country. As Gutierrez (2004) describes:

> Mexico became a close and convenient source of cheap immigrant labor. . . . One sector of the American economy after another called on Mexicans, first to mine the vast mineral deposits of the West, then to construct the railroads . . . and finally . . . as laborers to till, tend, and harvest the fields. (p. 266)

The interaction between the United States and Mexican laborers has been a tumultuous one for the immigrants, continuing into the 21st century. From unrestricted immigration to the encouragement of immigration for use for field labor, from restrictions on immigration to the actual physical removal of Mexicans and Mexican Americans, the policies of the United States toward Mexican immigration have been highly inconsistent. For example, in 1924, the U.S. Congress established for the first time the Border Patrol to monitor movement across the Mexico–U.S. border. This border had previously been open to free movement back and forth, but with the establishment of the border patrol in 1924, the United States created an immigration policy that physically limited the number of Mexicans who could enter the country. In addition to limiting the number of Mexican immigrants to the United States through the Border Patrol and the National Origins Act, both in 1924, the United States began to physically require that many Mexicans and Mexican Americans move to Mexico. It is reported that from 1929 to 1934, the United States "repatriated" more than 400,000 Mexicans, of which approximately 200,000 had been born in the United States and thus were U.S. citizens. This means that the United States illegally forced out its own citizens, based solely on their race and nationality. Of those who were so repatriated, 64,000 were forced to move to Mexico without any legal proceedings. But the discontinuous nature of U.S. policies regarding Mexican immigration swung again toward encouraging more immigration, this time in 1942 when the U.S. government became officially involved in intentionally bringing Mexicans to the United States. In what is called the Bracero Program, the United States and Mexico signed an agreement that authorized a number of Mexican immigrants to work temporarily in the United States in labor positions such as seasonal agricultural work. This was undertaken to fill the labor needs of the country due to the loss of workers during World War II. Under this new program, the United States offered protection of workers for the temporary time that they were in the country, but then the workers had to return to Mexico.

Portes and Rumbaut (1996) summarize these ever-shifting policies and practices:

> Contrary to today's portrayal of Mexican immigration as a movement initiated by individual calculations of gain, the process had its historical origins in U.S. geopolitical and economic expansion that first remolded the neighboring nation and then proceeded to organize dependable labor flows out of it. Such movements across the border of the reduced Mexican republic were a well-established routine in the Southwest before they become redefined as "illegal" immigration. (p. 274)

As can be seen from these highly swinging policies regarding immigrants from Mexico, the U.S. policy regarding such immigration has been inconsistent, has been based on the labor needs of the United States as well as on nativist sentiments, and cannot be easily defined.

Nativism

Although the image of the melting pot seems to be a positive one, in reality, the belief in and practice of nativism meant that people from many countries and regions are left out of this idealized version of America. Nativism had as its root belief the idea that "old" immigrants from western and northern Europe were significantly different from "new" immigrants who had arrived following the 1870s, along with the belief that only the "old" immigrants were "true" Americans (Feagin & Feagin, 2003, p. 64). These differences were proclaimed by people from all walks of life—from journalists, to political leaders, to scientists. Those with the power to make or influence policies proclaimed these differences as truthful distinctions that allowed differential treatment of immigrants.

In the mid- to late 1800s, much of the nativist sentiment was shown toward those who were not Protestant, especially Catholics and Jews. Despite the rhetoric of the American colonies being founded on religious and other freedoms, the freedom of religion was not guaranteed, nor was it respected by the population. In what was known as the Know-Nothing

Movement, around the period of 1840–1855, a number of secretive organizations attempted to enact these strongly anti-Catholic, anti-Southern, and anti-Eastern European feelings. In this movement, these organizations argued for an extension of the time required for any new immigrant to become an American citizen, and it promoted the election of only northern and western Europeans to political office. But it wasn't only secretive groups who argued for such restrictions. Each newly formed state varied remarkably in their policies regarding Jews, for instance. In Pennsylvania, only Christians were allowed to hold a state office. In New Jersey and North Carolina, the holding of a state office was restricted even more, to Protestants only. Maryland did not lift its restrictions against Jews living there until 1826. Later, during the Civil War, in December 1862, Ulysses S. Grant issued General Order No. 11, which expelled all Jews from Tennessee. Any Jews who remained would be jailed. Once President Lincoln heard of this order, he promptly directed Grant to cancel it. But that did not stop the anti-Semitism. Further examples in the 1860s and 1870s included attempts to deny Jews fire insurance and to exclude Jewish families from hotels. Similar nativist treatment was given to Catholics, when as early as the mid-1800s, Irish Catholics had become the targets of religious-based violence. As Feagin and Feagin (2003) noted, "By 1850 most large cities had seen anti-Catholic demonstrations and riots" (p. 81). And nonviolent but socially damaging discriminatory practices occurred in Pennsylvania, where Irish were not allowed to serve on the police force or to work in any positions within state agencies. An article in the 1851 issue of *The Massachusetts Teacher,* a magazine written for the teachers in the schools of that time, titled "The Defects of Irish Immigrants, 1851" indicates clearly that anti-Irish sentiment:

> [We should] by any means purify this foreign people, enlighten their ignorance, and bring them up to our own level. . . . Our chief difficulty is with the Irish. The Germans, who are the next in numbers, will give us no trouble . . . [the Germans] have, inherently, the redeeming qualities of industry, frugality, and pride, which will save them from vice and pauperism, and they may be safely left to take care of themselves. But the poor Irish, the down-trodden, priest-ridden of centuries, come to us in another shape . . . for the most part the simple virtues of industry, temperance, and frugality are unknown to them . . . [this problem] is one of pressing weight which we must overcome, or it will conquer us and contaminate our children.

As can be seen in this example, old immigrants are given "redeeming qualities" whereas new immigrants are considered to lack "simple virtues." Here we can see the clear sentiments of nativism becoming popular and publicized.

Americanization

The goal of the schools at the turn of the twentieth century, corresponding with the nativist feelings of the time, was the assimilation or Americanization of students. The goal was to teach students the specific values of the western European, middle-class culture within the United States. The curriculum of the schools was based on western European, especially Anglo-European, curriculum. The intent was to make students assimilate into the U.S. culture, even to the point of giving up their original cultures, traditions, and beliefs. The New York superintendent of schools described the intent of assimilation in 1918: educators should teach children "an appreciation of the institutions of this country [and] absolute forgetfulness of all obligations or connections with other countries because of descent or birth" (Tyack, 1993, p. 13). Cubberly wrote in 1909 about what these cultural values entail:

> Our task is to break up these groups or settlements [ethnic enclaves], to assimilate and amalgamate these people as a part of our American race, and to implant in their children, so far as can be done, the Anglo-Saxon conception of righteousness, law and order, and popular government, and to awaken in them a reverence for our democratic institutions and for those things in our national life which we as a people hold to be abiding worth. (pp. 15–16)

These societal beliefs were seen within the schools in the increasing emphasis on American citizenship training. Tyack (1993) reports that, "Whereas in 1903 only one state required the teaching of 'citizenship,' by 1923 39 did so" (p. 15). Tamura (1993) further describes that during this period there were "courses in American history and government, patriotic rituals as daily flag salutes and observances of national holidays, and English-only instruction" (p. 37). This phase of educational history can be called assimilation or Americanization, during which federal, state, and local school districts practiced policies that attempted to make students give up their beliefs, values, traditions, and language in order to be just like a person from the dominant culture, that is, to become an American.

With this fervent concern for Americanization of all students came the advent of the intelligence testing movement. With the educational system in the United States attempting to make every child know the same information and to think in the same way, the logical next step was to develop a measurement that would let educators know which students were getting the message and which were not. The Binet-Simon (later Stanford-Binet) intelligence test was developed for this purpose in the 1900s and was standardized by testing thousands of White students in the 1910s. The test began to be used to distinguish people of different national and racial origins in the 1920s, and by the mid-1920s, it was recognized that IQ scores could be used for political purposes. Intelligence tests were considered to be scientific examinations and helped lend credence to the idea of differences among different European immigrants.

National Origins Act

The clearest example of the political uses of intelligence test data came in the debate over, and the passing of, the Immigration Restriction Act of 1924. After a series of intelligence tests were given to men in the army, with higher scores received by those who spoke English and who had been in the United

States for a longer time, educators and politicians alike pointed to these intelligence test score differences as evidence of the superiority of the western and northern European heritage and the inferiority of all others.

These test scores added fuel to the nativist beliefs about the superiority of western and northern European culture and eventually were used as evidence in a political argument designed to restrict immigration. From 1921 to 1924, the U.S. Congress passed a series of Immigration Restriction Acts, the most egregious one being the Johnson-Reed Act, also called the National Origins Act of 1924. This act restricted the number of immigrants to a numerical percentage corresponding to the number of immigrants from any particular country who were already residing in the United States. The reason this resulted in heavier restrictions against southern and eastern Europeans, as well as against Asians, is that the percentages were to be based on the percentages of people in the United States from each country as of 1890. This setting of the year not at the most recent census of 1920 but rather at 1890 had the effect of leaving out the 15 million immigrants who came to the United States between 1890 and 1914, the 15 million who came from Southern and Eastern Europe. As stated earlier in this chapter, 98 percent of the American population in 1870 was from western and northern Europe. Thus these Immigration Restriction Acts of the 1920s, by setting the census year at 1890, assured that the only heavy immigration that could come into the United States would be from western and northern Europe. As Tozer (1995) writes, "For many nationalities the annual quota was cut by 99% below the peak years of earlier immigration" (p. 90). Fuchs (1995) gives some specific numerical limitations, pointing out that these numerical restrictions resulted in allowing only 4,000 Italians, 6,000 Poles, and 100 Greeks to enter the United States, during a time when millions of people were immigrating to the United States each decade. The U.S. commissioner of immigration illustrates one of the purposes of such restrictions by declaring one year after the National Origins Act of 1924 that "virtually all immigrants looked exactly like Americans" (Fuchs, 1995, p. 299).

Summary of Immigration Patterns and Policies to the 1920s

The history of immigration to the United States is one filled with an ebb and flow of immigrants from different regions of the world. In addition, the U.S. policies toward immigration have also been inconsistent. Owing to the ever-shifting policies regarding immigration, the numbers of people who were able to immigrate to the United States up to the early part of the twentieth century differ based on time period and on region of the world and nationality. U.S. policy has been inconsistent because of the needs of labor-based industries in the United States and because of nativist feelings.

The earliest immigrants to the land that is now the United States came from western and northern European countries. This critical mass of people was able to establish a dominant culture. Upon the further addition of immigrants from multiple countries and continents of the world, the dominant culture worked to strengthen and solidify its dominance. Through the creation of immigration restriction policies, the numbers of immigrants from eastern and southern Europe, from Mexico, and from Asia were strongly limited and restricted. And through the practice of Americanization, those immigrants who were already in the United States were encouraged to learn the traditions, beliefs, and language of the dominant culture of the United States. The impact of such practices of both immigrants and of the U.S. government upon the identities of immigrants will be discussed later in this chapter.

Patterns of Immigration and Immigration Restriction Policies: 1920s–21st Century

Immigration Policies and Statistics

The number of immigrants legally allowed into the United States each year has varied over time, as have the types of immigrants that have been allowed. As described earlier, the United States has set immigration restrictions based on regions of the world. From the 1920s to the 1990s, the immigration policies have varied also based on regions, but began to move away from nationality and in addition to deal with refugee and asylum policies. The National Origins Act of 1924 set the ceiling for immigration at 164,667 new immigrants each year. In 1929, that number was reduced to 153,714. After World War II, the U.S. government began to allow immigrants and refugees from selected countries to enter the country under special compensation. The Displaced Persons Act of 1948 provided for 100,000 "displaced persons" to enter each year, giving priority to those who had been displaced by the war. By 1951, the act was amended to allow 400,000 persons into the United States under this special clause. Then in 1952, for the first time, some of the nationality-based provisions were rescinded, while others were retained. For instance, the Japanese exclusion was repealed, and Asian nations were allowed small increases in quotas of immigrants. However, this act, the McCarran-Walter Immigration and Nationality Act, also maintained the general idea of a national origins quota system, still limiting immigration to a certain number based on nationality. In addition, this act described the type of person that could not enter the United States since it barred "radicals, communists, and subversives" from entering the country. Not until the Immigration Act of 1965 was the concept of restricting immigration based on national origin abolished. This act did, however, set different immigration ceilings from Western and Eastern Hemisphere immigrants. For the Western Hemisphere, the number of immigrants that could enter the United States was set at 120,000, whereas from the Eastern Hemisphere, the number was 170,000. But again making the practice of immigration and immigration policy more complicated, those from the Eastern Hemisphere were admitted based on a preference scale, with immigrants who had either family ties or occupational skills needed by the U.S. being given rights of entry. Immigration policy was changed again, this time in 1978, when the rate of immigration was finally not tied to region but rather was looked at as worldwide, and the ceiling for immigrants was set at 290,000.

Refugees

Another type of immigrant to the United States that has not yet been discussed is the immigrant who comes to the United States under refugee status. In the 1990s, the number of refugees accepted each year was set at approximately 140,000 per year, varying on a year to year basis. To gain acceptance as a refugee in the United States, which is to be given asylum in the country, a person must fit a specific description. Rytina (2005) gives the definition of a refugee used by the United States (as set forth in the Immigration and Nationality Act and the Refugee Act of 1980).

> A refugee is an alien outside the United States who is unable or unwilling to return to his or her country of origin because of persecution or a well-founded fear of persecution on account of race, religion, nationality, membership in a particular social group, or political opinion. (p. 1)

As Donahue and Flowers add,

> anyone fleeing a well-founded fear of persecution on account of the previous reasons is also a refugee. Persons who are deemed solely to be fleeing poverty and the lack of economic opportunity are *not* considered refugees. While immigration to the United States may be an option for such people, seeking refugee status or asylum is not. (1995, p. 13)

The situation of refugees is different from that of most voluntary immigrants. Many refugees to the United States did not come to the United States first. Rather, most refugees worldwide first flee to the closest country to their home country. Sometimes, they then continue to move from country to country, with some eventually arriving in the United States. In fact, according to Amnesty International, "The first choice of most refugees is to return home when conditions become safe" (Donahue and Flowers, 1995, p. 12). The following statements by a Salvadoran refugee in the United States, who was about to return to her home country, indicate the strong feelings about wanting to return to a homeland: "War is the ugliest thing I have ever seen! There is nothing like going back to one's homeland. It is a hundred times better to be living under a tree in one's own country than to be in a comfortable house in a foreign land" (Donahue and Flowers, 1995, p. 2).

Countries most commonly allowed political refugee status have been those that have either caused widespread harm to their citizens or have political systems with which the United States does not agree. Between 1880 and 1920, nearly two million Jews fled Russia and Eastern Europe. These immigrants were most often poor and isolated within their own countries, and they had been the victims of Russian policies such as "pogroms," which were basically peasant massacres. Then during the time of the Holocaust—the killing of six million people, mainly Jews—policies allowed Jews to claim political refugee status to enter the United States. The United States also allowed political refugee status to Cubans, during a time when the U.S. was staunchly anticommunist. The United States sponsored airlifts during different periods, and in 1980 it sponsored the Mariel boatlift. Many Southeast Asian immigrants have similarly fled to the United States under the protection of political refugee status. Southeast Asian immigration began strongly in the 1960s and 1970s, when many feared the abuse of power by communist governments. The countries from which refugees flee that the United States is most likely to allow as refugee status depends greatly on the relations between the United States and that country, or to be more precise, the relations between the democratic capitalism of the United States and the political system of that country. Since World War II, the countries with the greatest numbers of refugees allowed in the United States are the following: Cuba, Vietnam, Poland, Laos, countries of the former Soviet Union, and Cambodia. These are countries that have political systems that the United States has tried to change through war. On the other hand, people seeking refugee asylum in the United States from El Salvador, Guatemala, and Honduras have a very low acceptance rate. These countries have no historical connection with the United States as far as attempts to work with or against their governments and political systems. In 2004, out of 75,546 applicants for refugee status to the United States, 52,835 were admitted (Rytina, 2005). The largest percentage of refugees came from Somalia (25.2%), followed by Liberia (13.5%), and Laos, 11.4%). Immigrants from Laos include both Laotians and Hmong. Other countries with 5 percent or more of the refugees admitted to the U.S. in 2004 were, in order, Sudan, Ukraine, Cuba, and Ethiopia.

Immigration and Refugee Status

The United States officially recognizes only certain people as legal immigrants or formally accepted refugees. A student's family's immigrant or refugee status can have a great impact on all aspects of that student's life, including his or her education. Several court cases have set policies both allowing and denying people basic citizenship rights based on their immigration or refugee, documented or undocumented, status. The immigrants that are most strongly affected by these cases of immigrant status are those from Mexico, especially within the states of Texas and California. These court cases often conflict with each other, indicating the changing views of the impact of immigration to the United States. The following are some sample court cases that legislated the rights undocumented or illegal aliens can have. A U.S. Supreme Court case in 1971, *Graham v. Richardson,* set the tone for treatment of undocumented immigrants by deciding "that aliens could not be denied welfare benefits simply on the basis that they were aliens" (Fisher, 1995, p. 22). A crucial case in 1982 continued this path of allowing rights to all U.S residents. In the case *Plyler v. Doe,* "the Supreme Court ruled that undocumented children cannot be denied access to education solely on the basis of their immigration status" (Lucas, 1997, p. 7). This Court in this case further elaborated on their decision by finding that "children of people who came to this country illegally cannot be denied the same free public education available to other children. The Court expressed that it was especially concerned that these children would be forever 'second-class citizens' without an education" (Fisher, 1995, p. A-4). It is important to note the deliberate use of the word people in this case. The point here is that the U.S. Constitution protects people, not only those designated citizens. The history of this case was that noncitizens were required by the state of Texas to pay for public school or not be allowed to go to school. This requirement disallowed about 50 children of noncitizen residents from attending school because they could not afford to pay the tuition. The U.S. Supreme Court felt that without being able to receive an education these children would be forever harmed.

By the 1990s, though, there was a swing in the feelings about immigration, once again, with the passage of Proposition 187 in California, which denied noncitizens the rights of daily life in the United States. Proposition 187 prohibits illegal immigrants from attending any public school at any level. With this requirement, parents must prove their legal residence in the United States, and all school administrators and teachers must report to the government any students or parents that they suspect of being illegal immigrants. This proposition also denies nonemergency medical care, including childhood inoculations. In addition, it prohibits all illegal immigrants from receiving any funding for social services. Although the California courts have put a halt on the practices required by Proposition 187, the issue of legal or illegal, documented or undocumented, immigrant status is still being argued, supported, and challenged. Other similar laws are being enacted, and then overturned, in other states as well. Since 2006, towns in Pennsylvania, California, and Texas, for example, have enacted laws that will fine landlords for renting apartments to illegal immigrants. Similar to Proposition 187, these laws are being halted while further arguments about the issue can be heard.

New Patterns of Immigration

A unique type of immigration can be seen in the immigration patterns of Puerto Ricans. In 1917, the United States designated Puerto Ricans—both within the United States and in Puerto Rico—U.S. citizens. The concept of immigration is thus a bit different for Puerto Ricans since there is a legally allowed two-way flow of travel between the two countries. This type of movement is more appropriately called migration, and indeed has been called circulatory migration (Nieto, 2004b). Nieto describes the different life experiences for Puerto Ricans as a result of this circulatory migration concept:

> For one, in general Puerto Ricans have continued to identify with their culture and language more than was the case with European immigrants who arrived earlier. In fact, Latinos in general have resisted to a great extent the pressures of the assimilationist ideology that characterized the experiences of European immigrants. Circulatory migration has provided a cultural and linguistic continuity not afforded previous immigrants or even some recent ones, and this has been manifested by a

practical need for use of the Spanish language and familiar cultural patterns. . . . The second effect of the circulatory migration for Puerto Ricans has been to redefine immigration from "a single life-transforming" experience to "a way of life. (pp. 518–519)

In a somewhat similar pattern, some Mexican American families commonly engage in "border crossing," crossing back and forth between Mexico and the U.S. in order to maintain and strengthen family, community, economic, and cultural ties. In her description of her anthropological study of the Aguilar family that straddled the U.S. border, Browning-Aiken (2005) lays out the complex yet commonly accepted movement patterns for families. Aguilar family members lived in towns from Sonora, Mexico, to Tucson, Arizona, to Phoenix, Arizona. Browning-Aiken describes

> Family photos and María's reports of picnics and other excursions with her cousin's family in Tucson, the Aguilar family's summer visits to their uncles' families in Cananea [Sonora, Mexico], frequent trips to the border town of Nogales to see their father and other relatives, and occasional visits to the mining families in Southern Arizona, as well as the visits of many of these families to the Aguilar home, suggested long-term relationships based on both reciprocity and *confianza*, a sense of trust and faith in the support of one's friends. (p. 174)

As Browning-Aiken (2005) continues, we can see how children learn from these many different family members and family locations. She writes that "Myriam knew how to tend the little neighborhood store in Cananea [Sonora, Mexico] because of her aunts, how to take care of the farm animals in Cananea from her uncles, and how to get homework help from her older cousin in Tucson" (p. 174).

Two additional patterns of immigration have developed since the 1960s: the kin selective pattern and the enclave pattern. Both of these patterns involve immigrants entering the U.S. to join already established networks of either families or occupations, allowing for smoother entry and settlement into the new country. Zhou (2001) describes the kin selective process for one particular group, the Vietnamese, who migrated to the U.S. both as refugees and as immigrants.

> Adversarial conditions . . . in the late 1970s and early 1980s continued to send thousands of refugees on the rugged journey to a better life. Once the early refugee waves established communities in the United States, leakage of information from America to Vietnam provided impetus for a continuing outward flow. Upon resettlement in the United States and other Western countries, many Vietnamese refugees rebuilt overseas networks with families and friends. Letters frequently moved between the receiving countries and Vietnam, providing relatives in the homeland with an intricate knowledge of the changing refugee policies and procedures of resettlement countries. (p. 190)

Portes and Bach (1985) discuss further the importance of these and other factors within the immigrant community in the immigrants' adaptation to their new lives. They write:

> The ethnic community [is] a source of emotional support, protection against external pressures, and even economic gain. The dense networks of contact within the immigrant community function routinely as sources of employment, information about events in the host and home countries, and social support. . . . It is the real-world social relationships that immigrants establish that represent the decisive element in their long-term adaptation. (pp. 299–300)

New York City has many examples of kin-selective immigration. In fact, as of 2007, 72 percent of the immigrants in the city came to the U.S. through family ties, while 11 percent came through employer sponsorship. Two stories were told in the May 30, 2007, issue of the *New York Times*. One story is about the

> Good Locksmith Inc., on Grand Street, a business run by the Lai family from China, who finally unlocked their door to America, relative by relative, after being unwelcome by law for a century. . . . Steven Lai, 46, whose immigration at 23 depended not only on his mother's sponsorship, but on a long line of male forebears who endured 20-year family separations and exclusion from citizenship as they labored in the United States, first building railroads in 19th century California . . . (para. 7–8)

The article describes another immigrant family that developed ties to America over generations. "These days, in a Lower East Side neighborhood that has been a cradle of family chain migration to America for 200 years, the deli at Delancey and Allen Streets is a 24-hour operation run by a man from Bangladesh—one of about 70 relatives to follow a Bangladeshi seaman who jumped ship here in 1941" (para. 6).

Nationally, as of 2007, 58 percent of legal immigrants came to the United States through family ties, specifically through the granting of visas for family members of current U.S. citizens. Another 22 percent came through the avenue of employer sponsorship.

The ethnic enclave pattern of immigration is exemplified by Cuban immigrants. As Peréz (2001) explains, an ethnic enclave is not only a place where immigrants can live within the familiarity of others from their home countries, but it is a place where new business and enterprises are formed that enable new immigrants to find employment. In describing Cuban immigration to Miami, Peréz (2001) explains that

> recent Cuban immigrants may enter the U.S. labor market through the large number of firms that are owned and operated by members of their own group who arrived earlier. While compensation may not be higher in the enclave, ethnic bonds provide for informal networks of support that facilitate the learning of new skills and the overall process of economic adjustment. (p. 96)

Summary of Immigration Patterns and Policies, 1920s–the 21st Century

Immigration has been full of attempts to codify who counts as a legal immigrant, an accepted refugee, or an undocumented resident of the United States. There have been many shifts in policies, including encouraging immigrants and refugees from certain countries to come to the United States, but also disallowing undocumented immigrants to participate in certain features of U.S. daily life. With a number of immigrants already living in the United States, family members who still live in the countries of origin have begun to join their families in the United States. Immigration has become more inclusive in that there are immigrants from more countries now living in the United States. In the 1990s, approximately nine million immigrants and more than 130,000 refugees entered the United States each year.

Identity

Impact of Immigrant or Refugee Status

The immigrant or refugee status of students has a significant affect their lives. Commonly, families are afraid to go to the grocery store, to a clinic, or to pay bills in public because of the fear of being approached by the Immigration and Naturalization Services (INS). Especially for those children who are called illegal aliens, their official status affects their confidence in their right to participate in daily life. As Lucas (1997) states:

> The immigration status of a student's family can have a major impact on the student. Even when they themselves are legal residents or citizens, children of those with no official immigrant status bear the extra burden of fear that they and their families will be deported. . . . Such children are unlikely to participate in any school activities or to seek recognition or attention for fear that the undocumented status of their families will be discovered. (p. 11)

I would like to share an experience that illustrates the constant awareness that Mexican immigrants have that they may be asked to prove their identity. In this case, while riding a bus from San Diego to Los Angeles, the Border Patrol sent an agent onto the bus to check for citizenship. Since this was my first time on a bus between these two cities, I did not know what the procedure was. But the riders on the bus with me immediately began to pull out their identification cards or licenses. The Border Patrol agent asked each person to prove his or her legal residence status. Two things stood out in my experience. First, the Hispanic man next to me said, with a sort of resignation, that though he was born in Mexico, he had become a U.S. citizen 20 years ago and that he sure gets tired of being asked to prove himself in so many situations. In the meantime, the agent looked at me, saw that I was White, and said "Hey, how're you doin'?" I was not asked to show any identification or to prove my citizenship. The racial differences stood out in the practice of the Border Patrol in this situation. For the rest of the trip, then, the Hispanic man and I knew that we were perceived differently by government officials. We knew that I have the privilege of not having to prove who I am, whereas he is consistently questioned and challenged about who he is.

Impact of the Practices of Americanization

The process of becoming an American is very complex. Most often, a new immigrant must learn a complex set of rules and regulations, along with a myriad of living skills that are needed to negotiate daily life in the United States. Just think of all the daily living skills that people need to know to live in the United States. Figure 3.2 lists some of the daily processes that are needed for newly immigrated persons to get established in the United States. Attempting to construct identities so that people can both retain their already developed cultural identity and adapt to the new cultural identity that they are being asked to incorporate can be complex, confusing, and scary. As Lucas (1997) describes, "Immigration is a transitional experience that poses difficulties. . . . [Immigrants'] lives are disrupted. They experience culture shock as they leave behind the more familiar for the less familiar and begin to develop new identities that integrate their previous lives with their new ones" (p. 13). In attempting to deal with such practices and policies, immigrant adults and their children necessarily go through a time of turmoil and confusion over issues related to their identity, over questions such as who am I and how does who I am change upon moving to a new country, with a new language and a new culture.

Within such a complex transition of moving, or fleeing, to a new country and school system, there will clearly be an accompanying complex set of adjustments that both children and their families will experience. Lindborg and Ovando (1998) identify four stages of adjustment that recent immigrants to the United States will go through when arriving in the U.S.

1. *Arrival Survival.* During this stage, families will devote almost all of their time looking for a place to live, learning to find their way around their new community, and learning what has to be done to get all of the other basic necessities.

2. *Culture Shock.* "This is an emotionally stressful time during which families may find their energies drained from having to cope day after day with the new sociocultural environment. During this stage they may be disillusioned with American ways."

3. *Coping.* As families become more comfortable in their new surroundings, and more confident that they can become successful in navigating the systems, they may be interested in becoming involved in their children's schooling. They may also be willing to help newer families as they go through the process of adjustment to the United States.

4. *Acculturation.* At this point, families have become a part of the mainstream community and may take on leadership roles in immigrant

Immigration Law
Overview of immigration law
Sample immigration forms
Types of visas available

Government Functions

Courts	Attorneys
Licenses	Police
Immigrant rights	Firefighters

Employment
Overview of opportunities
Job search techniques
Employment services
Resumes and interviews
Corporations
Starting a business
Types of businesses
Banking for businesses

Finance and Banking
Services

| Currency | Credit |
| Investment | Taxes |

Insurance

Health	Rental
Automobile	Life
Homeowners	Choice of company

Housing
Buying
Selling
Renting
Establishing basic services
    like phone, utilities

Food and Shopping
Supermarkets and
    convenience stores
Department and
    specialized stores
Restaurants

Catalog shopping	Malls
Food shopping	Car purchases
Shopping by	Shopping
television	online

Health Care
Preventive and curative
    sources of care
Medication
Living wills
Emergencies
Medical professionals
Immunizations
Fire safety

Education
Levels
Library services
English instruction

Public Agencies
State Chambers of Commerce
Embassies and consulates
Immigration offices

Recreation and Travel

Entertainment	Sports
Activities	Organizations
Religion	Holidays
Climate	Tourism
Time zones	Metric conversions

Travel by car, plane, train

Communications
Telephone
Mail
Telegraph services

Source: Adapted from Access USA (1994), *The Complete Guide to Immigration and Successful Living in the United States,* Millington, NJ: Access USA.

**Figure 3.2   Processes of Daily Life That
Must Be Learned by New Immigrants**

communities. (Lindborg & Ovando, 1998, cited in Larson & Ovando, 2001, p. 15)

In attempting to deal with the many new changes in cultural expectations of the newly arrived immigration experience, a multitude of factors affect that experience, including the characteristics of the individual immigrant, the characteristics of the immigrant's family, and the relationship between the immigrant's original country and culture and the context of the United States. Some key factors related to the individual are age at the time of arrival, proficiency in the native or English language, and relationships with family members. Of key importance within the immigrant family is not only the level of proficiency in English but also the economic resources they bring with them to the United States and whether they have the knowledge and abilities needed to gain economic resources once they are here. And finally, the relationship between the immigrant's home culture and country and the United States has a crucial impact on the immigrant's experiences in the United States. For instance, the formal relationship between the two countries throughout history will play a big role in how well the immigrant is accepted by people in the United States. The formal relationship that has been developed will give the immigrant's country a particular status, high or low, within the United States. If the immigrant's home country is one that the United States has long held as friendly status, the acceptance of the immigrant will be much more likely than if the original country is one that the United States has at some point determined to be unworthy, put restrictions against, and waged a propaganda campaign against through movies, television, and journalism. In addition, once immigrants arrive in the United States, the presence of others from their native country, and the presence of others from their race or ethnicity, will affect their experiences as well.

Within such a complicated set of expectations, several types of identity relations may develop since the individual and the group must come to terms with how much of their home culture and the culture of the larger society will count as part of their identity. Four categories of identity related to the level of fit within one's ethnic and cultural group and the culture of the society at large have been distinguished. The terms of the categories presented here come from Locke (1998), who described minority identity categories in general; Hernandez and Carlquist-Hernandez (1979); and Chavez and Roney (1990), who use the terms specifically to describe Mexican Americans.

1. *Traditional.* Persons who can be considered traditional in terms of identity are those who identify strongly with their original culture, with their family and community, while rejecting many characteristics of the dominant culture. For some people, the choice of which culture to retain is truly their choice, whereas for others, the dominant society denies them access to the characteristics and practices of the mainstream culture.

2. *Bicultural* (Locke, 1998) or *Duotraditional* (Hernandez and Carlquist-Hernandez, 1979). Persons whose identities can be considered within this category are able to function equally well within both their original culture and the culture of the dominant society. They are equally tied to their families and communities and to the society at large.

3. *Acculturated* (Locke, 1998) or *Atraditional* (Hernandez and Carlquist-Hernandez, 1979). People who have been acculturated into mainstream society have adopted the characteristics of dominant society. They will have given up the characteristics of their culture of origin, will speak English as their primary language, and will have few connections with their families.

4. *Marginal* (Locke, 1998) or *Deculturated* (Chavez and Roney, 1990). As Locke (1998) writes, people with this identity are "neither completely at ease in the culture of origin nor minimally a part of the dominant culture" (p. 8). People are out of touch with their cultural heritage and are not a part of the larger society either.

Impact of Immigrant and Refugee Patterns on Families

For children, experiences in the schools often add an additional stress on the construction of identity. A common result is rifts in family relationships since parents and their children become assimilated at different rates. Since the schools serve as strong socialization agents, children often pick up on the patterns and language of the dominant society more quickly than their parents and may be more eager to break their ties with their family and their family's culture of origin. Portes and Rumbaut (1996) coined the terms "generational consonance" and "general consonance" to describe the relationships across family members once immigration to the U.S. has occurred. As Zhou (2001) describes,

> *Generational consonance* occurs when parents and children both remain unacculturated or both acculturate at the same rate or both agree on selective acculturation. *Generational dissonance* occurs when children neither correspond to levels of parental acculturation nor conform to parental guidance, leading to role reversal and parent-child conflicts. (p. 207)

Research has also shown that parents and children view the new country (the U.S.) in different terms. Zhou (2001) found that Vietnamese parents who immigrate to the United States do not perceive there to be much discrimination against them. However, their children indicate that they have both been the recipient of discrimination and in fact have come to expect discrimination in their lives. When asked whether there is "racial discrimination in economic opportunities," 1.6 percent of parents agreed strongly, but 31.6 percent of their children agreed strongly. And when asked if they have "expected discrimination no matter what," 8.2 percent of parents said yes, while 35 percent of their children said yes. Clearly there are different expectations and experiences, different perceptions of the world, between the generations within Vietnamese American families.

Thus the consequences of immigration for families may range from intergenerational support and stability among family roles to intergenerational conflict and confusion. In any case, the process of putting oneself into a new culture puts stress on the identity development of individuals as well as families.

The experiences of immigrant children have been documented in several books, including books by Santa Ana (2004), Igoa (1995), and Donahue and Flowers (1995). In working with children who had recently immigrated to the United States with their families, Igoa noted several key themes:

> More than 75 percent of the more than 100 immigrant children I have worked with in the past fifteen years have experienced gaps in their education because of travel, time needed for preparation of exit and entry documents, and moving around in search of a better home. Many children have skipped one grade or more. (p. 6)

Figure 3.3 presents the words of some of these children as they describe their experiences in immigrating to the United States. These stories portray the intense confusion that children can feel when they are so uncertain about the next phases of their lives.

Girl from Poland, age 12

My family is from Poland. I was ten years old when I came to Amerika. Before we came, we stopped at another country. I don't remember the name of it. . . . First they placed me in second grade. In second grade I was one week. Then I went to fourth grade. In fourth grade I was five months. Then I went to fifth grade. In fifth grade I was five months also. Now I am in the sixth grade. (Igoa, pp. 6–7)

Boy from Afghanistan, age 11

I was born in Afghanistan in a beautiful home. I lived there for five years. I went to school in Afghanistan up to second grade. I was eight. Then the Russians came so we had to move from Afghanistan to Pakistan. . . . I started school third grade in Pakistan. One day my mom came and said, "We are going to America." I was really shocked because she never told us that we were going to America. So we came. (Igoa, p. 41)

Girl from Mexico, age 12

I knew for two years that my family was planning to go to the United States. I came home from a fiesta late one night and I saw my mother packing. She said that the papers finally came and we were leaving the next morning. We packed until early morning. That was confusing and sad because I never got to say goodbye to my friends. (Igoa, p. 42)

Figure 3.3 Experiences of Leaving a Home Country

Figure 3.4 provides a series of stories by children who describe their struggles in trying to fit in to their new schools. From these students, we learn about the treatment given immigrants by other children, by teachers, and even by their parents. We learn about how their struggles to fit in lead to emotional struggles and cognitive dissonance. We learn how painful it is to have one's knowledge of a language taken away. And we learn that their identity cannot be based on their names anymore because their new educational system gave them new names that meant nothing to them, that instead were just reminders of how different they are. These are feelings related to identity that only those of refugee or immigrant status will have to deal with.

Imposition

Imposition can be seen in a number of practices by the dominant culture. In some cases, such as Native Americans and Mexicans, people who had for centuries lived on the land that is now the United States were invaded and had an outside culture imposed on them, on their long-established communities and societies. For Africans, the institution of slavery was imposed on their lives, denying them all rights to citizenship, including the rights to an individual identity. In all these series of contacts, the result was the imposition of a new culture, a new language, and a new identity on groups of people who often already had well-established communities and traditions and beliefs. Through the practice of nativism (discussed above) the dominant culture of the United States could choose whom to allow into the country and whom to keep out, essentially assuring the strengthening and solidifying of their culture. Then through the practice of assimilation, or Americanization, that culture imposed new cultural identities on people, sometimes with quite harsh means. Through legalized segregation, the dominant culture has been able to determine which groups can take part in which parts of daily life. Then there are combinations of practices affecting individuals' and groups' identities, such as segregating a group and then forcing that group to become Americanized. In this type of attempt, the result is a total destruction of a culture.

Imposition has been the term used here to describe the practices of the U.S. government and dominant culture toward these other groups. Another term that could be used, and in fact has been used in a number of pieces of literature, is colonization. In the practice of colonization, the dominant culture and legal system imposes an entire cultural and legal system onto the people who live in a country or on a continent. In colonization, the legal and cultural systems that have already been established by the residents of the land get overridden by a foreign system. Although citizens of the United States often think of other countries as colonizers, in fact the United States has practiced colonization in a number of instances and to a number of established groups.

Girl from Vietnam, age 10

I was always being pushed to adapt to be American. Do this and do that. While I was trying to adapt to one stage, it's time to move on to the next, and I was falling behind. It's hard—it's like fast-forward and you're in slow motion. Somebody was trying to fast-forward me. (Igoa, p. 63)

Girl from Vietnam, came to the United States at age 9, now in eighth grade

You don't know anything. You don't even know what to eat when you go to the lunchroom. . . . I was very shy and scared. I didn't know where to sit or eat or where the bathroom was or how to eat the food. . . . Now I know more, but I still sit and watch and try to understand. I want to know, what is this place and how must I act? (Donahue and Flowers, p. 128)

Girl from Laos, came to the United States at age 10, now in ninth grade

I didn't know anything. I didn't know the ABCs or the arithmetic and I felt so stupid. I should have been in 1st or 2nd grade, not in the 5th. I told my parents I want to change, but the teacher said no because it depends on your age. I cried because I didn't understand. (Donahue and Flowers, p. 128)

Girl from China, came to United States as an 8 year old, in high school she could speak only a bit of Chinese after being fluent until the age of 8

It's hard not to understand your own language . . . not to know your own language more than a second language, which is English for me. I probably forgot over 70 percent of what I learned since first grade. . . . So I don't feel very comfortable about not knowing more Chinese than I do English. (Igoa, p. 85)

Girl from Hong Kong, immigrated at age 7

When I first arrived in San Francisco from Hong Kong at age seven and a half, the only English I knew was the alphabet and a few simple words: cat, dog, table, chair. I sat in classrooms for two to three years without understanding what was being said, and cried while the girl next to me filled in my spelling book for me. . . . While other kids moved about freely in school, seeming to flow from one activity to the next, I was disoriented, out of step, feeling hopelessly behind. I went into a 'survivor mode' and couldn't participate in activities. (Quan, 2004, p. 14)

12th-grade Lao Mien boy, immigrated at age 14

The school was so big! There were students everywhere all the time—not just in classes. I didn't know how you were supposed to know where to go when. There was no one who could speak Mien and explain to me. My uncle had told me if I needed any help to go to the Dean. My teacher asked me something and I didn't understand her. So I just said "Dean, Dean," because I needed help. That is how I got my American name. She was asking me, "What is your name?" and I kept saying "Dean." Now everybody calls me Dean. Now it is funny, but it is also sad. My name comes from not knowing what was going on. (Donahue and Flowers, p. 128)

Figure 3.4 Experiences of Immigrant and Refugee Children in Schools

As with the discussion about immigration, the following discussion is not a complete history of imposition by the United States. Additional imposition has occurred over time. Again, selected examples of imposition are presented in order to lay the framework for understanding how imposition affects the identity of those who have had an entirely new and foreign culture imposed upon them. The themes presented here are intended to give an overall idea they not a complete treatise on the subject.

Practices of Imposition: Colonization and Segregation

Native Americans

The history of contact and interactions between Europeans and Native Americans is a clear example of the harmful and genocidal decimation of a group of people through imposition. Historians have estimated that the indigenous population of the North American continent at the time of the arrival of the Europeans in the late 1400s was anywhere between 3 million to 18 million (Snipp, 2004). But by the late 1800s, owing to the practices of imposition, war, disease, legal restrictions, and Americanization or assimilation, the Native American population had been decimated to approximately 250,000. The interaction between the U.S. government and the different American Indian tribes is an example of both the deliberate and the unintentional destruction of a set of traditions, cultures, and lands.

American Indian tribes were recognized by the United States as legitimate, sovereign nations, and as such, the imposition of the United States culture onto Native American cultures had to go through legal procedures. The United States set out on two basic paths: one was the signing of treaties and the other was forced relocation of Indians away from their homelands. As Snipp (2004) describes: "The political and legal status of American Indians in the United States is an extremely complicated subject, tangled in a conflicting multitude of treaties, formal laws, bureaucratic regulations, and court decisions" (p. 322). In the 1830s, Congress passed a series of Removal Acts that authorized the forceful removal of Indians from their homelands in the east to unwanted lands west of the Mississippi. Many tribes were moved to lands that were physically different from their ancestral lands: from warm humid lands of plentiful vegetation to the dry and cold northern plains, for instance. Many tribes tried ineffectively to resist the government order and to remain in their homelands. The Cherokee, for instance, tried to resist the forced movement for nearly ten years. When in 1838–1839 the Cherokee were forcefully removed from Georgia to what is now Oklahoma, 4,000 Cherokee died during the forced march. In what has been termed the Trail of Tears, one-quarter of the Cherokee population died.

The Blackfeet tribe, being similarly forced to live in a particular land area, went through a similar decimation of population. Table 3.1 lists some of the key dates in the history of Blackfeet–U.S. government interaction, and shows chronologically how an entire population could be decimated from 100,000 members to fewer than 2,000 over only 60 years.

Table 3.1   History of Blackfeet–U.S. Government Interaction

Year	History
1836	The Blackfeet tribe had an estimated population of 100,000 members.
1837	The smallpox disease, passed to the Blackfeet people by an infected boatload of blankets, killed four-fifths of the Blackfeet population.
1855	The first agreement with the U.S. government was signed.
1870	In what has been called the Baker Massacre, a winter camp of Blackfeet was attacked by 2nd Calvary troops. The massacre took the lives of 176 Blackfeet, of which 161 were women and children, and only 15 were men.
1884	The Blackfeet people were confined to a government compound.
1890	The Blackfeet people were confined to the reservation and could not leave without permission of the government-appointed Indian agent.
1894	The remaining Blackfeet population: 385 men, 480 women, 700 children.

Additional imposition on the lives and identities of Native Americans by the U.S. government came through the education provided and required for Native Americans. The United States fully determined the type of education that Native Americans would receive by providing governmentally funded schools: from mission schools in the early 1800s, to off-reservation boarding schools for American Indian youth in the late 1800s, to 25 off-reservation boarding schools, to on-reservation boarding schools by the end of the nineteenth century. These boarding schools had the single purpose of completely assimilating Native Americans into the European American culture, English language, and Christian religion. Indian students' hair was cut, their traditional clothing was burned, and they were beaten if they spoke their own language or practiced their own spirituality. Delphine Red Shirt (2004) describes the feelings of Native American students put into these schools: "I learned shame there. . . . I learned silence there. . . . I learned fighting there" (p. 57). Red Shirt continues "What I did learn, I still carry with me" (p. 57).

As stated by the founder of several schools and colleges for Indians, Eleazer Wheelock, the purpose of the boarding schools was "to save the Indians from themselves and to save the English from the Indians" (Axtell, 1981, p. 97). A number of boarding schools for Native Americans still exist today.

Mexicans

The history of Mexicans in the United States was similar to that of Native Americans in the imposition of culture by outsiders, but unique in the policies developed related to immigration. Until 1848, the area that is now the southwestern portion of the United States was part of Mexico. People living in parts of what is now called Texas, New Mexico, Arizona, California, Utah, Nevada, and Colorado were citizens of Mexico. After the

Mexican–American War ended in 1848, the United States and Mexico signed the Treaty of Guadalupe Hidalgo, in which Mexico lost nearly one-third of its territory. After the Treaty of Guadalupe Hidalgo was enacted, the 80,000 people who were Mexican citizens were now U.S. citizens overnight.

The imposition of a set of language and legal and cultural systems onto these new citizens began in full force at this point. Although many immigrants from Mexico entered for the purposes of agricultural field labor, many of the Mexicans who had just become U.S. citizens were also pushed into field labor. Even though many had owned their land for generations, because of the entanglements of a new language and a new set of regulations for land ownership, many lost their land and thus began to work for other landowners. Being stuck in this position, most often underpaid and mistreated, these Mexicans were now U.S. citizens, and thus began the tradition of migrant farm labor, moving from place to place to follow the crops' harvest seasons.

The impact of this vision of Mexicans and Mexican Americans began to affect the education of children as well. Many Mexican American children did not receive an education, and others were segregated into separate schools. As an example of the way that the educational officials viewed Mexican American children, Weinberg (1977) reports that in Texas in 1928, a school superintendent stated:

> Most of our Mexicans are of the lower class. They transplant onions, harvest them, etc. The less they know about everything else, the better contented they are. . . . If a man has very much sense or education either, he is not going to stick to this kind of work. So you see it is up to the white population to keep the Mexican on his knees in the onion patch. (p. 46)

In the practices of colonization, the dominant culture has the choice of how minority cultures can be educated. For Mexican American children, the dominant culture determined that the children need not receive an education and then later required that their families pay for their public education. In either case, these policies effectively restricted the number of Mexican students who could receive an education. The educational system, then, did not work in the best interest of Mexican students. It attempted to continue to fill the agriculturalists' need for laborers by providing no, or differential, education for Mexican children. Though the practice of legal segregation by race eventually ended, the way of life that was imposed upon Mexicans by the Americans virtually tied the Mexicans to this one way of life.

African Americans

The lives of African Americans in the United States began with the legacy of slavery. The legally sanctioned practice of slavery enslaved Blacks and denied them not only citizenship but also personhood until the Civil War and the legislative actions that resulted from it in the 1860s. In 1860, the population of Blacks in the United States was more than four million, most of whom had been born into slavery (Genovese, 1976). Slavery was most widely practiced in southern and largely rural locations; the free Black population was evenly split between North and South, and nearly half was urban. The experiences of most Blacks in the United States began with slavery, and their culture, communities, and identities have been impacted by the legacy of slavery. One of the effects on Black communities has been both legal and informal segregation. Following are a few examples of efforts to legally segregate Blacks—to deny this entire population the practices of daily life that were guaranteed to other citizens of the United States.

1. Before the Civil War ended slavery, in 1849, where public schools did exist, they were segregated based on race. In Massachusetts, White students attend "Whites Only" schools, whereas Blacks attended "Negro" schools. Documentation has shown that by the end of the 1920s, South Carolina recorded expenditures of more than $10 million for its White students, while spending only $1.5 million for its Black students (*The Road to Brown*, 1990). Teachers' salaries were similarly disproportionate, with White teachers getting seven times the salaries of Black teachers. Clearly, the facilities, curriculum, and teachers were qualitatively different for White and for Black students. *Statement of the case*: In the case *Roberts v. Brown*, in Massachusetts, the Roberts family brought the case to court claiming that their daughter was unfairly disadvantaged by having to attend a "Negro" school. In this case, the judge made several statements. First, he said that yes, Negro schools were inferior and should be improved. But, the judge claimed, segregation is best for both races. So, the family lost the case, and the schools remained segregated.

   Comments: In effect, then, this Massachusetts case can be seen as the first law requiring schools to be separated by race. This case represents the common approach to unequal schools during the mid-1800s and even through to the 1940s. The ruling affected only the state of Massachusetts, but it set an example to other states of how a case could be organized. This was still the time of slavery. The Emancipation Proclamation was still 14 years away, and African Americans were still designated property in the eyes of the law of many southern states.

2. Prior to the 1900s, not only were the schools segregated by race in many states, the public transportation systems were also segregated by law. Thus, on trains in Louisiana, there were separate "Whites Only" and "Colored Only" train cars.

   Statement of the case: In the *Plessy v Ferguson* case, in 1896, Homer Plessy, who was one-eighth Black, rode in the "Whites Only" train car and was arrested. He claimed that it was unfair for Blacks to have to ride on separate cars. The court also made several statements in this case. It ruled that as long as the train cars for Blacks were equal to the train cars for Whites, "separate but equal" was fine in transportation. So, Plessy lost the case, and the trains remained segregated.

Comments: This case went to the U.S. Supreme Court, so the ruling affected all states in the nation. Following the *Plessy* ruling, 21 states passed segregation laws under the protection of *Plessy*. These laws, and many others like them, are often called Jim Crow laws. The following are some of the Jim Crow laws—laws that required legal separation of the races—that were passed as a result of the *Plessy* case. Note that the effects of *Plessy* were so strong and long-lasting that the country still was suffering their effects into the 1950s:

• Oklahoma segregated phone booths.

• Mississippi segregated Coke machines.

• In Atlanta, a Black witness could not swear on a White Bible.

• Florida segregated not only the schools but even the textbooks in storage.

• Intermarriage was illegal in 38 of the 48 states until the mid-20th century.

• In Arkansas, White and Black voters could not enter a polling place together.

• In Alabama, a White woman would be forbidden to give nursing care to a Black man in a hospital.

• North Carolina required racially separate washrooms in its factories.

• Four states required separate washrooms in their mines.

• In six states, White and Black prisoners could not be chained together.

• As of May 1951, 17 states required the segregation of public schools.

(From *The Road to Brown*, 1990, and Kluger, 1976.)

Any hope of trying to change these segregation laws would be dashed by the lack of African American attorneys in the South. For nine million African Americans in the South, there were fewer than 100 Black lawyers in the 1920s. This was at a period when severe segregation was not only acceptable but actually required by the court system.

3. Finally, owing to the *Brown v. Board of Education* case in 1954, the U.S. Supreme Court ruled that the schools must for the first time become desegregated. Despite nearly a century of freedom for African Americans and increased U.S. citizenship of many races and nationalities, the years leading to 1954 saw an educational system that remained segregated by race. African Americans could not enter the public school systems in many states. Seventeen states and the District of Columbia required segregation by law, in many cases writing legal segregation into their state constitutions. By 1954, 40 percent of the students who attended public school in the United States were in legally segregated school systems. That included 8.2 million White and 2.5 million Black students who were affected by the segregated system.

Statement of the case: Unlike earlier cases, which claimed that separate schools were unfair because the facilities and equipment were inequitable, *Brown v. Board of Education* claimed that separate schools are "inherently unequal," and that the damage is psychological and may last for a lifetime and for generations. The U.S. Supreme Court ruled that yes, separate schools are inherently unequal and that the schools should be desegregated. Thus the ruling reversed the earlier damaging *Plessy v. Ferguson* case and upheld the equal protection of the 14th Amendment.

Comments: This was the most important case in the history of desegregation. There had been a buildup of legal precedents to the *Brown* case. State after state had dealt with issues of desegregation, each in a different way. The *Brown v. Board of Education* case was, in actuality, the combined cases from five different state rulings. Cases from Kansas, South Carolina, Virginia, Delaware, and Washington, D.C., were brought together under the umbrella of the name *Brown v. Board of Education.* Thurgood Marshall, later to be named the first African American Supreme Court Justice, was the lead attorney in the case. Working with eight other key attorneys on the case, he prepared the case. Their opponent was John W. Davis, who had won more U.S. Supreme Court cases than anyone else in history. At one point, he was the Democratic nominee for president. The arguments before the Supreme Court lasted for 17 months, with the team led by Thurgood Marshall winning the case and setting in motion for the first time the requirement that all children be given the opportunity to learn in the same school districts and buildings.

Summary of Imposition

Unlike immigration, in which people move to the United States voluntarily to become a part of the country, groups who either already lived on the land that is now the United States or were brought here forcefully without their consent had very different types of interactions with the dominant culture and with the U.S. government. In the case of Native Americans, Mexican Americans, and African Americans, the dominant culture imposed its legal system and cultural way of life onto preexisting cultures. Through the practices of colonization and segregation, the cultures of these groups were restricted; in some instances, they were changed completely. For many people who have been imposed upon, little to nothing is left of their original culture. Thus their traditions, language, and ways of life have been altered, sometimes completely.

Identity

Different Cultural and Legal Ways of Knowing

Having a different cultural and legal way of knowing hinders the ability of colonized and segregated groups to negotiate with the dominant culture, making it difficult to keep land, traditions, values, and one's very identity. Examples of the different ways of knowing and the resulting constructing of identities in Native American, Mexican American, and African American cultures and communities are described here.

Native Americans

Toward the end of the nineteenth century and into the twentieth century, the United States stopped creating legal treaties with Native Americans. Instead, the Bureau of Indian Affairs, the government body responsible for making policies with Native Americans, wrote policy "recommendations" regarding certain practices on Indian reservations. These written policies were counterintuitive to the traditional Native American ways of working with each other and with others, which were locally based and grounded in tribal communities; they were not based on written policy. In fact, many tribes did not even have a written language.

An example of governmental interference and the inability of a people to negotiate or understand the "policy" being presented can be seen in a governmental recommendation of 1923, regarding the "give away" ceremony. One of the basic and important parts of many American Indian ways of life is the practice of the "give away," often done during dance ceremonies. Begun hundreds or thousands of years ago, and continuing today, community members gather together and participate in the give away ceremony, which is done to honor a relative or community member. The words of a Blackfeet author illustrate the importance of these traditions:

> A long time ago Give Aways were held as a sacred event. Today, tribal celebrations and public events often feature a Give Away. The person who does the Give Away may do this with the help of his family and relatives. It is held sometimes in the name of a deceased relative or to honor a person who is going through a Sundance ceremony as a participant. Sometimes a Give Away is held when a prayer or vow has been granted. For example, somebody might have made a vow two years before and that vow has been fulfilled by that person and family. Therefore they honor that event and that person with a Give Away. Sometimes an individual may spend two years or more collecting and making the gifts: horses, blankets, money, shawls, automobiles and whatever else the person and his family deem appropriate to be given away. (Long Standing Bear, 1992)

It is clear from these words that give aways are important cultural events in the lives of many Native Americans. Now, with this strong sense of community and honor in mind, read the following proposal from the U.S. Department of the Interior:

1. That the Indian form of gambling and lottery known as the *ituranpi* (translated "Give Away") be prohibited
2. That the Indian dances be limited to one in each month in the daylight hours of one day in the midweek, and at one center in each district; the months of March and April, June, July, and August be excepted

3. That none take part in the dances or be present who are under 50 years of age
4. That a careful propaganda be undertaken to educate public opinion against the dance and to provide a healthy substitute
5. That there be close cooperation between the Government employees and the missionaries in those matters which affect the moral welfare of the Indians. (Long Standing Bear, 1992. Office of Indian Affairs. Supplement to Circular No. 1665: Indian Dancing. February 14, 1923)

This type of governmental intrusion affects an entire culture. In this case, by limiting the ability to pass on beliefs and traditions to the young members of the culture, those beliefs and traditions are not understood and are not able to be continued. Instead, they are lost. This is one of the factors that has contributed to the loss of so many Native American languages, cultures, and sense of who they are.

Another particularly deculturalizing practice during the time of the boarding schools was the re-naming of Native students by the English speaking teachers. Among most tribes, a young person is given a name based on an event or a characteristic that has been associated with that person. Ni-Kso-Ko-Wa, or Long Standing Bear Chief (1992), of the Blackfeet tribe, describes his own family's history of naming. His Indian name is Bear Chief. When he was given the name Bear Chief by a man named Many Guns, that name was given to honor Many Guns' grandfather. To recognize this honor, Bear Chief gave Many Guns blankets and other gifts in thanks for the name. But since a number of young people were also given that name over his lifetime, his name was changed later in his life to Long Standing Bear Chief, indicating that he has long been Bear Chief.

In his story about his "Name Giveaway," Phil George (2004) tells us through poetry about his own naming process.

> That teacher gave me a new name . . . again
>   She never even had feasts or a giveaway!
> Still I do not know what "George" means;
>   And now she calls me: "Phillip."
>   TWO SWANS ASCENDING FROM STILL WATERS
> must be a name too hard to remember. (p. 31)

Another case of renaming comes from a young man named Ah-nen-la-de-ni. Ah-nen-la-de-ni described that he "had been proud of myself and my possibilities as 'Turns the Crowd' (Ah-nen-la-de-ni), but Daniel La France [his new name] was to me a stranger with no possibilities. It seemed as if my prospect of a chiefship had vanished" (Coleman, 1993, p. 83). As Coleman (1993) explains, "The Indian system of naming was held to be related intricately to traditional cultural attachments which the boarding school was intended to erase in the young Indian's mind" (Coleman, 1993, pp. 101–102). The results in each of these cases are the imposition of a non-Native name, given by a culture that was trying to eradicate the Native American way of life, with the result of the diminishment of a history and context associated with their original names.

Mexicans and Mexican Americans

Like Native Americans, the imposition of a different cultural and legal way of knowing hindered the Mexican Americans' ability to negotiate with the dominant culture to keep their land, their language, and their identity. Meier and Rivera (1972) describe the confusion in this sudden imposition of new rules and regulations. People who went from being Mexican citizens to U.S. citizens overnight were guaranteed as part of a formal treaty to protection of their property rights, their rights to speak their native language of Spanish, and their rights to U.S. citizenship. What they were not prepared for, however, was how the Anglo-American culture defined the term "rights." Meier and Rivera write:

> Although they were left in their same geographic and cultural setting, these new citizens were now exposed to unfamiliar legal, political, and social institutions. . . . Guaranteed full protection of property rights, they soon became enmeshed in a web of confusing Anglo laws which required proof of ownership unfamiliar to them. (p. 71)

Banks (1997) describes further some of the legal restrictions and maneuvers imposed by the U.S. courts in order to gain the land of these Mexican Americans:

> The Anglo-Americans were able to obtain most of the land owned by the Mexicans by imposing a series of legal and financial restraints. Land boundaries in Mexico had been rather loosely and casually defined. Many Mexicans had to appear in Anglo courts to defend their rights to the land they owned. Often they did not have the legal papers proving ownership of their land, and Mexican legal papers did not conform to superimposed U.S. law. In many cases they had to sell their land to pay taxes imposed by the new government or exorbitant fees to Anglo lawyers to argue their cases in court. Legal battles over land titles often dragged out in the courts for years and became expensive. Tactics such as these and the Congressional Land Act of 1851, which required U.S.-recognized proof of land ownership, had the ultimate effect of making the Mexican largely landless and poverty stricken. (p. 344)

African Americans

The impact of generations of people born into a system of slavery is the long-lasting effect of being denied basic human rights. Bennett (2006) lists the governmentally and socially determined denial of rights for slaves: denial of property, civil, and legal rights, could not make a will or inherit property, could not get legal rights to marriage, could neither buy nor sell property.

Additionally, slaves were not even allowed to keep their names; instead they were given the surnames of the slave owners. Thus, the families of slaves since then have had to carry the name of the people who owned them, who kept them as property.

Another devastating long-range result of slavery was mass hangings, known as lynching. There were nearly 3,500 recorded hangings of Blacks by Whites between 1882 and 1951, but the number of actual hangings, including those not documented, is believed to be more than 6,000 (Franklin and Starr, 1967). In 1919, ten of the hangings were of Black men who were wearing their military uniforms from when they were soldiers in World War I.

The legacy of the *Plessy v. Ferguson* case of 1896, discussed earlier, was the presence of two separate societies: one with the freedoms guaranteed by the U.S. Constitution, the other with no freedom to pursue education or the many other public functions enjoyed by the dominant members of society. Much of the work to end segregation culminated in the *Brown v. Board of Education* case in 1954, and work after this ruling was aimed at enforcing the ruling. The *Brown* case, which will be described later in this chapter in much greater detail, was the first ruling by the U.S. Supreme Court to recognize the debilitating effects on students of being legally segregated:

> To separate them [African American children] from others of similar age and qualifications solely because of their race generates a feeling of inferiority as to their status in the community that may affect their hearts and minds in a way unlikely ever to be undone. (Browning, 1975, p. 5)

Self-Determination

Prior to the arrival of the Europeans, Native American tribes were self-governing nations that had their own languages, laws, traditions, and cultures. By the end of the 1920s, though, many Native Americans were restricted to reservation lands, while being denied their original rights to having their own local governments. The social and educational history of Native Americans in the United States from the 1930s to the 1990s is a history of attempting to regain control over their own lands and governments. An important step in the direction of self-government was taken in 1934, with the passage of the Indian Reorganization Act, also known as the Wheeler-Howard Act. This act ended the breakup and outside allotment of lands; it made it possible for tribes to acquire additional lands; and it allowed reestablishment of local governments. This crucial act set the tone for many policies that came after 1934, and it can be seen as a positive action. However, it can also be seen as a way for the United States to avoid addressing and redressing past injustices. Snipp (2004) describes the positive and negative results of the Wheeler-Howard Indian Organization Act (IRA):

> The IRA permitted tribes to organize their own governments to handle a limited number of issues on their reservations. However, tribal governments wishing to organize under the IRA legislation were required to adopt a system of representative democracy similar in form to the federal government; other forms of government, such as traditional theocracies, were not permitted. For many years, these tribal governments had little real power and very circumscribed jurisdictions. (pp. 323–324)

Further, as Feagin and Feagin (2003) write, even with the passing of the Indian Reorganization Act, "serious problems persisted" (p. 147). "Some Indian lands were sold to pay taxes, and many Indians fell deeper into poverty as land resources were depleted. For many years, Indian lands have also been taken for dams, national parts, and rights-of-way for roads" (p. 147).

The 1960s through the 1990s involved the passage of a number of acts that gave governmental approval of continued movement toward self-determination by Indian peoples. In 1968, Indian peoples, among others, were allowed to use their native languages in their education by the passage of the Bilingual Education Act. In 1975, with the passage of the Indian Self-Determination Act, the U.S. government reinforced the movement toward Indian self-determination by recognizing the autonomy of tribes. Freedom to practice religion, guaranteed by the U.S. Constitution but not granted to Native Americans, was officially granted in 1978 with the passage of the Indian Freedom of Religion Act. And in 1990, a deeply personal and emotional issue in the lives of American Indians was finally resolved. For generations, scientists and anthropologists have been recovering the physical and human remains of Indian tribes and displaying them in museums around the country. The Native American Graves Protection and Repatriation Act of 1990 requires federal agencies to return human remains of ancestors to tribes that request they be brought back to their own lands.

In 1990, there were approximately 500 recognized Native American tribes with approximately 200 native languages spoken. The issue of native languages is of crucial importance to the lives of Native Americans, indeed to the very survival and continuation of Native American tribes. For Native Americans, the issue revolves around whether native languages, and the lives, traditions, and cultures that they describe, are to exist in the future. Some native languages have seen a resurgence due to attempts by school systems, whereas other languages have completely disappeared. Snipp (2004) describes the patterns of native languages:

> The use of American Indian languages and the number of native speakers have increased significantly in recent years. . . . The number of American Indians who do not speak English, especially among those under age 40, is very small. Despite the widespread use of English, about a fourth of the American Indian population also regularly use a native language, and there is some evidence that this may be on the increase. One reason for this insurgence is that many tribes are engaged in active efforts to encourage native-language use. In areas where there are large concentrations of native-language speakers, such as the Navajo reservation, it seems likely that these efforts to preserve the language will be successful. However, some tribes such as the Catawba in South Carolina have all but lost their language (the last two native speakers died in the 1950s). (pp. 327–328)

A number of Native American tribes have made strides toward keeping their original languages. As Lomawaima (1995) describes, "Since the passage of the Bilingual Education Act of 1968 . . . at least 70 native communities have developed language-education programs" (p. 341). One example is the Blackfeet tribe, which has established a Blackfeet language kindergarten in the hope of passing on the language to future generations. Additionally, in the 1990s, there were 27 tribal colleges that helped teach adults language and culture. Not only is the language to be continued in this way, but also the very culture from which the language arose.

Similarly, African Americans went through a series of different types of educational institutional practices. Blacks in the United States went from not being allowed to enter any schools in some parts of the country prior to the Civil War, to a U.S. government idea called the Freedman's Bureau, which from 1865 to 1872, established night schools and industrial schools for African Americans. However, concurrently, African Americans had been establishing their own schools, with an estimate of more than 500 schools specifically for African Americans already in operation by 1866. Additionally, a key effort by African Americans to establish educational opportunities came through church-operated schools called Sabbath Schools. These schools operated in the evenings and on the weekends, and by 1869, there were estimates of 1,500 such schools, with 6,000 teachers and 100,000 pupils (Anderson, 1988). However, beliefs about the most appropriate education for African Americans have varied. Some African American as well as European American educators encouraged assimilation of Blacks into White, middle-class society as much as possible. Others, though, believed that it was more important for African Americans to gain political and civil rights from an education that didn't primarily focus on their assimilation into a White-dominated society.

At the conclusion of the Civil War in 1867, the U.S. government (the Union) established what became known as the first Reconstruction Act. As is common in a war, the victor imposed restrictions on the losing side. Thus, the North, which was now officially the federal government, sent federal troops into the South to establish new policies and practices. The Reconstruction Era in the South lasted from 1867 to 1877, with a number of fairly dramatic changes. Some key changes were the establishment of a number of prestigious Black colleges. Additionally, Blacks now had the right to vote, and indeed Blacks won political offices during this period. Tozer (1995) describes the rapid changes that occurred during Reconstruction: "Remarkably, more black U.S. senators were elected from the South in the first fifteen years following the Civil War (two) than in the next hundred years (one)" (p. 156).

And in the 1990s, the arrangements that have been set up by a number of African American communities include the establishment of schools that are for Black children only. These schools attempt to bring back some dignity to Blacks' experiences of life since the teachers are all African American and the curricula are geared toward promoting the role of African traditions in the development of the world as it is today.

Oppositional Identity

As stated earlier, the identity development of people who have immigrated to a new country will proceed in a different pattern from the identity development of those who have had a culture imposed on them. Or in Ogbu's terms, voluntary and involuntary minorities will have different sets of expectations and different types of identity development. Some of the types of identity patterns described in the immigration section also apply to involuntary minorities. Ogbu (2004) describes "the existing system of majority-minority relations," applying to groups who are not part of the dominant society.

1. *Involuntary incorporation into society.* Usually these minorities do not become minorities by choice. Rather they are forced into minority status against their will by conquest, colonization, enslavement. . . .

2. *Instrumental discrimination.* For example, denial of equal success to good jobs, education, political participation and housing.

3. *Social subordination.* For example, residential and social segregation, hostility and violence; prohibition of intermarriage; requirement of the offsprings of intergroup mating to affiliate with one group with no choice. In some cases oppressed minorities are forced against their will to assimilate into the dominant group, although this assimilation usually results in marginalization.

4. *Expressive mistreatment.* For example, cultural, language, and intellectual domination. Dominant group members stigmatize minorities' food, clothing, music, values, behaviors and language or dialect as bad and inferior to theirs. (p. 4)

As Ogbu (2004) explains:

> These four mechanisms are used by the dominant group to create and maintain the collective identity of the minorities; i.e., to "carve them out" and maintain them as a separate segment of society with a distinct identity. The existence of the minorities with distinct collective identity remains as long as these mechanisms or mistreatment of the minorities remain. (p. 5)

An additional discussion of how individuals' identities are affected by society's treatment of them was presented in the chapter 2 discussion of racism. To reiterate the ideas there, when members of minority groups, an involuntary minority, have to deal with consistent negative depictions of themselves, they may react in several ways: They may internalize all the negative ideas about themselves, or they may more strongly turn inward and try to build up their own ethnic group. This second strategy, the formation of an *oppositional identity*, will be elaborated on here. The research on this concept has mainly been on the identities and strategies of African Americans.

Ogbu (1988, 1992, 2004) has provided much of the research on an oppositional identity. He points out that the identities of involuntary minorities, such as African Americans, will develop very differently from that of immi-

grants. Ogbu (1988) lays out the key factors involved in developing an oppositional identity:

> A very significant factor is that blacks did not come to occupy their sub-
> ordinate relation to white Americans voluntarily in the belief that this
> was a starting point of a new opportunity to achieve a better life for them-
> selves and/or for their children. Rather, blacks were initially forced to
> occupy their subordinate position involuntarily through slavery, relegated
> to menial status, and after emancipation from slavery were denied mate-
> rial resources for advancement and denied true assimilation into the
> mainstream of society. Moreover, under this circumstance blacks had no
> "homeland" to return to like immigrant minorities; nor could they easily
> "pass" [appear to be part of the dominant culture] physically to escape
> their subordination. (p. 172)

Ogbu describes the barriers, responses, and strategies involved in the
development of an oppositional identity. He proposes that there have been
both instrumental and expressive barriers to daily life and advancement of
minority groups. Instrumental barriers include all the barriers that have denied
minority groups equal access to education, housing, and employment—that
is, segregation laws. Expressive barriers are emotional or psychological barriers—that is, the scapegoating and cultural derogation of minorities.

In response to these barriers, minority groups have created a set of strategies to deal with their treatment. Ogbu describes these as responses to barriers that help them maintain their sense of self-worth and their sense of
identity. The reason that these responses are oppositional is that such groups
never had a chance to develop a positive sense of identity within the United
States. They know that members of the dominant group have been their
oppressors since the initial periods of contact. Not wanting to be like their
oppressors, then, these individuals will be likely to attempt to develop identities that are in opposition to those of the dominant group. The more that an
identity is developed that is in opposition to the dominant group's way of
being, the more that identity can be protected from harmful and negative
insertions into the dominant identity. Ogbu (2004) explains:

> Under this circumstance, involuntary minorities respond collectively as a
> group and they also respond as individuals in ways that reinforce their
> separate existence and collective identity. Furthermore, their response
> often makes their oppositional collective identity vis-à-vis their percep-
> tions of the collective identity of the dominant group. That is, their very
> attempts to solve their status problem lead them to develop a new sense
> of who they are, that is in opposition to their understanding of who the
> dominant group members are. (p. 5)

Resulting actions can be seen at the community level, such as engaging
in collective struggle to eliminate segregation or to provide a new system of
education for the community. Actions can also be seen at the family level, by
keeping children out of particular activities or educational systems that

would be degrading to their identity. And finally, actions can be seen at the individual student level, by engaging in behaviors either that are in opposition to those expected within the dominant culture or that give up one's identity by trying to pass as a member of the dominant culture.

Summary

The United States is made up of countless groups of people—their cultures, their traditions, and their identities. Immigrants have come to the United States from all regions of the world, bringing with them their hopes for a positive future for themselves and for their children. Their efforts, though, are often complicated by the reactions of the people of the United States and the policies of the U.S. government regarding immigration. Virtually every group of immigrants, other than Protestants from western and northern Europe, has been restricted from immigrating at some point during the last 150 years. Through exclusion and restriction acts, immigrants from most countries have been restricted from coming to the United States. These restrictions are based in part on economic fears of loss of jobs and in part on perceived superiority of the dominant culture. The impact of these perceptions is felt by students of immigrant families. Although wanting to fit in and to be accepted by classmates from their new country while holding the traditions and beliefs that are part of their original culture, immigrant and refugee children face difficult challenges in trying to construct their identities in their new country.

When the first immigrants arrived on the land that is now the United States, they encountered Native Americans who already had established their own cultures, traditions, and languages. Thus began the practice of imposition and segregation. The dominant culture of the United States imposed its legal and cultural systems onto Native Americans, even setting up boarding schools purposefully to change Native American children into "Americans." African Americans also were imposed on thorough the legacy of slavery. African Americans and Mexican Americans, among others, have been segregated away from mainstream society through legal and informal policies. The impact of these impositions is that individuals may react to them by developing what is called "oppositional identity." In the attempt to keep their sense of who they are as positive human beings, many people will develop a way of living, believing, and perceiving the world that doesn't necessarily align with that of the dominant culture but allows them to maintain their self-respect. The behaviors that result can be seen in language, communication styles, appearance styles, and expectations for education and employment.

Hernandez (2004) summarizes the key trends in immigration and imposition that need to be considered and studied as we move through the twenty-first century.

First, attention needs to be paid to the role of racial and ethnic discrimination and intergroup relations as they affect children and youth in immigrant and native-born families, either similarly or differently. Second, particular attention should be paid to neighborhood and cross-national social networks, to family traditions and expectations, and to connections to ethnic communities and resources tithing the United States. Third, these issues must be addressed in the context of the great diversity of children and youth in immigrant and native-born families regarding their economic opportunities, their race and ethnicity, their family structure, their socioeconomic status, their economic opportunities, their race and ethnicity, their family circumstances, the social contexts in which they live, and their language and culture. (p. 416)

Reflective Writings

1. *History of the Treatment of a Specific Ethnic Group.* The majority of people in the United States have been treated in a number of different and often conflicting ways throughout the history of the United States. Using examples and discussion from this chapter and from any knowledge you have from other sources, describe how one specific group has been treated throughout U.S. history during different periods, in terms of immigration policies, Americanization, and segregation.

2. *Crucial Events in the Social History of the United States.* Make a chart of what you feel are the ten most crucial events in the social history of the United States that help explain why our educational system is the way it is today. These may be specific educational court cases; they may be incidents of social and racial tension; they may be proclamations by the U.S. government regarding a specific group of people. Explain why you feel that the events you have selected have played such an important role in multicultural education.

3. *Examining a Current Issue throughout History.* Select an issue of concern within your community or school system (for example, bilingualism, concerns over jobs, immigration). Describe how that issue has been treated throughout the last 150 years in the United States using discussions from the chapter or from your own knowledge and experiences.

4. *Classrooms throughout U.S. Educational History.* The educational system has been organized in several different ways over time, specifically to encourage the results desired during different periods. From Americanization, to segregation, to the school of today, reflect on or imagine what the classrooms might have looked like over different times in history. You may reflect on a number of classroom components, such as the following: goals of education, who is to be taught, materials used in the classroom, perspective from which the materials and the teaching is drawn, physical arrangement of the classroom, assessment techniques. How do these descriptions of the classroom reflect the goals for the period?

5. *Traditions within Your Community.* Think about a traditional gathering in your culture or your community (for example, Fourth of July or Día De Los Muertos). Now imagine if you were barred from holding that community event or, if it were to be allowed, that no persons under the age of 50 could take part. Make a list of the traditions, beliefs, and values in your community that would be altered or lost as a result of community members not being allowed to continue the festivities, of not being allowed to pass those traditions on to the younger generations. Then describe how your culture would be changed in the long run by losing the traditions that have been banned.

6. *Ethnic History in Your Community.* Do some research and find out the different ethnicities of groups of people who have lived in your community throughout history. Has any particular group moved in and then moved out over time? Have certain groups held certain positions in your community more than others? Can you trace the current practices or institutions within your community that began with the traditions of a particular group?

7. *Deciding Who Should Be Admitted to the United States.* Assume you have the responsibility for setting the standards for acceptance of refugees into the United States. Here are some suggestions that you have received from your constituents:

— The educational background and skills of refugees

— The wealth or poverty of refugees

— The refugees' ability to speak English

— The religion of refugees

— The race of refugees

— The age of refugees

— The refugees' family connections to the United States

— The refugees' belief in democracy

— The refugees' belief in capitalism

— The number of refugees for which the United States feels a special responsibility because it contributed to the refugee problem (for example, the Vietnam War)

— The number of refugees for which the United States feels a special responsibility because it wants to end a certain type of political system (for example, Communism)

For each, indicate whether this standard: 1 = should not be considered; 2 = don't know or can't decide; 3 = maybe should be considered; 4 = should definitely be considered.

Once you have completed this checklist (1) lay out the profile of the type of person who you would allow into the United States with refugee status; (2) describe how U.S. society would be affected by the types of refugees who could and could not enter the country, and (3) if possible, discuss your results with classmates.

8. *Revisiting the Development of Prejudice.* In chapter 2, a number of theories were proposed to help explain the development of prejudice: racial and cultural difference theory, economic competition theory, traumatic experience theory, frustration-aggression theory, and social control theory. Reflect on how the development of prejudice has affected the treatment of people over time within the United States. Selecting one specific group of people, discuss how prejudice toward that group over time may have developed based on as many of the theories of prejudice you feel apply in the case of that group.

9. *Ideas for Working with New Immigrants.* Reflect on what would be required for new immigrants to fit into either your community or your school. What resources are available within your community or your school that would be helpful for people new to the community? Prepare a guide for possible new immigrants to your community or your school, listing and describing the information and resources that are available for their use if needed.

Chapter Four

Classroom Orientations and Learning Styles

Identity Development Related to Classroom Orientations and Learning Styles

Much of the relation between practices in schools and the social construction of identities has been discussed in the preceding three chapters. In discussions of culture, for instance, it can be seen that there are multiple cultural ways of life, which include communication, organizational, and intellectual styles. These cultural ways of life are what children know and understand as they enter school. Within the school, though, there has been an insistence that students learn the dominant culture's way of life. From speech patterns and language, to ways of thinking, to views of time and space, the educational system in the United States has privileged and promoted one set of styles and patterns over all others. When adding in the access to power held by those of the dominant culture, the issues of prejudice and race also enter into the schools' practices that affect their students' identity development.

This chapter looks at an additional variable in the social construction of identities: the attitude of teachers toward their students. Since students spend thousands of hours with their teachers over their lifetime, the ways that the teachers view and perceive their students will have an initial impact that will continue for years on those students' identities. Sometimes teachers will have preconceived notions of how well they believe a student will achieve. These notions are often based on race, gender, or income level. The important point here is how teachers will treat students who have characteristics that are different from their own. Be it cultural ways of thinking or physical appearance, the teacher has the opportunity to judge each student, and whether that judgment is negative or positive will have a great impact on the student's identity development.

In addition to characteristics such as culture and race, another set of characteristics will become visible in the classroom. Those characteristics are the learning styles and the various different intelligences used by students in their learning processes. Although schools traditionally have required students to learn in a very structured environment, with patterns of participation and ways of thinking already preestablished, not all students fit into that traditional teaching–learning setting. Some learn better with different types of settings and methods. These differences in learning styles are some of the main reasons for misunderstandings and for the mislabeling of student achievement. When the teacher rigidly adheres to only one style or pattern, many students are left out, unable to achieve or to develop a positive sense of accomplishment and self-esteem. Teachers, it will be argued here, need to look at student differences in learning, in cultural background, and in race, gender, and income, not as problems to be overcome, but rather as positive resources from which draw in their development of new knowledge and in fostering positive effects on an ever-developing identity.

Preliminary Activities

Individual Activity

For this activity, you will need to think about your own teaching practices. If you are currently in teacher education courses preparing to become a teacher, reflect on what you believe your practices will be. When you have a student or students who are struggling in your class, what reasons would you give for their failure or their struggles? On what would you focus your efforts to explain their failure? Here are three possibilities that will be discussed in this chapter. Do you assume that they lack the characteristics needed to succeed in your class? Do you assume that their home life is lacking in the proper educational experiences or encouragement? Do you consider the possibility that your school or classroom is not meeting the learning needs of those students?

Small Group Discussion

Discuss the views that you just reflected upon. What are the implications of each of these different assumptions or considerations for how your classroom would operate? What would be the implications for the students in your classroom? Extend the discussion of the different assumptions to society as a whole. What are the implications of each of these different assumptions or considerations for how society operates, and for the different people in society?

Teachers' Attitudes toward Students

Deficiency Orientation and Difference Orientation

There are many ways that teachers view students, depending on the teachers' orientations toward culture, race, learning styles, and so on. Since the 1960s, however, two main ways to view students have emerged: the deficiency orientation and the difference orientation. These two views of students are similar in that they are both attempts to understand why a student is learning or is struggling in the classroom. However, they are distinct in a number of ways. The key distinctions involve *who* is seen as needing to change or improve and whether or not there is a belief that there is *one way* of learning or solving problems to which all students must adhere.

Deficiency Orientation

The deficiency orientation can be defined by its own name—deficiency. A teacher holding the deficiency orientation believes that a student is deficient in something, is lacking something, something that the teacher feels the student should have in order to succeed properly. When the deficiency orientation is used to explain the behaviors of individuals in society or of students in the classroom, the emphasis is placed on assumed deficiencies within the individuals or within their family and community. This orientation became popularized in the educational literature of the 1960s, when writers such as Frost and Hawkes (1966) wrote about children who were failing or struggling: "The impoverishment of their lives is so severe that failure is a natural consequence." Beck and Saxe (1969), in the same vein, claimed: "These are socially disadvantaged children because they are denied the experiences of normal children."

What is it that the teacher thinks is lacking in the student? Generally, the assumption of the teacher is that there is a single standard of knowledge, a single way of knowing. If a student does not think or perform in that way, then that student is deficient. Thus, there is always a comparison between what the teacher knows and expects and what the student knows and expects. This is almost always a comparison between the abilities, ways of thinking, and cultural resources that the teacher has and with which he or she is familiar. Teachers who use this orientation in their thinking about students believe that there is a mainstream way of thinking and acting, and they then go on to focus on students' comparative deficiencies in these areas. Nieto (2004a) lists some of these "so-called deficits."

> Singled out for blame were children's *poorly developed language* (more concretely, the fact that they did not speak standard English); an *inadequate mother* (the assumption being that low-income Black mothers were invariably poor parents); *too little stimulation* in the home (that their homes lacked the kinds of environments that encouraged learning); *too much stimulation* in the home (their homes were too chaotic and disorganized or simply not organized along middle-class norms); and a host of other, often contradictory hypotheses. (p. 255)

The result is often a lowered set of expectations. If the teacher believes that a student is deficient in some "normal" area, then the teacher will believe that it is not possible for that student to succeed in that area.

This strategy of claiming a deficiency in the student's home or community life has become widespread since the 1960s. In both school and societal settings, there are outcries over the lack of family values and the impact of this on the schooling of children. In fact, much of the outcry is over how "those" students harm the education of "normal" students. Furthermore, some teachers who hold the deficiency orientation have great concern for the insidious nature of poverty. These teachers end up blaming the child's failing in school on poverty rather than trying to discover and address the learning needs of these children.

In short, the deficiency orientation allows teachers to put the responsibility for the students' failure on the students and then to ask the students to change. A response that I have received from several of my preservice teacher education students represents this deficiency orientation, when they write, "When in Rome, do what the Romans do. When students are in my class, they do what I do." A statement that encapsulates this belief is *I could teach these students better if they were just more like me.*

The story of Bing's classroom, described in Figure 4.1, gives an example of some of the characteristics of a deficiency-oriented classroom. As you read Figure 4.1, note the way that the teacher treats Bing's written work and ideas. Also note the way the other students in the class treat Bing in a similarly degrading way, possibly taking the lead from their teacher. The effects on Bing's identity include his almost crying out for someone to recognize his linguistic strengths, and the limiting of his future possibilities by denying him access to creative learning. As a result, note how the teacher's deficiency orientation toward Bing has affected her treatment of him, Bing's classmates' treatment toward him, and the resulting effects on Bing's identity. The next section describes a different way of viewing a student, a way that allows Bing's strengths to be encouraged in the classroom.

Difference Orientation

Another approach to use with a struggling student is called the difference orientation. In this orientation, the teacher does not assume that the student is wrong or deficient. The teacher does not blame the student's family life or community. The teacher who holds the difference orientation, instead, sees the student's characteristics as different, not deficient. This teacher will see the differences not as wrong but rather as possible strengths that could be built upon in the teaching–learning situation.

Teachers who hold this orientation carefully examine their own ways of teaching and also take responsibility for examining the curriculum of the classroom and the structure of the school to find a way to build upon the unique strengths of students who do not fit the mainstream profile. A statement that encapsulates this belief is *I could teach these students better if I just knew*

Bing is a fourth grader in a suburban elementary school. He speaks his native Chinese fluently and speaks English well, though with a Chinese accent and some nonstandard grammar. His English vocabulary is not as large as many of his native English-speaking classmates. He is proud of his ability to speak two such different languages. He attends Chinese school on weekends and is learning to read and write Chinese.

His teacher heavily corrects all Bing's written work in red pen and constantly corrects Bing's grammar, vocabulary, and accent in class. His classmates have adopted the same pattern. Bing wishes his teacher and classmates acknowledged and appreciated his bilingual strengths rather than being critical of his mistakes in English grammar, vocabulary, and pronunciation. When he looks at the papers he gets back, he is distressed to find so much emphasis on the mistakes he has made rather than on the content he has written about. He wants to know what his teachers think of what he has written, not just of the mistakes he has made. He also wishes there was somewhere in school where the fact that he is bilingual would be seen as an asset, as something special and important about him. He wants other students to listen to his good ideas in games and appreciate how well he draws and figures things out.

When students in his class were selected to work with a visiting poet-in residence, Bing was not selected. His teacher said that was because his English was not strong enough. Bing would love the opportunity to work with the poet and believes that his understanding of two languages helps him have a better feel about using language and could be a real help in learning to write poetry.

Reprinted with permission from *Open Minds to Equality: A Sourcebook of Learning Activities to Affirm Diversity and Promote Equality, 3/E* by Nancy Schniedewind and Ellen Davidson, 2006. Published by Rethinking Schools. www.rethinkingshcools.org

Figure 4.1 The Deficiency Orientation in the Classroom

more about them. In looking again at Bing in Figure 4.1, what could the teacher have learned about Bing that would let her see his characteristics as strengths rather than as deficiencies?

This orientation requires the teacher to take action—not to "fix" the deficient child or family, but rather to examine his or her own teaching practices to determine how to teach in a way that includes the experiences of all learners. One of the first critics of the deficit orientation, Ryan (1972), describes this shift in what the teacher puts the effort into changing:

> We are dealing, it would seem, not so much with culturally deprived children as with culturally depriving schools. And the task to be accomplished is not to revise, amend, and repair deficient children, but to alter and transform the atmosphere and operations of the school to which we commit these children. (p. 61)

Jeannie Oakes and Martin Lipton (2007) give us descriptions of teachers who use the difference orientation rather than the deficiency orientation when working with their struggling students. Judy Smith, a teacher in a low-income, diverse school in Los Angeles, describes how she utilizes the difference orientation within her teaching.

> The diversity of the 37 students in my first period economics class gives the class incredible energy. They represent countries such as the Philippines, Tonga, Vietnam, Hungary, Egypt, Mexico, Dominican Republic, Guatemala, Peru, and El Salvador. Although 77 percent speak another language at home (Spanish, Arabic, Hungarian, Tongan or Tagalog), approximately half speak English fluently. A quarter of the students are black, but not all are African American. Often students gravitate toward other students of the same race and heritage. Most English learners hesitate to speak in front of their peers.
>
> To address these realities, my students and I co-construct a positive, respectful learning community. We discuss openly the benefits of a learning community where we all learn and feel respected and valued. I consciously plan lessons that include a number of activities that ensure that the students' voices and languages are heard.
>
> The students provide me with the opportunity to learn mores about the content, the issues that affect their lives, the truths and the impact of various societal problems, and, most important, the reason teachers teach. Together we make meaning of content, day-to-day issues, and grow as human beings. (p. 63)

As we can see, rather than assuming something was wrong with the students in her class, and trying to "repair" the deficiencies, Judy takes note of the unique characteristics that the students bring to the classroom, builds on them, and takes the time to learn from her students more about their lives.

Effects of Teachers' Orientation on Students' Construction of Identities

The orientation that a teacher holds toward students in the classroom will have a major impact on each student's identity. The label of "deficient" can affect the construction of identity in similar ways as those described in the earlier chapters. These effects may range from a student developing low self-esteem to a system that puts students into tracks that prepare them for lower-status lives. By seeing students as lacking in some "normal" characteristics, almost always considered to be the cultural characteristics of the dominant culture, the teacher either ignores or overlooks the cultural characteristics that are present in every child. In effect, the teacher in this orientation looks at the student every day as someone who lacks the cultural background that the teacher feels all students should have. That is a difficult hurdle for a student to overcome.

Students feel the effects of these orientations that are held toward them. Many students, depending on their race and income level, are targeted with the deficiency approach not only in school but in society. Several authors, including Jonathan Kozol (2005) and Evans-Winters (2005), during their observations in very high-poverty areas, talked to many students who felt the impact of deficiency orientation. In her interviews with Evans-Winters (2005), an adolescent Black girl conveys that

> I think Black teachers would treat us different from White teachers, because I think some of them prejudice at that school. Like this one teacher hate to see me coming. . . . That school can't help me. They sick in the head. They can't help ghetto people. They scared. Our principal and assistant principal are scary. (p. 86)

Many students face similar identity struggles as Nicole when they are told by the media that their family or community is lacking in something. Many students whose parents do not speak English, or who are in the lowest income levels, or who live in violent communities, struggle with trying to either explain or understand that they and their parents are not really the causes for their treatment. Rather, it is the perceptions of others toward them that are negative. As Nieto (2004a) points out, it is not the student or the family that is deficient, but rather "it is the school's *perception* of student's language, culture, and class as *inadequate* and *negative,* and the subsequent devalued status of these characteristics in the academic environment, that help to explain school failure" (p. 256).

A Native American student in my class wrote to me that in attending the school on the reservation where his Montana tribe lives, with virtually all White teachers, he was easily able to distinguish deficiency-oriented from difference-oriented teachers. Deficiency-oriented teachers, as he describes them, would teach without any reference to or consideration of the culture of the Indian people of the community. These teachers made him constantly feel stupid, by not taking any time to learn about the strengths of the students and their families. The single difference-oriented teacher, on the other hand, asked parents and elders to come into the classroom to help her learn more about the culture in which she now lived. This public recognition that Indian students had strengths from which the teacher could learn, as would be expected, gave the students a sense of respect for themselves, for their culture, and also for the teacher.

Summary of Teachers' Attitudes toward Students

The deficiency orientation and the difference orientation represent two ways to view students who are failing or struggling in the classroom. A key distinction between the two is that the deficiency orientation holds that something is lacking in either the student or the student's family and community life. A teacher who holds this view will expect the student to undertake all the changes in order to be more like the cultural expectations that the teacher holds. The teacher who holds the difference orientation, on the other hand, sees the struggling student as having strengths that can be used to build upon in constructing knowledge. Rather than trying to make the student or the student's family take the blame, the difference-oriented teacher takes the more difficult path of taking the time to get to know the student, the family, and the community. This teacher will take the responsibility to provide a classroom and a school setting that will recognize the student as having valuable contributions to make to the classroom and to his or her own learning.

Very important to changing to a difference orientation is to reexamine the components of culture presented in chapter 1. By recognizing the different ways of communicating, of thinking, and of living in society as just that, as different yet equally valid, the teacher can help give meaning to students' lives. Additionally in the classroom, teachers and students can work together to construct knowledge and understanding by recognizing how the different ways of knowing can be used in the classroom. In particular, the difference-oriented teacher will work to understand and examine the learning styles, strategies, and intelligences of students in the classroom.

Learning Styles and Intelligences

Preliminary Activities

Individual Activity

Think about the setting that you most prefer when you are studying. Do you like to work with other people? Do you need silence? Do you feel you learn better sitting at a desk? On a comfortable chair? On the floor? Write down as many characteristics of your preferred learning environment as you can.

Small Group Discussion

In a small group, list all the components of the learning settings of each person in the group. Which characteristics are preferred by several people in the group?

There are many different ways of approaching the learning environment. For some people, learning takes place more naturally in nonstructured environments. Some like to explore and come up with, on their own, the meanings of events and ideas. For some people, the structured and task-oriented environment provides a better learning setting. Some like to have guidance from an authority in their learning process. The deficiency-oriented teacher will see people who veer from the mainstream ways of learning as lacking in the characteristics needed to succeed in the classroom. The difference-oriented teacher, in contrast, will recognize that there are many different preferred ways of learning, and that these styles may not be what are expected.

Instead of deeming the learning style of student as inappropriate, then, this teacher will learn about the student's way of approaching learning and will provide opportunities for the student to be successful by providing a variety of learning environments in the classroom.

Learning Styles and Strategies

The terms *learning styles* and *learning strategies* refer to the ways that students approach a learning situation. Whether it is learning in the classroom, studying for an exam, or gaining new information from a community or from work, individuals tend to display fairly consistent patterns of learning behaviors. Once these patterns have been established, we tend to stay with these styles and strategies and to feel uncomfortable if we are asked to learn in a different style. We actually learn better if our learning is consistent with our learning styles and strategies.

The purpose of studying learning styles and strategies is for teachers to ensure the most effective teaching strategies for all students. As Brown (2003) explains, "When students' learning preferences match their instructors' learning styles, student motivation and achievement usually improve" (abstract). The rest of this chapter, then, describes the components of learning styles, learning style inventories, and how teachers can teach in ways that will address the multiple learning styles and strategies held by students in their classrooms. The result for teachers will be the opportunity to use the difference orientation to provide the optimum learning environment for all students.

The definitions of learning styles and learning strategies are different, but they share some key basic points. Think again about your preferred setting for learning. Does that remain fairly consistent? Has it changed over time? Is it different for different subject matter? These questions get at the heart of the differences between styles and strategies of learning.

Learning styles are considered to be consistent over time. The definition of learning style adopted by the National Task Force on Learning Style is "that consistent pattern of behavior and performance by which an individual approaches educational experiences." The definition continues: "It is the composite of characteristic cognitive, affective, and physiological behaviors that serve as relatively stable indicators of how a learner perceives, interacts with, and responds to the learning environment" (Keefe and Languis, 1983, p. 1). This consistent, stable nature of our patterns of learning is what is referred to as our learning style.

Learning strategies, on the other hand, are defined as "the techniques or skills that an individual elects to use in order to accomplish a learning task" (Fellenz and Conti, 1993, p. 1). The key phrase in this definition is that "an individual elects to use" a learning strategy. In other words, the idea is that we have several learning strategies available for our use, and we, knowing the situation, will select the one that best works for us at that particular time.

Learning styles and learning strategies are similar in that they both describe the ways that an individual approaches a learning situation. There is some debate over whether these learning approaches are formed in our genetic makeup and are part of our biological nature. Learning styles are considered to be more of a stable part of our personality, whereas learning strategies are selected based not only on our internal characteristics or style but also on the external situation or the context. But in both types of learning approaches, it is clear that our learning has been in large part shaped and molded by our experiences.

Components of Learning Styles

Physical Settings

The physical setting is one critical component of the study of learning styles. From your group discussion, you can recognize that a large number of characteristics of physical settings will differ from learner to learner. These characteristics of learning settings can be described as environmental. Many characteristics of the learning environment can be placed under the categories of light, temperature, design, and sound. These characteristics of the learning setting have a range of meanings that vary from individual to individual. For instance, the type of light a learner prefers when studying can be described in a continuum of very dim to very bright. Furthermore, that light can be natural sunlight or it can be artificial light either indoors or outside at night. The preferred temperature of a learning setting can range from quite cool to quite warm. In thinking of the design of the preferred learning setting, there are a number of variables. For instance, some learners will prefer to study in a formal setting that is designed specifically for the purposes of studying, such as a library. Others will like to work in an informal setting, such as a cafe or dormitory lounge. Relating to the sound characteristics of the learning setting, some learners prefer to learn in silence, whereas others prefer to have some noise while studying. But the type of noise can vary widely, from music playing in the background, to the noise of nearby conversations, to the sounds of a nearby river. Additionally, some learners will regard these noises as background to their learning, whereas others will interact with the noise, for example, by singing along to a song.

Have you identified some of these characteristics as part of your preferred learning setting? Some of these characteristics may be crucial to your learning setting, whereas others may play no role at all. On the other hand, you may prefer all these at one point or another. Can you describe the type of light, temperature, design, and sound you prefer when studying?

Social Settings

When you imagined your preferred learning setting, did you imagine other people present within that setting? Several social groupings are common for learners who are studying. One grouping is to work with other people while learning. But this social arrangement can be met with several combinations. Do you like to share your studying with other people? If so, do you work with one partner, sharing the responsibilities for learning? Or do you like to work within a group where members support one another but do not require any particular level of commitment to consistently work within that group? Or do you work in groups in which every group member has a specific role to play to contribute to the final group project? In each of these examples, the learner prefers to work with other people while studying.

Another social grouping is that a learner prefers to study alone, not sharing any of the studying with other people. This characteristic can have several meanings for learners, since different arrangements allow the learner to study alone. Do any of the following arrangements describe your preferred learning social grouping: Totally alone in a room while studying? Studying in a public place with other people in the room, but sitting alone at your own table? Sitting with others at a table but studying individually at that table? In each of these examples, the learner prefers to work alone, without sharing or giving any responsibility for learning to any other people.

Learning Senses

Although the environmental and social factors of learning styles help set a pattern for learning related to the environment in which we study, equally important are the senses used by the learner. In this section, we examine the senses, or modality preferences, that we use when learning. Learning occurs through all of our senses, often with multiple senses simultaneously and on occasion through a single sense. The senses referred to most often in education are visual, auditory, kinesthetic, and tactile. These learning sense describe how we interpret the subject matter and the presentation of material.

- Visual: reading, watching a video
- Auditory: listening
- Kinesthetic: practicing, role playing
- Tactile: writing, building, or constructing

Can you determine which learning sense is the most effective for you in your learning? Remember that combinations of these learning senses are extremely common. For example, I use the visual and tactile learning senses concurrently when I take notes while reading or watching a video. I seem to need to use both reading and writing in conjunction with each other in order to learn and reinforce information most effectively for me. Another combination is when someone uses both visual and auditory learning senses, when they repeat verbally what they are reading concurrently. Which of the learning senses do you feel are the most effective for you? In what combination? Which learning senses are most commonly stressed in schools?

Cognitive Learning Styles

The basic idea behind cognitive learning styles is that learners approach new information in different ways. Some learners like to learn in a step-by-step process, moving in a sequential order through the material.

These learners would prefer to begin with the details of the information, moving toward the end goal, which they plan to reach at the end of their work. Some terms used to describe this type of cognitive style are analytic, sequential, left-brained, and concrete. Other learners prefer to think of the whole picture, desiring to have a grasp of the overall goals and ideas to know where they are headed before they begin learning. Some of the terms used to describe this cognitive style include global, relational, right-brained, and holistic.

Learning Style Inventories

Over the last several decades, at least 30 different instruments for assessing learning styles have been developed, analyzed, used in classrooms, and criticized. Some of these instruments measure the physiological aspects of one's learning style, such as those involved in the physical setting. Some instruments measure the cognitive styles of approaching learning. Some instruments measure affective or emotional involvement in learning, including attention and motivational factors. And a few other instruments attempt to determine how these aspects combine to create a learning style. Table 4.1 gives a list of some representative types of learning style inventories that are often used to determine learning styles.

Discussions of four sample learning style inventories follow here. First, the Edmonds Learning Style Identification Exercise (ELSIE) is an inventory that can be used in the classroom to determine students' perceptual modality preferences, or learning senses. Second, the Kolb Learning Style Inventory helps understand the learners' cognitive style and the types of experiences that different students find most helpful in their learning. Third, the Witkin Hidden Figures Test gives a measure of the students' cognitive styles as well, focusing on the students' relation to their learning and social environment. And fourth, the Dunn and Dunn Learning Styles Inventory provides a way to understand the students' learning styles as a whole, looking at the complex mixture of the many multiple components of learning. These sample learning style inventories provide examples of what learning style research attempts to offer to teachers in their efforts to meet the needs of all of their students.

Edmonds Learning Style Identification Exercise (ELSIE)

The ELSIE helps teachers and learners recognize learners' strengths in what is called perceptual modalities, or what in this chapter is called the learning senses. In this exercise, students are read a list of 50 common English words. Students are then asked to write on their answer sheet their reactions:

1. Visualization: a mental picture or image
2. Written word: imagining the word spelled out
3. Listening: the sound of the word with no visual image attached
4. Activity: a physical or an emotional feeling about the word

Table 4.1 Representative Learning Style Inventories

Edmonds Learning Style Identification Exercise (ELSIE)

- Helps determine students' strongest areas of perceptual learning.
- Reinert, Harry. "One Picture is Worth a Thousand Words? Not Necessarily!" *The Modern Language Journal, 60* (1976).

Kolb Learning Style Inventory

- Helps determine the type of activity and experience most commonly used by the learner when learning something new
- Kolb, David A. *The Cycle of Learning*. (McBer and Company, 1993).
- Kolb, David A., Experiential Learning: Experience as the Source of Learning and Development (Englewood Cliffs, NJ: Prentice-Hall, 1984).

Hidden Figures Test

- Helps determine a learner's areas of cognitive preference, focuses on relational and analytic styles of learning.
- *Kit of Factor-Referenced Cognitive Tests* (Princeton, NJ: Educational Testing Service, 1962).
- Described further in Witkin, H. A., Moore, C., and McDonald, F. J. "Cognitive Style and the Teaching/Learning Processes." Paper presented at the annual meeting of the American Educational Research Association, 1974.

Learning Styles Inventory

- Helps determine students' holistic learning styles, including areas of strength in environmental, emotional, sociological, physical, and psychological components of learning.
- Dunn, Rita, Dunn, Kenneth, and Price, Gary E. (Lawrence, KS: Price Systems, 1989).
- Described further in Dunn, Rita and Dunn, Kenneth. Teaching Secondary Students through their Individual Learning Styles: Practical Approaches for Grades 7–12 (Boston: Allyn & Bacon, 1993).

Paragraph Completion Method

- Helps determine the amount of structure students prefer when learning.
- Hunt, David E. *Assessing Conceptual Level by the Paragraph Completion Method* (Toronto: Ontario Institute for Studies in Education, 1978).

Gregorc Learning Styles Model

- Helps determine students' cognitive styles, focuses on concrete, abstract, random, and sequential patterns of learning.
- Gregorc, A. "Learning/Teaching Styles," in *Student Learning Styles: Diagnosing and Prescribing Programs* (Reston, VA: National Association of Secondary School Principals, 1979).

This exercise is known for being especially useful in the classroom since teachers can administer the exercise during class in approximately 30 minutes. Another interesting aspect of the ELSIE is that students can write their own answers and do their own scoring, providing all with immediate feedback about the ways that students tend to learn most easily. A profile sheet is provided along with the exercise, which gives a visual representation of the learners' strengths in a graphic form. This exercise is useful in that teachers can come to understand their students' learning strengths, making it more possible for teachers to develop teaching strategies that will be most beneficial for each of the perceptual modalities indicated in the profile sheet.

Kolb Learning Style Inventory

Kolb (1984) developed a model of learning styles that focuses on the types of experiences that students engage in when learning. In his model, he lays out the experiential nature of learning. His model proposes a cycle of learning that includes the activities of concrete experience, reflective observation, abstract conceptualization, and active experimentation. In everyday terms, these activities translate to feeling, watching, thinking, and doing. Kolb proposes that, ideally, a learner will have the opportunity to learn through each of these types of activities, but that each learner will have a strength in a particular type of learning activity. Figure 4.2 lays out the characteristics of each of these learning styles within Kolb's experiential learning style cycle.

In determining which of these activities you are most comfortable with in learning, think about the following questions: Do you prefer to have personal involvement in an experience? If so, you might prefer the first link in the cycle, which is feeling or concrete experience. Do you want to observe and reflect before taking an action? This would indicate the watching or reflective observation component of the learning cycle. Do you prefer to base your thinking in theoretical and logical concepts? This would be the thinking or abstract conceptualization learning style. And finally, do you feel the need to take action and apply what you have learned to a practical situation? If so, you would most likely have the learning style of doing or active experimentation.

Table 4.2 on page 140 gives some example items and responses in the Kolb Learning Style Inventory. As Kolb describes, the Learning Style Inventory describes the way that people learn and how they deal with daily situations in life. Which of the learning styles proposed by Kolb do you feel are most effective for you? Which learning styles are most commonly stressed in schools?

Hidden Figures Test

One learning style test that has been highly researched and actively used in learning styles research is the Hidden Figures Test, which is used to determine learners' cognitive styles of learning. This test, made popular among learning styles researchers by Witkin and Moore (1974), asks learners to attempt to recognize a series of shapes that are hidden within complex pat-

Concrete Experience
— Feeling —

The learner who prefers the
concrete experience
learning style:

· Learns by intuition
· Learns through experiences
· Is sensitive to feelings
· Relates to people

Active Experimentation
— Doing —

The learner who prefers the
active experimentation
learning style:

· Learns by doing
· Has the goal of
  "getting it done"

Reflective Observation
— Watching —

The learner who prefers the
reflective observation
learning style:

· Learns by observation
· Is cautious, reflecting
  carefully before
  making judgments

Abstract Conceptualization
— Thinking —

The learner who prefers the
abstract conceptualization
learning style:

· Learns by thinking
· Prefers logical analysis
  of ideas
· Undertakes systematic
  planning

Source: Adapted from David A. Kolb, *Experiential Learning: Experience as the Source of Learning and Development* (Englewood Cliffs, NJ: Prentice-Hall, 1984).

Figure 4.2 Kolb's Experiential Learning Style Cycle

terns of lines. According to this testing procedure, those who are easily able to distinguish the selected shapes from the background patterns can be considered to be "field independent" learners. These learners are able to look at patterns—and conduct their learning—independently of their surrounding environment. Another term that is used to describe this learning style is analytical. The second learning style that can be determined by this test is the field dependent or relational learner. A basic first description of these different learning styles is that relational or field dependent learners are equally concerned with the personal relations and interactions among people as they are with the content that is covered. Relational learners "place an emphasis on affective and reality-based learning, a broad and personal approach to the

---

Table 4.2   Example Items and Responses from the Kolb Learning Style Inventory

---

The following are example items and possible responses from the Kolb Learning Style Inventory. How would you rank the choices for each situation? Can you determine which response in each case most likely would represent the concrete experience, reflective observation, abstract conceptualization, and active experimentation learning styles?

1. I learn best when:
   a. I listen and watch carefully.
   b. I rely on logical thinking.
   c. I trust my hunches and feelings.
   d. I work hard to get things done.
2. I learn best from:
   a. observation
   b. personal relationships
   c. rational theories
   d. a chance to try out and practice
3. When I learn:
   a. I like to see the results from my work.
   b. I like ideas and theories.
   c. I take my time before acting.
   d. I feel personally involved in things.

Concrete experience (feeling)	(1c, 2b, 3d)
Reflective observation (watching)	(1a, 2a, 3c)
Abstract conceptualization (thinking)	(1b, 2c, 3b)
Active experimentation (doing)	(1d, 2d, 3a)

Source: Adapted from David A. Kolb, *Experiential Learning: Experience as the Source of Learning and Development* (Englewood Cliffs, NJ: Prentice-Hall, 1984).

processing of information, a search for relevance and personal meaning in what is taught, and a need for qualitative feedback" (Anderson and Adams, 1992, p. 22). Analytical or field independent learners, on the other hand, are task and content oriented, learn well from impersonal methods, and show analytic and sequential thinking. These learning styles result in different needs for students who have these different learning styles. Table 4.3 lays out some of the key characteristics of these two different learning styles. From your own experiences in schools, do you feel that one of these learning styles is more commonly stressed within classrooms? Do you feel that any subject matters could be taught by addressing one or the other type of learning styles or through a blending of styles?

Table 4.3 Characteristics of Field Dependent or Relational and Field Independent or Analytical Learning Styles

Field Dependent or Relational Style	Field Independent or Analytical Style
• Perceive information as part of overall, global picture	• Perceive discrete parts in detail in separation from global picture
• Exhibit improvisational and intuitive thinking	• Exhibit sequential and structured thinking
• More easily learn materials that have a human, social content and that have an experiential or cultural relevance	• More easily learn materials that are inanimate and impersonal
• Prefers verbal presentations of ideas	• Prefer abstract presentation of ideas
• More person oriented	• More academic and task oriented
• Influenced by other people, works in groups	• Not greatly affected by the opinions of others, individualistic
• Externally motivated	• Internally motivated

Source: Adapted from "Acknowledging the Learning Styles of Diverse Student Populations," *New Directions for Teaching and Learning,* by James A. Anderson and Maurianne Adams. Copyright by Jossey-Bass, Inc., Publishers. Reprinted by permission.

Dunn and Dunn Learning Styles Inventory

As can be seen thus far in this chapter, numerous components make up a learner's preferred style of learning. Dunn and Dunn (1993), in recognizing these many parts of learning style, have created a learning style inventory that measures these components in the intent to gauge learning style in a holistic manner. In their work, they describe that "learning style encompasses at least 21 different variables" (p. 31). In their Learning Style Inventory (LSI), they distinguish the elements of learning styles into the different types of impact that they have on the individual. Table 4.4 lays out the different types of com-

Table 4.4 Dunn and Dunn Learning Styles Model

Environmental:	Sound	Light	Temperature	Design
Emotional:	Motivation	Persistence	Responsibility	Structure
Sociological:	Self Adult	Pair Varied	Peers	Team
Physiological:	Perceptual	Intake	Time	Mobility
Psychological	Global & Analytic Impulsive & Reflective		Hemisphericity (right–left brain)	

Source: Rita Dunn and Kenneth Dunn, *Teaching Secondary Students through Their Individual Learning Styles: Practical Approaches for Grades 7–12.* Boston: 1993 by Allyn & Bacon.

ponents that the LSI measures, including environmental, emotional, sociological, physiological, and psychological components. Environmental components include the physical setting of the learning setting, such as the level and type of sound, of light, of temperature, and the impact of the design of the room or learning setting. Emotional components involve the individual learner's sense of how much to be involved in the learning task, such as motivation, persistence, responsibility, and structure. The sociological components of learning style refer to the people that a learner prefers to work with when learning, including both the number of people and the comparative age groups of the people with whom learning will be shared. Physiological components of learning style are the perceptual preferences of the learner, or the learning senses; both the type of intake needed and the time of day in which intake is preferred (intake referring to food or drink); the time of day in which learning is more easily accomplished; and the amount of mobility that a learner would prefer during learning. And finally, the psychological aspects of learning refer to the cognitive aspects mentioned earlier in this chapter, such as whether a learner is global or analytic in approach to learning, whether the learner tends to use the left or right hemisphere when learning, and whether the learner tends to be impulsive or reflective when learning. Table 4.5 gives a few examples of the range of variability in some of these components when tested through the Learning Style Inventory. As can be seen, there is wide variation in the level and type of learning characteristics of a learner.

Learning Intelligences

When we think of the term *intelligence,* we may think of a person's IQ score. Or we may imagine a student's grade point average to indicate a certain level of intelligence. On the other hand, we may point out that although some people do not seem "book smart," they seem to have common sense.

Table 4.5 Range of Variation within Dunn and Dunn's Elements of Learning Styles

Sound while learning:	Always needs quiet when learning	Usually needs quiet when learning	It depends on what is being learned; sometimes needs quiet and sometimes does not	Often works with some kind of sound: radio, records, TV, conversation	Always or usually works with sound: radio, etc.
Design while learning:	Always does best thinking on a bed, lounge chair, floor, or carpet	Often does best thinking in an informal environment	It depends on what is being done	Thinks best on a wooden chair and desk, as in a library or a classroom	Always works in a formal setting; does not do best work unless in a "hard" chair
Persistence while learning:	Starts many things that are not finished; enjoys working on several tasks simultaneously	Only occasionally has tasks that have been started but not completed	Whether or not the learner completes what is started depends on the level of interest in that task	Usually completes the things that are begun	Always completes the things that are begun; it bothers the learner not to complete them
Learning alone:	Works best alone and gets more things done that way	Prefers doing most things alone	It depends on what needs to be done—and with whom	Prefers doing things with someone else	Likes working with others and could serve as the leader
Mobility while learning:	Can sit still for long periods when interested in what is being learned	Sitting still is not much of a problem	If interested, can sit still; if bored can't sit still	Finds it difficult to sit still for long periods	Finds it impossible to sit still for long periods

Source: Rita Dunn and Kenneth Dunn, *Teaching Secondary Students through Their Individual Learning Styles: Practical Approaches for Grades 7–12.* Boston: © 1993 by Allyn & Bacon.

And some people may seem to have special talent in one area, such as music, but are not particularly strong in other areas. A key turning point in the recognition of these different types of strengths of individuals has come with Howard Gardner's (1983) proposal of seven different types of intelligences. According to the theory of multiple intelligences, there are many different ways to approach and to learn from the stimuli within the world. Some of these are what have been traditionally considered intelligence, as measured by the IQ test, and others are what have often been considered the more creative types of thinking. Gardner (1991) describes his theory of multiple intelligences in general:

> I have posited that all human beings are capable of at least seven different ways of knowing the world—ways that I have elsewhere labeled to the seven human intelligences. . . . Where individuals differ is in the strength of these intelligences—so-called profile of intelligences—and in the ways in which such intelligences are invoked and combined to carry out different tasks, solve diverse problems, and progress in various domains. (p. 12)

As can be seen, Gardner emphasizes that we will all have some level of each of these intelligences, but we will each have our own unique pattern of strengths within the different intelligences. Table 4.6 outlines the seven different learning intelligences, and the following paragraphs describe each of the intelligences in more detail.

One of the intelligences that is specifically measured with standardized tests is linguistic intelligence, or, the ability to use words effectively. There are many different opportunities for an individual to use linguistic intelligence, since so much of U.S. society is based on the written and the spoken word. Gardner (1983) points out some of the main uses of linguistic intelligence:

> First of all, there is the rhetorical aspect of language—the ability to use language to convince other individuals of a course of language. . . . Second of all, there is the mnemonic potential of language—the capacity to use this tool to help one remember information. . . . A third aspect of language is its role in explanation. . . . Finally, there is the potential of language to explain its own activities—the ability to use language to reflect upon language. (p. 78)

A poet, a trial attorney, a comedian—these are all individuals who display a keen linguistic intelligence. Such people have a sensitivity to the meanings, patterns, and rhythms of language. They, and anybody who shares a strength in linguistic intelligence, know of the potential of language "to excite, convince, stimulate, convey information, or simply to please" (Gardner, 1983, p. 77).

A second type of intelligence that is often measured through standardized tests is logical–mathematical intelligence. This type of intelligence is described as "skills related to mathematical manipulations and discerning and solving logical problems" (Sadker and Sadker, 2003, p. 43). Logical–mathematical intelligence is obviously exemplified by the mathematician, but it is also displayed as a great strength by people who work with logic and

Table 4.6 Outline of Learning Intelligences

Linguistic Intelligence
- The ability to use words effectively—orally or in writing
- The understanding of the potential of language to convince, to remember, to explain, or to interest others
- A sensitivity to the meanings, patterns, and rhythms of language
- A poet, a trial attorney, a comedian, a journalist

Logical–Mathematical Intelligence
- An understanding of logical patterns and relationships among statements, propositions, numbers, functions, and other abstractions
- Patterns and chains of connections are sought, discovered, and put into an order
- A mathematician, an analytic philosopher, a computer programmer, a scientist

Spatial Intelligence
- A sensitivity to the visual world and the ability to recreate or interpret that mental image
- The ability to transform or modify an image into something new
- The ability to manipulate the form or the object, to appreciate how the object would be viewed from another angle, or how it would look (or feel) were it turned around
- An artist, an interior designer, a surgeon, an engineer

Interpersonal Intelligence
- The ability to understand other people and their feelings
- An ability to read the desires, intentions, and motivations of other people
- A counselor, a teacher, a salesperson

Musical Intelligence
- The ability to discern meaning and importance through music
- A recognition of the components that make up music—pitch, rhythm, and metric—and the use of those components to communicate with others
- Hearing tones, rhythms, and larger musical patterns and constantly be monitoring and reworking these patterns
- A composer, a singer

Bodily Kinesthetic Intelligence
- The ability to solve problems or communicate using the body or parts of the body
- Control over the physical movements of the body, but also an ability to get across information or feelings to others through using body motions
- The perception of the world is affected by position and status of the body
- A dancer, a mime, an athlete

Intrapersonal Intelligence
- The ability to understand one's own emotions and being able to draw upon them as a means of guiding one's behavior
- The ability to apply lessons learned from the observation of other people to oneself
- A counselor, a therapist

Naturalist Intelligence
- The ability to recognize and classify types of living things, such as plants, animals, rocks, flora, and fauna
- The ability to recognize patterns in science, as well as in everyday life
- A botanist, a farmer, a chef

Sources: Gardner, 1983; Checkley, 1997; Lazear, 1999; Sadker and Sadker, 2003.

with patterns, such as analytic philosophers and computer programmers. Individuals who have a strong logical–mathematical intelligence will be interested in and efficient at following lines of argument, the ordering of symbols, and the relationships among objects or statements. This type of individual, as Gardner (1983) writes, is "more able to appreciate the actions that one can perform upon objects, the relations that obtain among those actions, the statements (or propositions) that one can make about actual or potential chains, and the relationships among those statements" (p. 129). When the world is approached using logical–mathematical intelligence, patterns and chains of connections are sought, discovered, and put into an order by the individual who is attempting to make sense of the world.

Spatial intelligence is a third type of intelligence: "This domain involves uncanny sensitivity to the visual world and the ability to re-create or interpret that mental image" (MILS). A few key abilities seem to be most strongly attached to this type of intelligence. This intelligence revolves around being able to create or re-create an image and not only to see an image but to transform it or modify it into something new. In what Gardner calls the "spatial realm," a person with spatial intelligence will be able to manipulate objects either physically or in the mind. An individual who has a strength in spatial intelligence will be able to "manipulate the form or the object, appreciating how it will be apprehended from another viewing angle, or how it would look (or feel) were it turned around" (Gardner, 1983, p. 174). People in such varied professions as artist, interior designer, and surgeon display spatial intelligence every day in their practices. Artists are able to transform a physical object or a mental image into a new interpretation. An interior designer can look at an open space and imagine how that space could be filled to effect a pleasing visual result. And a surgeon must both imagine and be able to physically manipulate various tools within a complex set of physical objects within an enclosed space.

A fourth intelligence is musical intelligence: "the abilities of individuals to discern meaning and importance through music" (Gardner, 1983, p. 101). Anyone who performs musically, either in public or in private, is displaying musical intelligence. People with musical intelligence can recognize the components that make up music—pitch, rhythm and metric—and can also use those components to communicate with others. They can vary pitch and alter rhythm in order to communicate different feelings. But Gardner defines composers as exemplars of musical intelligence. For the composer, as Gardner (1983) describes, "is always, somewhere near the surface of his consciousness, hearing tones, rhythms, and larger musical patterns . . . constantly to be monitoring and reworking these patterns" (p. 101). This strong sense of musical intelligence means that the person approaches the world by translating many of the ideas and objects into musical patterns that can then be understood and appreciated in a musical sense.

Bodily kinesthetic intelligence is "the ability to solve problems or communicate using the body or parts of the body" (MILS). As Cook (1997) writes,

"This special ability includes physical skills such as coordination, balance, dexterity, strength, flexibility, and speed." Although dancers and athletes are often considered to have high bodily kinesthetic intelligence, the consummate user of this type of intelligence would be the person who performs as a mime. The general characteristic of this intelligence is "the ability to use one's body in highly differentiated and skilled ways, for expressive as well as goal-directed purposes" (Gardner, 1983, p. 206). To have a strength in this intelligence means that not only is there control over the physical movements of the body, but also that there is an ability to get across information or feelings to others through using body motions. This use of the body to actually give information is the reason the mime is considered to be such a strong possessor and user of bodily kinesthetic intelligence. But Gardner also points out that not only is the body used to communicate to others, it is also a filter through which the world is perceived. Gardner (1983) writes: "the individual's perception of the world is itself affected by the status of his motor activities: information concerning the position and status of the body itself regulates the way in which subsequent perception of the world takes place" (p. 211).

The next two intelligences fall within the realm of what Gardner calls personal intelligences. Both interpersonal intelligence and intrapersonal intelligence involve a sort of social reading of people, of being able to understand how people feel, behave, and what they desire. Interpersonal intelligence is "the ability to understand other people and their feelings" (MILS). For people such as teachers or counselors, there is a strength in the ability to read the desires, intentions, and motivations of other people. In addition to recognizing the feelings of others, though, people who have interpersonal intelligence have the potential to use that knowledge in order to help others strengthen themselves. Intrapersonal intelligence involves the same sorts of abilities, but this time in relation to oneself. Gardner (1983) describes this type of intelligence as having "access to one's own feeling life—one's range of affects or emotions . . . [and also the ability] to draw upon them as a means of understanding and guiding one's behavior" (p. 239). These two types of personal intelligences are inexorably tied together because knowledge of both oneself and of others requires the same type of understanding of emotions and motivations. Gardner (1983) describes how these are tied together:

> These two forms of knowledge are intimately intermingled in any culture, with knowledge of one's own person perennially dependent upon the ability to apply lessons learned from the observation of other people, while knowledge of others draws upon the internal discriminations the individual routinely makes. (p. 241)

And finally, Gardner later added the Naturalist intelligence as an eighth type of intelligence (Checkley, 1997; Lazear, 1999). Gardner describes in an interview with Checkley that he began to wonder about the great biologists throughout history, such as Darwin. He wondered how they could classify natural items or living beings with such great ease. Creating and enlarging taxonomies, he began to realize, required a type of intelligence that he had not yet considered. Because of the facility with which these naturalists dealt with the natural world, Gardner (naturally!) labeled his eighth intelligence the Naturalist intelligence. But it was not only famous scientists that could be considered as having this type of ability. In our human past, hunters were able to distinguish animals and birds, and hunters and gatherers were able to distinguish plants that would provide human nutrients as opposed to those that would be toxic to humankind. Currently, Gardner includes botanists and chefs as exemplars of the Naturalist intelligence.

Can you determine which intelligences are strengths for you? Do you approach your daily life with any of these particular intelligences consistently at the forefront?

Gardner suggests that the assessment of learning intelligences should be done under natural circumstances. One possibility for assessment is to determine which types of patterns an individual is more likely to use and to remember. Strengths in different intelligences should be apparent in the different patterns that people remember and use consistently. For instance, a musical intelligence would be shown when an individual continues to replay a musical pattern in his or her mind. Spatial intelligence would be seen when an individual is able to recognize a spatial pattern, and even a rotated or transformed pattern, over time. Bodily kinesthetic intelligence would be shown in the ability to learn motor patterns quickly and to be able to transform them into new movement patterns. Gardner suggests that the best way to determine strengths in learning intelligences in the classroom is to observe the way that children interact within the classroom, with such things as puzzles, games, objects, and people. If a child enjoys telling stories or doing crossword puzzles, that may indicate a strong linguistic intelligence. If a child seems to enjoy using blocks to construct objects, that may indicate a strong bodily kinesthetic intelligence. And if a child consistently tries to comfort other children in the classroom, that may indicate a strong interpersonal intelligence.

Recognition of Learning Styles and Intelligences

One way for schools and teachers to avoid considering the possibility that they may need to change their teaching strategies is to adopt the deficiency orientation. By doing this, teachers can "place complete responsibility for children's failure on their homes and families, effectively reducing the responsibility of the school and society. . . . [thereby] blaming the victims of poor schooling rather than looking in a more systematic way at the schools in which they learn (or fail to learn) and the society at large" (Nieto, 2004a, p. 3). This can be seen in the story of Bing, where the teacher did not question the teaching and assessment methods used in the class. Had the teacher examined her teaching practices, she may have found some creative ways to help Bing use his linguistic strengths in the classroom. For instance, she could have set up cooperative groups in which students could teach each other in their own languages. She could have assigned creative writing projects that allow students to use metaphors or folklore from their own language or dialect to enhance their Standard English writing. Perhaps she could have set up learning centers around the classroom at which students could investigate many different styles of writing—summaries, restatements of main ideas, poetry, biographical writing, and so on. These and numerous other ideas could have been developed if the teacher had shifted away from the deficiency orientation and toward the difference orientation. It is likely that not only would Bing have benefited from such a reexamination of teaching practices but other children would have benefited as well. Perhaps if the teacher had made an effort to address the various learning styles, intelligences, and interests of each student in her classroom, *all* students would have had the chance to maximize their learning opportunities and outcomes.

It is clear that there are many different ways of learning. Now, are there ways to meet all these different learning approaches and needs of students in the classroom? Think of all the teaching strategies that you have seen from being a student from kindergarten to the college level. Of those many teaching activities, do some match more closely to specific learning styles and strategies? Can each teaching strategy be altered to address the multiple needs of all the students? Teachers can develop their own ideas for matching teaching strategies with learning styles and strategies by determining the learning styles and strategies of their students. By then reflecting on their own teaching strategies, teachers can make the alterations in their approaches to make sure they address the needs of all of their students.

Questions and Concerns about the Learning Styles Approach

Ladson-Billings (1992) explains some of the criticisms of the learning styles approach in the classroom. These basically revolve around whether there is sufficient evidence to warrant the use of the learning styles approach as a way to improve students' academic achievement. She writes:

> The learning styles research is open to criticism on several levels. First, only a few styles (for example, field-dependence/independence, reflection/impulsivity) have been extensively researched. Second, this research is rarely linked to issues regarding teachers' learning styles and/or teaching styles. And, perhaps most importantly, there is little evidence to suggest that distinguishing students according to their learning styles makes any significant differences in their academic performance. Each of these areas requires further exploration before we can accept or reject the saliency of learning styles as a way of addressing the educational needs of students. (p. 108)

Critics of the learning styles approach suggest that perhaps more important than the learning styles of students is the attitude of the teacher, that the awareness of the teacher should be focused more on the teachers' style rather than on the learning styles of the students. Gregorc (1979) has even found that teachers who attempt to teach with teaching styles that are different from their own preferences for learning have levels of discomfort when teaching. As he writes, "Teachers whose teaching styles closely approximate their *major learning preferences* report comfort, ease, and authenticity. . . . Those who consistently instruct via minor styles report feelings of awkwardness, lack of efficiency and authenticity, and pain—mental and physical" (p. 24). Several key questions about the importance of both learners' and teachers' styles arise from these criticisms.

Do Learning Styles and Strategies Develop as Part of the Learner's Culture?

For people who answer this question yes, they believe the learning styles and strategies of individuals are tied in part to the cultural group of which they are a part. More specifically, the cultural patterns and traditions of individuals and groups have led people to have culturally specific ways of looking at the world. As described in chapter 1, the way people understand their world is shaped by their culture's history, traditions, and ways of thinking. In addition, each culture provides its own particular styles of communication, patterns of interaction, and ways of knowing. It is the complex interaction of these patterns of living that shape how people act and how they expect others to act. In addition, these cultural backgrounds, styles of communication, patterns of interaction, and ways of knowing play a part in shaping the learning styles and strategies of the individual student as well—as Anderson (1988) describes it, "Different cultures produce different learning styles." Anderson continues: "It would seem feasible that different ethnic groups with different cultural histories, different adaptive approaches to reality, and different socialization practices would differ concerning their respective cognitive/learning styles" (p. 4). Irvine and York (1995) describe the interaction of culture, group, and individual:

> Although it is clear that culture, particularly ethnicity, is a powerful force that influences students' predispositions toward learning, it must be emphasized that cultural practices are learned behavior that can be unlearned and modified. . . . Consequently, culture affects individuals in different ways . . . culture is constantly evolving and that although some students may share the same cultural background and predispositions, not all members of the same cultural group behave in identical ways. (p. 492)

In general, then, "it appears that culture and ethnicity are frameworks for the development of learning-styles preferences" (Irvine and York, p. 492).

However, as in the previous discussion, there have been challenges to the view that learning styles are tied to culture. Nieto (2004a) summarizes some of the reasons why this view has been challenged:

> Some of the early research in this field concentrated on ethnic and racial differences in learning, a perspective that can skirt dangerously close to

racist perceptions of differences in IQ. As such, it has been the subject of some controversy and criticism. There are vast differences among learners within ethnic groups, and these differences may be due not just to culture but to social class, language spoken at home, number of years or generations in the United States, and simple individual differences. Social class, for example, has been proposed as equally or more important than ethnicity in influencing learning. (pp. 149–150)

Should Teachers Attempt to Match Their Teaching Strategies to Their Students' Learning Styles?

A key criticism of the learning styles approach is that not enough research has been conducted to claim that this approach is helpful in improving academic achievement. Dunn and Dunn (1993), however, list more than 100 research studies that study the relationship of learning styles to school performance (pp. 453–469). These range from studying the effects of using the learning styles approach in the classroom on students' attitudes, academic achievement, and study habits. These studies examine the effects of learning styles approaches ranging from the ages of K–12, to the university level, to employees in business.

Another concern in this area is over whether teachers should discover each student's learning style and then provide each student primarily with the teaching that matches the student's particular learning style. If this were to happen, students would always have the opportunity to learn with the learning styles and strategies that are most beneficial for them. On the other hand, perhaps if students were allowed to learn in only one way consistently, they might miss some experiences that could teach them something new. Perhaps, the argument goes, students can learn about the perspectives and experiences that many people share. Students should not become static in their learning, so perhaps they should be exposed to different types of learning. And finally, even if one teacher is able to meet the learning styles and strategies of a specific student, it is not certain that future teachers will be able to do so or even desire to do so. The question, then, is should students learn only from the style that is theirs, or should they be encouraged to develop strengths in additional settings, senses, intelligences, styles, and strategies?

Summary

The orientation that a teacher holds toward the students in the classroom depends a great deal on how much the teacher knows about the students and their cultural backgrounds. When teachers do not recognize, and make no attempt to understand, the students' cultures, teachers will be more likely to consider students' behaviors as deficiencies if those behaviors do not match the dominant model. Not understanding why the students do not fit in the expected cultural models that the teacher has constructed, those students will be seen as lacking in some key characteristics. They will be seen as deficient. Or their families and communities will be seen as not providing the appropriate educational preparation for their students.

The difference orientation, on the other hand, lends much more to the recognition and understanding of identity and of unique ways of acquiring knowledge. Oakes and Lipton (2007) illustrate how learning about students and their communities can help teachers learn best how to teach students.

> Many teachers, on their own and with the support of like-minded colleagues, do reach out in caring and sympathetic ways. They work to establish relationships that allow them to gain a deep understanding of their students and communities, and they respond by demonstrating that knowledge in their lessons and relationships. (Oakes and Lipton, 2007, p. 400)

An example of a difference-oriented teacher, like Judy who was described earlier, is the now famous math teacher from Los Angeles, Jaime Escalante. Escalante worked in an inner-city school where students were rarely encouraged to become academically successful. Further, the students' cultures and styles were rarely considered in classroom teaching. In this setting, Escalante began an advanced placement math program, out of which students scored well above average on their standardized achievement tests. His story has been popularized in a movie called *Stand and Deliver.* When Escalante was asked how he recruited students into the advanced math class, he responded:

> I often chose the rascals and kids who were "discipline problems" as well as those who simply liked math. I found that the "class cut-ups" were often the most intelligent, yet they were extremely bored by poor teaching and disillusioned by the perceived dead end that school represented for them. (Escalante and Dirmann, 1990, p. 409)

Another example of a teacher who did not succumb to the deficiency orientation is Erin Gruwell, former teacher and author and creator of "The Freedom Writers." In her book *The Freedom Writers Diary* (1999), which was turned into a movie, Gruwell describes how she was tired of hearing teachers assume the worst about their students and decided to work together with her class to fight for social justice through writing. It was not only the teacher, Gruwell, who heard and felt the negative attitudes of the teachers in the school and of the educational system itself. One of her students wrote in his journal:

> Who would have thought of the "at risk" kids making it this far? But we did, even though the educational system desperately tried to hold us down. By labeling us at an early age, they were almost able to affect our school record for life. . . . Four years ago, it would have been unimaginable for us, a group of diverse kids, to work together in class discussions, and today, we learn together, we laugh together, we cry together, and we wouldn't have it any other way. (Gruwell, 1999, p. 269)

Here are examples of the recognition that a teacher can have that students may not seem to be academically proficient, but that these same students have strengths that just may not have been discovered.

A multitude of different learning styles and even more combinations of the different aspects make up individuals' learning styles and strategies. Each student in a classroom will present a unique learning profile, with different preferences for settings, senses, intelligences used, styles, and strategies for learning. By considering the possible learning styles and strategies represented in the classroom, the teacher can adapt the strategies and activities used in the classroom in order to best meet the needs of all students in the class. By closely and carefully examining the learning styles and intelligences, the language and communication patterns, the cultural backgrounds, and other characteristics that a student brings to the classroom, the teacher can take responsibility for providing an educational experience that is respectful of the students' identities while helping them learn in the ways that are most conducive to their approaches to learning and living.

Reflective Writings

1. *Revisiting Chapter 1—Cultural Discontinuities and the Attitudes of Teachers.* Look again at the components of culture presented in chapter 1 and summarized in Tables 1.1 and 1.2. These are different ways of communicating, thinking, and being that have been developed through families and communities. The stories presented at the end of chapter 1 give examples of how students who have cultural discontinuities between home and school cultures can be misunderstood and devalued. In light of the discussion in this chapter (4), how can cultural discontinuities be discussed using the framework of deficiency and difference orientations?

2. *Recognizing Deficiency and Difference Orientations in Your Own Teaching.* In what circumstances or settings, and why, do you believe that you do or you will use the deficiency orientation in the classroom? The difference orientation?

3. *Recognizing Deficiency and Difference Orientations in Society's Descriptions of People.* Examine three days of the newspaper in your town to look at how various people are being described. Especially good places to look are editorial columns and letters to the editor. Can you determine which orientation, deficiency or difference, is being used to describe people? Is there a distinction between the orientations used toward different groups of people?

4. *Revisiting Chapter 2—Implications of the Deficiency Orientation for the Development of Stereotyping, Prejudice, and Racism.* Discuss how the beliefs that are held in the deficiency orientation can lead to the

development or continuation of stereotyping, prejudice, and racism. Reflect on this issue in relation to schools and to society as a whole.

5. *Relation of Orientations toward Students and Orientations toward People in Society.* Discuss whether you believe there is a relation between the orientations held toward students in the classroom and the orientations held toward people in society.

6. *Analyzing Terms.* Analyze each of the following terms for their meanings. These terms are often grouped together. Is this an appropriate grouping? What makes them similar? In what ways does each term provide a new distinction on the topic?

   • Culturally deficient
   • Culturally deprived
   • Culturally disadvantaged
   • Culturally impoverished
   • Culturally inadequate
   • Culturally unready

7. *Balancing Deficiency and Difference Orientations in the Classroom.* Using the description of Ms. Vanderbilt's classroom, in Figure 4.3 (below), examine the description to determine the use of the deficiency and difference orientations. First, indicate the ways that Ms. Vanderbilt uses the deficiency orientation in her classroom. Second, write some ideas for how a teacher could use the difference orientation to enhance the education and identity development for students in Ms. Vanderbilt's classroom.

8. *Create Your Own Learning Profile.* Examine your own learning and studying. Keep a learning diary for several days in which you record all of your behaviors while you are learning and studying. In examining your preferred learning settings, describe what you prefer in each of the following: lighting, temperature, design, sound, and presence of others. In examining your preferred learning senses, record any activities that you do that involve the following: visual, auditory, kinesthetic, or tactile behaviors. As a result of this examination of your own learning patterns, you should be able to create a profile of your own learning.

9. *Learning Styles and Intelligences Emphasized in Schools.* Which learning settings, learning senses, learning styles, and which of the multiple intelligences are most commonly stressed in schools? What examples can you give of the physical arrangement of the classroom, the curriculum used, and the methods used that emphasize the specific learning styles and intelligences you have indicated?

10. *Matching Teaching Strategies with Learning Styles, Strategies, and Intelligences.* In 15 minutes, write down as many examples of teach-

ing strategies and activities as possible. These teaching strategies should range from kindergarten through university levels. Which of these strategies and activities would be most useful for the different learning settings, senses, styles, intelligences and strategies? In other words, are there some teaching strategies that are most beneficial for certain learning styles, and others most beneficial for other styles?

11. *Should a Teacher Focus on a Students' Learning Styles?* Earlier in this chapter, a debate over whether teachers should use learning styles approaches in the classroom was described. A key question is whether students should learn only from the style that is theirs or be encouraged to develop strengths in additional settings, senses, intelligences, styles, and strategies. Discuss this debate.

12. *Creating Activities for the Learning Intelligences.* One approach to addressing learning intelligences in the classroom is to set up learning centers for each of the learning intelligences. In this type of classroom, there will be seven centers around the classroom, each focusing on the developing of a particular learning intelligence. Thus, there would be a learning center for developing musical intelligence, another for developing logical-mathematical intelligence, and so on. A unit on dinosaurs, for instance, would need to include activities that address dinosaurs from a spatial perspective, from a linguistic perspective, and the like. Create a series of seven learning centers, each with activities that are designed to help students learn about a specific topic through the different learning intelligences.

Ms. Vanderbilt has been teaching a Head Start class on Chicago's southwest side for 3 years. This teaching assignment was her first after acquiring her teaching certificate from a large university in the Midwest. The class this semester is typical of classes she has taught since she began. Her students are Black and Hispanic residents of a poor socioeconomic community. The community members, including the parents of Ms. Vanderbilt's students, respect the school and look on it as the main institution that will improve life chances for their children.

There are 28 students in Ms. Vanderbilt's class. There are 16 girls, 10 Black and 6 Hispanic. Two of the Hispanic girls are Spanish-speaking. Of the 12 boys, 8 are African American; of the 4 Hispanic boys, 1 is bilingual. On entering Ms. Vanderbilt's classroom, you are struck by the richness and warmth of the environment. Colorful bulletin boards, colorful posters (mostly of nature), bushy plants in decorative pots, two aquariums, and two hamsters (in cages) capture your attention. Three learning centers, a library corner with the "big books," or the so-called classics, and Great Books for children, a rocking chair, and a large yellow carrel that students can climb up into are also prominent features of the room.

As you bring your gaze back from the room's artifacts to the teacher and students, you learn that the class is preparing for a field trip to the Art Institute, with a stop in nearby Grant Park for a picnic lunch. The class is discussing the lunch arrangements, and several of the students are calling out what they are planning to bring to eat. Ms. Vanderbilt calls their attention to the "basic four" food poster on the side wall and reminds them of the nutrition unit that concluded the previous week. She tells them that she expects their lunch to consist of the food categories that are pictured in the poster. She also tells them to review the worksheet on the three French painters—Monet, Manet, and Renoir—whose work they will see on the field trip. She has students pair up to review this information, explaining that her students work better cooperatively than alone. The recess bell rings, interrupting the discussion; Ms. Vanderbilt quickly gets the students ready for one of their favorite school activities and leads them out to the playground. She asks you, as she leaves, to meet her later for coffee in the teachers' lounge.

When the two of you meet, she tells you that this class is really super, and this field trip is their fourth time taking in a cultural event downtown. She adds that next week they are going to attend the youth symphony. She says that, given time and an active enrichment program, most of the students will have a good opportunity for academic success in school. Her curriculum is geared to exposing the students to a way of life they have not been privileged to know; she points out that the information on the bulletin boards and posters is designed to help students learn about life on the other side of the tracks. In her classroom, every boy and girl learns the same things—academically and socially—that students in the suburbs learn. She makes active use of after-school tutoring programs to get students up to grade level in basic skills, and she works extensively with parents on homework-monitoring strategies.

Source: *Making Choices for Multicultural Education*, 3rd ed., by Sleeter/Grant. Copyright © 1999, Prentice-Hall, Inc. Reprinted by permission of John Wiley and Sons, Inc.

Figure 4.3 Ms. Vanderbilt's Classroom

Chapter Five

The Identity
Construction Process

Throughout this book, you have been asked to reflect on your identity—on how your cultural background has affected and shaped your identity; on how prejudice and racism impact your identity; on how relations of power within assimilation, immigration, imposition, and segregation have affected your identity; and on how practices and attitudes within the schools have given you views of who you are. You have also been asked to consider how these same aspects of society and schools affect the identities of colleagues and your current or future students.

This chapter addresses directly the processes by which individuals construct their identities, in relation to others and in relation to their roles in society. The focus on identity construction within multicultural education is on developing within each person the understanding of how their cultural and ethnic identity affects their views of themselves, of others, and of the world in general. As a result of a long history, the United States is populated by people from a variety of cultural backgrounds. However, practices within the country have essentially been determined by the members of a dominant group who share similar characteristics and have been based on prejudice and racism. Thus, people from cultural and ethnic groups outside of the dominant group may view who they are in different ways at different times in their lives. The ideas and activities presented in this chapter discuss how our identities might develop in a multicultural society—how individuals might go through their recognition of who they are in a multicultural society. As you read about the process of identity construction, think about your own sense of identity to see if you can identify some of the steps you have taken along the way. In addition, think about how you will, as a multicultural educator, have the opportunity to help students understand themselves and how their identities are being constructed, as well as how you can help them have a positive sense of who they are culturally and ethnically.

Preliminary Activities

Review your answers to the first reflective writing in chapter 2. Have your answers changed since first reflecting on the questions? Have further reading, further reflecting, further discussing, and further experiencing changed your sense of identity? The questions from the reflective writing are listed again below. Reflect carefully on your understanding of your own identity, and comment on each of the following questions.

— Do you believe that you are in the identity versus role confusion stage, in which you are just beginning to ask, "What do I believe?"

— Have you been operating at the identity diffusion stage, which means that you have not begun to make an attempt to understand your identity?

— Do you feel that you are in the stage of ethnic identity clarification, in which you understand who you are and what that identity means in relation to other people in the world?

— Are you in the contingency stage, during which you are constantly and consistently attempting to further clarify your understanding of who you are and what you believe?

— Do you recognize yourself as being located within one of the particular ethnic identity stages for your ethnic group?

Stages of Identity Construction

The information presented here comes from the discussions of a number of different researchers of cultural and ethnic identity development. A common approach used by these researchers is to present identity construction as a process consisting of a number of stages as the person goes through his or her life. These "stage theories" imply that people tend to move between and through these stages at some points in their lives. The spectrum of the identity construction theories goes from a lack of awareness of one's own identity, to a sense of clarification of one's identity, to the use of one's identity to help make positive changes within society.

There seem to be three views about the process of identity construction. One is that we do not undertake any reflection about our identity and therefore make no changes in our understanding of who we are. A second is that we go chronologically through a series of stages moving from lack of awareness of our own identities to a fully integrated sense of cultural and ethnic identity. And a third, proposed by Parham (1989), is that we go through cycles in the process of our identity construction; we may repeat several of the stages at different points in our lifetimes, based on new experiences and interactions with others. Thus, within the cycling idea, we will continuously be reexamining our own sense of cultural and ethnic identity. Although these three views of identity construction are posed as possibilities, the research does not clearly identify any of them as the ultimately correct view. As Helms (1989) explains, "It is not clear from racial identity theories whether stages are additive and build successively upon one another or disjunctive such that each stage represents a unique restructuring of experiences" (p. 241).

Important to any discussion of the identity construction process is that many variables in one's life can affect a person's identity and the active construction of that identity. Discussions of identity construction, as Helms (1989) writes, "portray a changing process, a process that is influenced by individual characteristics as well as situational or environmental factors" (p. 227). Helms goes on to describe some of the factors that may interplay with each other during the construction of identity:

> (a) any individual's identity can potentially be influenced by members of his or her own racial group . . . as well as other groups with which he or she comes in contact . . . ; (b) social environments are the result, at least in part, of the racial identity characteristics of the people in the environment; (c) individuals exist in many environments, not all of which are equally potent influences on their racial identity development; and (d) environments, like individuals, are changeable. (p. 232)

Within this complex mix of interactions, experiences, and personal reflections, an individual can engage in the process of identity construction. In this section, six different stages of identity construction will be examined and are presented in Table 5.1. Of key importance here is that identities are, in large part, actively constructed by persons in relation to society and community. The belief underlying this discussion is that some individuals may identify a chronological pattern underlying their identity construction; others may recognize themselves as being in some stages but not in others; and some may see a continuous cycle of repeating various stages in the process based on additional life experiences. Finally, the discussion will include how a teacher's sense of identity within the identity construction process will affect his or her understanding of the meaning and purpose of multicultural education.

Unexamined Identity

For many people, the idea of understanding their own identity, and how that identity has been shaped by historical, societal, and community factors, has never been considered (see Table 5.2 on page 161). For people in this stage of identity construction, there are several reasons for this lack of recognition. For some, there is a lack of interest in the whole field of identity studies and identity construction. For others, there may be recognition that other

Table 5.1   Examining Cultural and Ethnic Identity throughout a Lifetime

1. Unexamined Identity	Lack of interest in or concern with identity, views of identity based on the opinions of others
2. Search for Identity	Active questioning and seeking to understand one's cultural or ethnic identity
3. Construction of Identity Based on Devaluation of Others	Basing one's cultural or ethnic identity on the devaluation or exclusion of others
4. Clarified Identity	Clear sense of and acceptance of own cultural or ethnic identity, with all its positives and negatives
5. Expanded Sense of Identity	Recognition of an identity that is based on multiple factors and that includes multiple characteristics of multiple groups
6. Use of Clarified Identity to Achieve Societal Change	Using the understanding of one's identity to help achieve positive changes in society

people have concerns about identity, but they themselves do not share that interest. For people with an unexamined identity, their views about identity—in themselves and in society—are formed based exclusively on the opinions of others. Now there are variations on this theme. Nevertheless, for all who are at this stage, there is a lack of recognition of racial issues within society, with a corresponding dismissal of discussions of such issues.

The work by Helms (1990) and Tatum (1994) helps describe further how this type of identity construction is expressed. Their idea of a contact stage is intended to more closely describe the identity construction of Whites within the United States and is unique as a stage because of the relationship of race to power within this country. Being White allows for a lack of need to be interested in ethnicity; Whites are not confronted with "ethnicity" as a signifier on a daily basis. The contact stage clearly demonstrates how persons can have unexamined identities: individuals are unaware of their own racial identity; they do not think of themselves as "White" but rather as "normal." Furthermore, they will tend to view racism as "individual acts of meanness" rather than as an institutionalized system. They typically do not recognize or acknowledge White privilege. They may have a naive curiosity or fear of people of color, usually based on stereotypes. Often, they will perceive themselves as completely free of prejudice, unaware of their own assumptions about other racial groups. This unexamined identity can be seen clearly within the statements of several teacher education students (Noel, 1995a):

"I'm just normal."

"We don't have racism here because we don't have any minorities."

"Why can't we treat people as human beings? Why must we distinguish between cultural background or skin color?"

Table 5.2 Unexamined Identity

Identity Diffusion

The individual has not yet begun to examine his or her own identity. (Marcia, 1980)

Identity Foreclosure

The individual has made a commitment to an ethnic or cultural identity, but has made that commitment based on the expectations of others without doing his or her own explorations. (Marcia, 1980)

Contact

The individual is unaware of ethnicity, has a naive curiosity or fear about people of other groups, and will consider himself or herself as free of prejudice. (Helms, 1990; Tatum, 1994)

Personal Identity

The individual has a sense of self and of others that is independent of and unrelated to ethnicity. (Poston, 1990)

Individuation

The individual lacks awareness of any other's views of himself or herself, and never questions the perceptions of others. (Myers et al., 1990)

Ethnic Psychological Captivity

The individual internalizes the negative ideologies so often heard about his or her ethnic group, has a low self-esteem, and tries to be like a dominant group member. (Banks, 1994)

Pre-encounter

The individual's knowledge of ethnic identity is totally influenced by the dominant culture. (Cross, 1971)

But an unexamined identity is not limited only to Whites in this country. According to Poston (1990), some individuals who are biracial, whose parents or grandparents are of different races, may also have unexamined identities. Poston states that people who do not have an awareness or interest in their ethnic identity may have a sense of self that is unrelated to ethnicity. This is often seen in young children of all races and ethnicities.

According to Banks (1994), some minority persons who have not examined their identity tend to form conceptions of their identity based solely on the opinions of others. These are opinions that often have been informed, developed, and reinforced in a society that encourages and expects all people to "fit into" the dominant culture. In what Banks calls "ethnic psychological captivity," individuals internalize the negative ideologies and beliefs that are commonly stated about their ethnic group. They will believe these statements and have a low self-esteem. They may be ashamed of their ethnic group and may try to either avoid members of their group or become more like members of the dominant group. Following is a description of this type of unexamined identity, from the identity story of Gaye Williams (1998):

> In elementary school, I thought the white kids would not know I was Black if I did not tell them, although I am not at all light enough to pass. I made myself invisible and pretended I was someone else, for protection from the self-hatred that I had learned from somewhere. The fact that my imaginary self was always male, and more often white than Black, says something about the effects of curriculum, climate, and the availability of suitable role models to my sense of self-validation. Very little in my pre-college schooling gave me an alternative to hating my Blackness and femaleness, although at the time I am sure I would not have spoken of it that way. I retreated into identities I felt were safer, more attractive than my own. (p. 350)

How Our Identity Construction Affects Our Understanding of Multicultural Education

Gaye Williams writes about the effects of curriculum, climate, and role models on her construction of identity, on her inability to examine her own identity while retreating into other identities. This turns our attention to the teachers in the classroom. How will having an unexamined identity affect the teacher's view of multicultural education, of how the classroom climate should be developed? Sleeter (1992) writes that such teachers, those who have unexamined identities, tend to see multicultural education as irrelevant. After all, persons who do not reflect on identity within themselves, or who see identity as an unimportant issue, do not see the need to address such issues in their own thinking about their own teaching or in their interactions with their students. These teachers generally try to ignore the races of the students in their classes; they claim that they are color-blind. Sleeter (2005) describes this lack of awareness of race as "denying the salience of race" (p. 247). These teachers do not see themselves as unaware or in any way biased because they believe that everyone has had an equal opportunity within society. Following are comments from teachers and future teachers indicating the belief that multicultural education is irrelevant.

> "I will be teaching in a Class C [high school with fewer than 125 students total] school so I don't need to learn about multicultural education" (Noel, 1995a).

> "What's the big hang-up, I really don't see this color until we start talking about it. . . . don't see the color until we start talking multicultural" (Sleeter, 2005).

These teachers display characteristics that D'Andrea and Daniels (1990) describe as falling within the "culturally entrenched stage." During this time of unexamined identity, there is an assumption that all teachers and students share the same basic assumptions about normality, appropriateness, and personal needs. Teachers and counselors at this stage are genuinely unaware of culturally contrasting worldviews; thus, they are apt to teach in ways that encourage students to be like the teachers themselves. They are likely to deny that race or ethnicity plays any part in the development of the child, and they dismiss the idea that discussions with children about race and ethnicity are important within the classroom.

Search for Identity

In contrast to unexamined identity, many people at some time in their lives undertake a search to understand their cultural, ethnic, or sexual identity (see Table 5.3). For many people, their first experience in understanding comes as a moment in time that jars their sense of awareness. This has been called by Cross (1971) an "encounter," in which the individual has an experience that causes him or her to think about cultural or ethnic identity for the first time. This has also been called an "ah-hah!" moment, a moment that may actually startle or confuse us. On the other hand, for some people, the search for identity is just a part of their approach to their lives, and they consistently undertake such a search without a particular triggering event. In either case, the resulting emotions that the individual may feel can throw the person into confusion and a sense of incongruity.

In Cross's (1971) description of what he calls an encounter experience in the search for identity, the individual has an experience or event that shatters his or her current feelings about ethnicity. It is often a particular experience that calls attention to the negative connotations that have been expressed about one's ethnic group and that cause the individual to think deliberately about his or her ethnicity for the first time. The result can be a sense of confusion—sometimes referred to as "dissonance"—over how to perceive his or her own identity. The following statement, from an African American woman attending a predominantly White university, displays the sense of dissonance that a person can feel when encountering these perceptions for the first time. She describes how her roommates reacted when her boyfriend, a young Black man, visited her dorm room.

> They put padlocks on their doors and their dressers. And they accused
> me of drinking their beers. And I was like, "We don't drink. This doesn't
> make any sense." So what really brought me to move out of that room
> was when he left, I came back, they were scrubbing things down with
> Pine Sol. I was like, "I couldn't live here with you. You think we have
> germs or something?" (Tatum, 2003, pp. 78–79)

The theory of identity development by Myers and colleagues (1990)—the Optimal Theory Applied to Identity Development (OTAID)—presents a very similar type of experience in the individual's search for identity. In the OTAID, the person begins to question who he or she is. The person starts to explore those parts of himself or herself that others may have devalued. Often this triggers a conflict between a prior sense of security in self and a new sense

---

Table 5.3   Search for Identity

Encounter

The individual has an experience that causes him or her to think about cultural or ethnic identity for the first time. (Cross, 1971)

Moratorium

The individual has begun to examine his or her own identity. (Marcia, 1980)

Dissonance

The individual begins to question who he or she is, sometimes triggering a conflict between a previous sense of security about himself or herself and a newer sense of the negative perceptions held by others about him or her. (Myers et al., 1990)

Identity Confusion

The individual may for the first time feel incongruity over what he or she should be and what he or she is. (Cass, 1979)

Identity Comparison

The individual begins to accept his or her homosexuality but learns to try to hide it to fit into the social structure, while feeling isolated. (Cass, 1979)

Identity Tolerance

The individual accepts his or her homosexuality, but only at a basic level, and may try to join with other homosexuals to reduce the feeling of isolation. (Cass, 1979)

Disintegration

The individual begins to recognize the presence and impact of racism and often tries to persuade other people to abandon racist thinking. (Tatum, 1994; Helms, 1990)

Choice of Group Categorization

The individual is pushed to pick one race or group on which to base his or her identity, often leading to crisis and alienation. (Poston, 1990)

---

of inferiority. Sleeter (2005) includes the words that one White teacher wrote on September 12, 2001, the day after two planes flew into the World Trade Center Towers. Some teachers had been discussing globalization and how the world sees America. On the basis of that discussion one of the teachers wrote:

> Looking at this time of horror in America within the scope of culture and power is very unsettling to me. Maybe the bottom line is that I am not ready to examine it this closely. I find myself turning a deaf ear when someone gives a negative opinion that we had it coming, and I find myself walking away from that source.

The words above describe a person who rejects negative views of her culture and possibly her ethnicity. However, if people internalize the negative views of their culture or ethnicity, they may want to dissociate themselves from the parts that are described as negative. Following are examples of the search for identity that fit within these patterns, and the accompanying emotions that come with the search for identity.

In the story of Odie, a Native American youth who was encouraged to search for his identity by a teacher who helped him learn about his Native American heritage and traditions, Odie went back and forth between his mother's life on the reservation and his father's life in the city, and identity confusion ensued. As he learned more about the traditions on his mother's side of the family, he gained confidence in himself but became alienated from his friends. Odie says that, "I was having an identity crisis: do I want to be an Indian, do I want to know my culture, or do I want to be like everybody else [who] don't give a shit about culture, [who] can raise hell and talk back to their elders and don't think about a future?" (Cleary and Peacock, 1998, p. 67). Although Odie felt these tensions in identity construction, he was later able to come back to the schools on the reservation to work with teens that were going through similar crises.

The following identity story comes from Arturo Madrid, a professor of Humanities:

> I spent the first half of my life downplaying the significance and consequences of otherness. The second half has seen me wrestling to understand its complex and deeply ingrained realities; striving to fathom why otherness denies us a voice or visibility or validity in American society and its institutions; struggling to make otherness familiar, reasonable, even normal to my fellow Americans. (Madrid, 1998, p. 21)

The discussions by Cass (1979) help illustrate the complexities of feelings during this time of search for identity. In writing about the process of coming to understand one's identity as a homosexual, Cass describes that when a person is searching for identity, he or she has for the first time an awareness of possibly being homosexual. That individual then must adjust a number of pieces of his or her life. The individual must learn how to hide these feelings, how to avoid the sense of isolation, and how to move from a lack of awareness of identity to the acceptance of that identity. The emotions within this process include confusion, turmoil over inner feelings and external expectations, the sense of incongruity between a previously known sense of self and the new recognition of self, and most especially, a sense of isolation and alienation.

How Our Identity Construction Affects Our Understanding of Multicultural Education

As predicted by common sense and by research in this area, the search for one's identity can set the tone for an emotional reaction (Noel, 1995a). This reaction may range from cognitive dissonance to emotional shock. This is seen especially clearly in White students who are members of the dominant group. Lehman (1993) ties the emotions involved to the power structure that has suddenly become questioned: "Loss of power or of one's self-image, caused by information presented through a different perspective, can result in a dramatic emotional upheaval" (p. 134). In some cases, this encounter with a new perspective interrupts or disturbs the sense of security that one's knowledge is standard and normal. Kimball and Garrison (1994) describe this process in a concept that they call "hermeneutic listening":

> Interacting with others different from us can interrupt our habitual, unreflective, "normal" ways of believing, valuing and acting. Giving up or suspending prejudices is difficult, maybe even dangerous, because it disturbs our very identities and alters how we relate with others. (p. 2)

Discussions from teachers and future teachers who have begun this search for identity incorporate phrases such as "eye opener" to describe the impact on their understanding of teaching. A teacher education student's discussion portrays this sense:

> The discussion of . . . cultural socialization was a real eye opener to me. I had never before thought of schools as trying to conform everyone to the social norms. This probably was due to the fact that I fit into the norm of a working-class culture. I had never viewed it from another culture's perspective. However, after reading this discussion, I could see the truth of it. What hit me so hard was that it made sense. I could recognize these patterns in the school system. I was concerned that I would fall into the same trap, since it is the established way of doing things. Another thing that I realized is that most teachers probably don't even realize that they're doing it. (Noel, 1995a)

Construction of Identity Based on the Devaluation of Others

Sometimes, people will actively take part in constructing their identity, but only in relation to their perception of the worth of other groups. In other words, the construction of identity does not come from within, but by comparison to others (see Table 5.4). As with the other types of identity construction described here, not everyone will take part in this stage. Why do some people take part in devaluing other groups in order to construct their own identities? There is probably no exact answer. But reasons that have been posited revolve around people getting tired of hearing negative opinions expressed about their cultural or ethnic group. So a possible reaction is the total immersion in their own culture while withdrawing as much as possible from other cultures. Withdrawal ends up creating an "us" and "them" dichotomy. Carlson and Schramm-Pate (2005) report an example of devaluing another culture.

> I don't see how the blacks can call us white people racist when they are too. They get mad when we call them the "n" word, but is it right for them to call us a "cracker" and "white trash"? The confederate flag don't

mean slavery or hate. . . . To me I can't understand why they are so down on the Ku Klux Klan when the NAACP is the same thing—Negroes Against All Caucasian People. (p. 227)

Once this dichotomy has been achieved, it becomes easier to devalue people from cultural or ethnic groups different from one's own. An additional component of this construction of identity based on the devaluation of others is blaming other groups for problems—scapegoating—and includes blaming victims for their own lot in life, rather than understanding the historical, social, and political components that contribute to the victims' circumstances.

Banks (1994) terms this type of identity construction as ethnic encapsulation, in which a person believes that his or her ethnic group is superior to all others. Such an individual will practice separateness and try to exclude all others from his or her life sphere. Members of these "other" groups will be considered enemies by the encapsulated person. There is an extreme and highly exaggerated sense of ethnic importance.

Banks's idea is intended to relate directly to minority groups in the United States. But this sense of superiority is also felt by some Whites in their identity construction process. Helms's (1990) and Tatum's (1994) concept of reintegration describes how Whites may put responsibility for problems on other groups of people while denigrating the moral and ethical character of those "others." As Tatum explains, an individual at this stage may feel pressured by others to "not notice" racism. Whites may turn to explanations for racism that put the burden of change on those who are the targets of racism.

Table 5.4 Construction of Identity Based on the Devaluation of Others

Ethnic Encapsulation

The individual believes that his or her culture or ethnicity is superior to all others, with an exaggerated sense of how others are enemies. (Banks, 1994)

Reintegration

The individual accepts the pressures from others to ignore racism and to put the responsibility for racism on the victims of racism. (Helms, 1990; Tatum, 1994)

Identity Pride

The individual separates the world into "us and them," devaluing heterosexuals. (Cass, 1979)

Immersion

The individual totally embraces his or her own culture or ethnicity while withdrawing from other cultures. (Myers et al., 1990)

Immersion/Emersion

The individual focuses on his or her own culture or ethnicity only. (Cross, 1971)

Race-related negative conditions are assumed to result from minority people's inferior social, moral, and intellectual qualities. The individual will usually choose to avoid the issue of racism, if possible, rather than struggling to
define a nonracist identity. The following comment indicates a person who is
constructing his identity based on the devaluing of another ethnicity:

> Today's class was hard for me to sit through. I have never liked indians
> since I moved to Montana. . . . All indians ever do is whine about how
> the white man came and took their land. Hasn't anyone ever heard of sur-
> vival of the fittest? Maybe if indians were smarter and more civilized they
> would have stood a chance. (Noel, 1995a)

In these and many other examples of basing one's construction of identity on the devaluation or exclusion of others, we can see that the individual
who is in this particular part of the identity construction process has chosen
to proclaim his superiority over people of other races. Even though the first
example given here was the result of feeling years of oppression, and the second example was the result of feeling years of cultural and political dominance, the end result on identity construction is similar: the devaluation of
another race.

How Our Identity Construction Affects Our Understanding of Multicultural Education

Sleeter (1992) documents the responses of teachers to the idea of multicultural education. Some teachers describe their students in terms of devaluation. In the example that follows, the devaluation is specifically on the nature
of socioeconomic status of the students in the classroom:

> Where are they coming from? . . . What's going on in their brains, you
> know? . . . [my husband and I] have been very strong disciplinarians and
> we encourage the work ethic . . . [they] have a totally helter-skelter house
> where there is nothing regular and the people who are your parent figures
> come and go and—you don't know . . . just what is going on in their
> brains and where they are coming from. (Sleeter, 1992)

Examples from my own observations indicate how the construction of
identity based on the devaluation of a cultural other can lead a teacher to publicly devalue that other group by verbally excluding a student from that group
in the classroom. From my informal surveys, it appears that teachers might
be more likely to publicly devalue others when the differences displayed by
those others are culturally determined, but that more teachers tend to want to
hide their beliefs when the differences are based on ethnicity or race.

Clarified Identity

The basic description of the clarified identity is that a person has recognized, considered, reflected on, and reconsidered his or her identity, and as a
result has been able to clarify for himself or herself what makes up that iden-

tity (see Table 5.5). Terms used by identity researchers to describe a clarified identity include identity achievement, acceptance, appreciation, and internalization. At this point in one's construction of identity, the person has reflected on his or her identity and feels comfortable with who he or she is. As Maldonado (1975) describes:

> The phrase *ethnic self-identity* refers to the integration of ethnicity or race into the self-concept or self-image. It is the full recognition of one's ethnicity and the subsequent self-identity that flows from the values, ways, and styles of that ethnic background, instead of from a self-concept based upon the opinions and prejudices of the larger society toward that ethnic group. Ethnic self-identity is identity that develops from within the experience of the ethnic life instead of an image that is imposed from without. (p. 621)

Table 5.5 Clarified Identity

Identity Achievement

The individual has explored issues of identity and has made a commitment to his or her own constructed identity. (Marcia, 1980)

Ethnic Identity Clarification

The individual has clarified who he or she is culturally or ethnically, and accepts positives and negatives about his or her own and other cultural or ethnic groups. (Banks, 1994)

Internalization

The individual feels comfortable about self and about others, recognizes both the positives and negatives about what makes up his or her identity without feeling his or her identity threatened. (Myers et al., 1990)

Internalization

The individual has a sense of security and satisfaction with his or her own cultural or ethnic identity. (Cross, 1971)

Identity Acceptance

The individual accepts his or her homosexuality and begins to take part in cultural expressions of that identity. (Cass, 1979)

Appreciation

The individual begins to accept and appreciate his or her multiple group affiliations, while attempting to learn more about each of those heritages or cultures. (Poston, 1990)

Pseudo-independence

The individual develops an understanding of the effects of White racism, specifically, and of his or her own responsibility for helping to dismantle racism. (Helms, 1990; Tatum, 1994)

As Banks (1994) writes in relation to ethnicity, individuals are able to clarify personal attitudes toward their own ethnic identity. They will be able to accept both the positive and negative attributes of their ethnic group, and thus of other groups as well. Importantly, as laid out in the OTAID (Myers et al., 1990) model, these individuals both know and accept how others perceive them. They know which parts of themselves are associated with positive perceptions from others, and they can incorporate those positive perceptions into their constructed identity. At the same time, they can also accept that other people do not share all aspects of their identity, and their sense of identity does not become threatened by others who are different.

Depending on the cultural or ethnic group that one's identity is a part of, individuals will express their acceptance of themselves in a variety of ways. For Whites, the clarification process necessarily includes not only the recognition of one's whiteness, but also the recognition of the presence of White privilege that goes along with whiteness in the United States (Helms 1990; Tatum 1994). For homosexuals, the acceptance of identity is linked to the ability to and interest in taking part in the cultural expressions that go with that identity since for the first time they have been able to accept their identity (Cass, 1979). And for persons who are biracial, the clarification of identity can be called appreciation (Poston, 1990), during which time they learn to appreciate the multiple heritages that make up their identity while actively learning more about each of those heritages or cultures. Across all these identities, though, is the sense of acceptance and of commitment to the constructed identity.

An interesting example of the clarification of identity comes from the writings of Samantha, a student identified as learning disabled in the eighth grade, after years of being told that she could not learn as a regular student. She writes:

> In eighth grade I was finally recognized as learning disabled. . . . Special education changed my life. It was the best thing that ever happened to me. I could raise my hand in that class, even when being taught the most elementary concepts, and say, "I don't get it." It was the most wonderful feeling in the world. Eighth grade was my best year at the junior high. . . . Remember that if you have trouble in school, it might not be because you don't fit the school, it might be because the school doesn't fit you. (Abeel, 1998, pp. 139–140)

How Our Identity Development Affects Our Understanding of Multicultural Education

D'Andrea and Daniels (1990) refer to teachers and other professionals who are working with others while having their own sense of a clarified identity as having cultural integrity. Such people emphasize the cultural integrity of people from different backgrounds more than those whose identity has not been clarified. Many teachers will present material in such a way as to intentionally eliminate much of the false information about different cultural groups that is often developed through a lifetime of experiences and media.

Teachers at this point in the identity construction process, according to Sleeter (1992), will be likely to include human relations efforts in their classrooms. These teachers will have as part of their goals for their students the ability to respect, appreciate, and understand each other. Teachers who hold these beliefs will be comfortable thinking in terms of race and color and will attach positive feelings and images to racial diversity. They will also recognize a connection between race, student self-image, and student-student relationships.

Expanded Sense of Identity

Often, once individuals have a clarified sense of identity, they will want to continue to learn more about themselves and their relationship to others and to the world (see Table 5.6). There are a variety of ways that individuals show their expanding sense of identity. For some, there is a more complete emersion into one's own culture or ethnicity in order to understand its full complexities. For others, there is an integration of the several different components of one's identity, including culture, ethnicity, sexuality, and other pieces that make people who they are. And for still others, the expanded sense of identity is seen in the increasing numbers of cultures and ethnicities within which a person feels comfortable.

Table 5.6 Expanded Sense of Identity

Integration

The individual recognizes and values all of his or her ethnicities, with a sense of integration among all of them. (Poston, 1990)

Identity Synthesis

The individual begins to see that homosexuality is just one part of his or her identity, and begins to integrate sexual identity with other aspects of identity to develop a more holistic identity. (Cass, 1979)

Integration

The individual has so much inner security about one's heritage that his or her sense of community is broadened to include more people who share similar interests. (Myers et al., 1990)

Immersion/Emersion

The individual starts asking himself or herself more deeply what it means to be white, and may join with others who are asking the same sorts of questions in the same antiracist stance. (Helms, 1990; Tatum, 1994)

Biethnicity

The individual can function effectively in two different cultures. (Banks, 1994)

Multiethnicity

The individual can function within several cultures, including their values, symbols, and institutions. (Banks, 1994)

Cass's (1979) description of "identity synthesis" is an example of how a person with an expanded sense of identity may be able to integrate the many different parts of his or her identity. Here, relating to sexuality, the individual realizes that some heterosexuals accept his or her identity as a homosexual. The individual accepts the possibility of considerable similarity between himself or herself and heterosexuals and also realizes that there will be some dissimilarity between himself or herself and others who are homosexual. The result is that the individual no longer needs to have a created sense of an us–them dichotomy. The individual can now integrate his or her sexual identity with the other aspects of his or her life to form a more complete identity. The individual's identity is no longer dominated by only one aspect of his or her life.

The following story, written by a man whose father was Black, whose mother was White, and whose family was Jewish, illustrates the process of identity synthesis.

> I searched for simplistic solutions. I tried to be "White" for six months. I ended up hating all White people. I tried being "Black" for a similar span of time and ended up hating Blacks just as much as Whites. To be a Jew had a specific meaning to me, something different from just being White. There were a lot of rules that had to be obeyed and followed. Anyone can be White. I tried to be Jewish and failed at that also. When I was in my late teens the remedy became clear. Be nothing. Identify with no one and no group.

[After a teacher in college inspired him]

> From that day, I kept on the main track with only some minor digressions. She helped me understand who I was, from a human point of view. And when it comes down to it, race is not human; it's an artificial categorization employed to justify what is inherently human: weakness, fear, diffidence and timidity. By focusing on the human side—my family, my relationships with my father, mother, brother and sister—I was able to make some substantial progress in consolidating a genuine identity. (Jeffries, 1996, pp. 219 and 224)

Tatum (1994) gives an example of the process of more fully immersing oneself in one's culture in order to understand its complexities. In what Tatum describes as immersion-emersion, an individual who has a clarified sense of being White is actively seeking to redefine whiteness. The individual will ask himself or herself questions such as, "Who am I racially?" "What does it really mean to be White in the United States?" He or she will seek support from other antiracist Whites who have asked similar questions. The focus is on developing a positive White identity not based on assumed superiority. He or she takes pride in an active antiracist stance.

Banks (1994) has laid out two themes that demonstrate a person's expanded sense of identity: biethnicity and multiethnicity. Individuals at these stages of identity construction have clarified their identity, have positive attitudes toward other ethnic and racial groups, and are self-actualized. These individuals have increasingly developed the skills and psychological characteristics needed to function effectively in two or more ethnic cultures. For example, a person may function within one ethnic group at home but can also function within the expectations of another ethnic group at work. He or she will tend to see the United States as a multiethnic nation, while being able to understand, appreciate, and share the values, symbols, and institutions of these several ethnic groups within the nation. Pollock (2004) documents a conversation about multiethnicity, as interpreted by a group of high school students talking to each other and to the interviewer about each others' identities:

> "Does that girl over there look Mexican to you?" he asked. "I don't know, do you think she does?" I asked. "Don't you think she looks Mexican?" he repeated. "I guess so, why?" I asked. "'Cause she's not Mexican, she's Samoan!" he said smiling. "Samoan and white, with some black," he added. . . . "How do you know so much about her?" I asked him. "She's my cousin. And she's his cousin too, and he's mine!" he said, pointing to a guy sitting next to him who was somewhat bigger, with curlier hair, less freckles, and a wider nose. "So are you Samoan too?" I asked. "Yeah, Samoan . . . and part white, and part Chinese," he said. "So do you call yourself Samoan?" I asked. "Yeah . . . and part white, and part Chinese!" he said, laughing. (p. 38)

I would like to add a story about a similar type of identity-laden conversation that took place in my car as I was driving a group of five elementary school boys to a mathematics competition at the local university. These boys all live in subsidized public housing and attend a school where 100 percent of the children receive free or reduced cost lunch, meaning that the school serves only children in poverty. As the boys began a conversation about PSP® systems (hand-held devices that, among their many features, is the capacity for music to be downloaded and played), they talked about not being able to afford to buy one. At that point, the boy whose family had emigrated from Mexico to the U.S. said to the boy whose family had emigrated from Vietnam, "You should buy one when you go to Vietnam again to see your family. They're cheap there." In reply, the Vietnamese-American boy responded, "You should buy one when you go to Mexico for Christmas. They're cheaper there." I listened as these boys expressed comfort and confidence in their identities. But further, I marveled as they demonstrated a basic understanding of global economics!

How Our Identity Construction Affects Our Understanding of Multicultural Education

Teachers who are involved in expanding their own sense of identity actively seek information that helps them see themselves within the larger society. One way to describe this practice is with Gadamer's concept of horizon (1975). Gadamer writes, "To acquire a horizon means that one learns to look beyond what is close at hand—not in order to look away from it, but to see it better within a larger whole and in truer proportion" (p. 272). When individuals have acquired such a horizon, they learn that their perspective is informed by their own specific communities, and that gaining a new perspective from another culture can serve to deepen their own understandings.

Burbules and Rice (1991) describe how the specific practice of dialoguing with others can provide the impetus and information needed to help teachers and their students expand their own sense of identity. First, if individuals dialogue with others who have different beliefs, traditions, and perspectives, "one's identity will be more flexible, autonomous, and stable to the degree that one recognizes one's self as a member of various different subcommunities simultaneously" (p. 404). In other words, the teachers and their students recognize that perhaps they are not simply one culture or ethnicity, but rather they are important parts of a number of different cultures and ethnicities. Second, as Burbules and Rice continue discussing the benefits of dialogue when constructing identities, "We can broaden and enrich our self-understanding by considering our beliefs, values, and actions from a fresh standpoint" (p. 405). When individuals begin to reconsider their own beliefs as informed by the perspective of another culture, they come to see the "value of incorporating that perspective into a more complex and multifaceted framework of understanding" (p. 405).

Teachers who are actively involved in constructing their identities by developing an expanded sense of their identities will ask their students to be involved in the process, believing that both teachers and students can benefit from discussing and learning from each other. A future teacher stated it this way: "The only way one progresses in society is by being exposed to levels of thinking other than your own" (Noel, 1995a).

Use of Clarified Identity to Achieve Societal Change

Most researchers on identity development claim that an individual will need to have a clarified identity before being able to recognize or address societal change (see Table 5.7). As Banks (1994) describes, this person will have internalized the ethical values and principles of humankind, and will then be able to have the desire to take action to make the world a better place. He or she will have the necessary delicate balance of ethnic, national, and global identifications, commitments, literacy, and behaviors, as well as the skills, competencies, and commitment needed to achieve societal change. Cross (1971) states that the person at this point in the identity construction process will have both internalization of values and commitment to changing society. According to Cross, the person at this stage will be committed to changing his or her community. The person will try to liberate those who have been oppressed or marginalized and will have developed a long-term commitment to changing the oppressive and racist institutions. Tatum (1994) adds that this individual will be actively antiracist within his or her own sphere of influence, will become increasingly aware of how other forms of oppression (for example, sexism, ageism) are related to racism, and act

---

Table 5.7   Use of Clarified Identity to Achieve Societal Change

---

Transformation

The individual's sense of self includes all people and all the world, recognizing an interrelatedness of all people and things. (Myers et al., 1990)

Globalism

The individual can function well not only within several cultures in one's own nation but also within the world, and can work to end social concerns such as oppression. (Banks, 1994)

Internalization-Commitment

The individual wants to work within the community to change oppression and racism. (Cross, 1971)

Autonomy

The individual continually undergoes self-examination in the effort to eliminate racism. (Helms, 1990; Tatum, 1994)

---

accordingly to eliminate them as well. Comments from teacher education students portray this process:

> I realized that it was possible to simply go through life totally oblivious to the entire situation or, even if one realizes it, one can totally repress it. It is easy to fade into the woodwork, run with the rest of society, and never have to deal with those problems. So many people I know from home are like this. They have simply accepted what society has taught them with little, if any, question. . . . I don't think I could ever justify within myself simply turning my back on the problem. I finally realized that my position in all of these dominant groups gives me power to make change occur. (Tatum, 2003, p. 100)

Fine, Weis, Centrie, and Roberts (2000) describe how students have been able to find ways to work together to improve society. Often, however, this must occur outside of the school, where students are free to go beyond structural and socially reinforced barriers. Fine et al. write:

> Young men and women are "homesteading"—finding unsuspecting places within their geographic locations, their public institutions, and their spiritual lives to sculpt real and imaginary corners for peace, solace, communion, personal and collective identity work. These are spaces of deep, sustained, community-based educative work, outside the borders of formal schooling. (p. 132)

How Our Identity Construction Affects Our Understanding of Multicultural Education

Tatum (1994) clearly defines the goal for education that is adopted by teachers who are using their clarified identity to achieve societal change: "the abandonment of individual racism and the recognition of and opposition to institutional and cultural racism." Teachers show the initiation of such social action in small but important steps. D'Andrea and Daniels (1990) have found that some teachers and counselors enroll in courses in areas such as ethnic studies, social work, and race and prejudice to further sensitize them to the needs of minority group persons. Some teachers enroll in these courses, expressing the desire to learn more about the conditions of minorities and the historical antecedents to those current conditions; some teachers scan the newspaper for evidence of prejudice and discrimination and share the articles in class; and other teachers work with their students to make sure that they are more aware of the interactions of race, politics, media, and the identities of individuals. Several examples from teachers describe the initial starting point in their desires to achieve social change:

> I . . . taught in the highest minority school I've ever been in, it was 95 percent Black. And to my surprise, that's when my commitment began. I didn't like the fact that the university community didn't know there was a Black school there. And they didn't. And I knew there was something wrong. (Sleeter, 1992, p. 47)

A teacher education student identified the particular moment in her realization that she was committed to achieving social change: "When a professor asked us at what point we would be willing to take responsibility for changing the world, I realized that that is where I am at" (Noel, 1995a).

Within their identity stories, several writers have pinpointed activities that helped initiate their interest in achieving social change. Some describe how teachers create opportunities for them to examine and construct their own identities and how these events led them to become involved in activities to achieve societal change. Or, as you will see in the following example, some students on their own seek opportunities to join others who wish to learn more about and construct their own identity. A student named Amir illustrated a new ethnic self-identity as he took part in the *Echoes* Institute, designed to bring people of many generations together to discuss identity and education (Weis & Fine, 2005). He describes his experience:

> When you break someone's spirit, not always will they be able to be strong and be able to get through things. You can really cripple someone like that. I know that being in my school, my grades didn't go up until I started getting into my history, and I actually found, you know, about what made me great. You know what I mean? . . . Me and my friends we're in this organization, Messengers of Black Cultural Awareness, that we all put together ourselves, with that purpose. But we all had to go back and get these things on our own, you know, and learn about ourselves,

and now we're bringing it to the table, and we're still learning with other people. But at the same time, like I said, I had to go to the black bookstores and talk to black people about our history. You know what I mean? With my own people, and then I can go back out there and share with everyone. (p. 252)

While his teachers at his school did not provide a space for learning about identity, he sought out others seeking the same purpose, and they did their own discovery through talking with others. Only then could Amir bring this new clarified sense of identity to the table to join with others to work toward societal change.

Complex and Transitional Perspectives

Although these stages of identity construction have been presented as if there were smooth shifts both within a stage and across stages, in reality the identity construction process is quite complex. It often proceeds in short spurts, with movement in all directions. Sleeter (1992) writes that the teachers whom she has observed who recognize this complexity were in the process of active growth. Their insights came in fits and jumps. Their discussions were less systematic than those of other teachers, since they were continuously trying to understand their own and their students' identities. The following identity story of Beatriz (interviewed by Rosalie Rolón-Dow) illustrates the complexity of trying to define one's identity.

Well, really [I am] Mestiza which means I'm Puerto Rican but American Puerto Rican. Sometimes I say Mestiza, sometimes I say Boricua. My parents are Boricua and that makes me Boricua, the only thing is that I was born here. (in Rolón-Dow, 2004, p. 13)

Rolón-Dow goes on to introduce us to Beatriz's concept of her own social class. When Beatriz's mother would tell her they were poor, Beatriz would react "by indignantly stating, 'We're not poor'" (p. 13). However, when asked to compare herself to her teachers, Beatriz said:

They're [the teachers] working class so they don't really understand until like you get to my point where my dad don't work, my mom don't work, I have to live off welfare. My dad gets SSI [Social Security income]. That's called poor. (p. 13)

Beatriz has several visions of her national and ethnic identity, based on her parents' versus her own place of birth. She also holds several concepts of poverty, claiming not to be poor in one instance and clearly understanding poverty in the next.

This next identity story is from a White man, who undertook the process of identity construction in a university course on social equity.

Being a de facto member of the dominant culture, I stayed blissfully ignorant of racial issues far longer than most minorities would. As I grew . . . I thought my struggles were pretty darn hard. Of course, I had a white male face to show employers, never giving a thought to what a colored or female face would have implied in trying to get hired. . . . Once I learned to see that . . . the advantages of my white maleness became more apparent. (Noel, 1995a)

Summary

There are many approaches to identity construction: it can be a chronological, step-by-step process in which one gradually gains a complete understanding of who one is culturally and ethnically; it can be a process that some people will engage actively in, whereas others do not engage in it at all; it can be a lifelong examination of who one is culturally and ethnically, with no clear-cut steps but with certain markers along the way. In any case, the process of identity construction involves views of self that come from within, that come from the perceptions of others, and that come from knowing the social and historical factors that affect identity. Students recognize this early in their life, as can be seen from the following interview of a middle school student about identity construction:

> Student: "I hate classifying people, even though it's something that's geared into my head."
>
> Interviewer: "Uh-huh. When did it get into your head?"
>
> Student: "In junior high."
>
> Interviewer: "Do you know why?"
>
> Student: "Because it's what everybody else was doing, you know. I hated junior high. I did. I hated it because it was like—it's a total identity crisis, or it was for me, you. Just trying to figure out where you belong . . . ok, seventh grade, day one, Jocks and the Burnouts."
>
> Interviewer: "Boom. Right at the beginning of school."
>
> Student: "That fast. That fast." (Eckert, 1989, pp. 76–77)

The process of identity development discussed in this chapter includes six components (see Table 5.1):

1. *Unexamined Identity.* In this stage of the process, the individual has a lack of interest in or concern with identity. When the individual exhibits his or her own identity, it is usually based on the opinions of others, without reflection on what it means to have an identity that has been created by the perceptions of others.

2. *Search for Identity.* When an individual actively begins questioning and seeking to understand his or her cultural or ethnic identity, we can say that he or she has begun the search for identity. For some, this search begins as a specifically identified moment, an encounter that causes the person to examine who he or she is for the first time. For

others, this is part of a process that is continuous and has no particular trigger points but continues throughout a lifetime.

3. *Construction of Identity Based on Devaluation of Others.* Some people, possibly because of their anger at being oppressed or blamed for problems based solely on their race or culture, will base their identity construction on the devaluation of others. They will hold up their own ethnicity as the positive one, while denigrating others based on their perceived lack of moral or ethical virtue. Often at this point, an us–them dichotomy is constructed.

4. *Clarified Identity.* Once a person has constructed a clear sense of self, that person will be able to accept both the positives and negatives of that identity. He or she will be able to hear the perceptions of others without creating a feeling of anger and will accept both the positives and negatives of both self and others.

5. *Expanded Sense of Identity.* Persons at this stage will recognize that their identities are based on multiple factors. They will realize that much of their identity is shared by people from multiple groups, and they will incorporate the characteristics of others into their own sense of identity. Their identity will be a synthesis of the many different components that make up who they are.

6. *Use of Clarified Identity to Achieve Societal Change.* Once a person has a clarified and expanded sense of identity, he or she will be able to actively attempt to achieve social changes in the world. He or she will at this point share the attitudes, skills, and interests in removing oppression and racism from the world.

I would like to end this chapter and this book with a final quote that I believe points out the efforts that are needed to take part in the identity construction process: "Given the difficulty of this process, it's no wonder so many stumble in the process or stop midway through" (Mura, 1995, p. 706). It is our role as teachers to help students through this identity construction process, supporting their efforts at every step along the way.

Reflective Writings

1. *Possible Patterns of Identity Construction.* Three possible patterns of identity construction were presented early in this chapter: that we move chronologically through stages, that we remain in an unexamined stage, and that we go through cycles in the process of identity construction. Discuss the implications of having each of these patterns represented in your classroom.

2. *Difficulty of Movement through Stages.* Based on your own experiences and reflections on identity development, do you feel that any of the particular parts of the identity construction process would be

more difficult to make a change in? In other words, would it be more difficult to move between certain proposed stages than others?

3. *Simultaneous Identity Stages.* It has been proposed by some that an individual could be within the different stages of identity construction related to different ethnic or cultural groups at the same time. For example, a person could have clarified her identity when related to certain ethnic groups, but at the same time base her identity on the devaluation of homosexuals. For another example, a person could use his clarified identity for societal change on behalf of one particular ethnic group, such as African Americans, but not take part in any efforts toward societal change for Native Americans. Discuss this idea.

4. *Moving into Different Stages.* Assuming that one can move among the various stages of identity construction, what types of experiences do you believe it would take to move in the different directions?

5. *Helping with Transitions.* Select one of the transitional statements laid out earlier. Discuss what could be done in the classroom to help further along this transition.

6. *Identifying Identity Construction.* Look back at the identity story presented in the introduction to this book. Identify the different types of identity construction that the author has discussed within different points in her life.

7. *Beginning the Search for Identity.* Talk either to friends or to students in your own K–12 classrooms in which you currently work to find out if they have begun the search for identity stage. How would you recognize an active search for identity? What questions might you ask?

8. *Must Clarified Identity Precede Social Change?* Discuss the idea proposed that it would not be possible to engage in behaviors that would help create societal change until one has a clarified identity.

9. *Becoming Involved in the Community.* What types of activities could you and your students in your K–12 setting be involved with in your community that would help each of you to use your clarified identity to help make societal changes?

10. *Examining Your Own Identity Construction.* Look back on all of your reflective writings that you have written in response to the various issues presented in this book. Can you identify within your writings the presence of one or more of the types of identity construction presented in this chapter? Discuss.

Appendix

Suggestions for the Multicultural Classroom

This textbook has encouraged you to examine your own beliefs, attitudes, perspectives, and ideas about multicultural issues such as culture, prejudice and racism, history, and individuality of learning styles. As you have read through this book and have taken part in the suggested activities and reflective writings, you have been clarifying your own views and perspectives. In a sense, you have taken part in the same types of activities that are recommended for use in the K–12 classrooms. In this Appendix, you will have the chance to develop your own approach to teaching a classroom that is multicultural in its spirit. The ideas gathered from your work with this book so far can now be applied to the classroom.

In this Appendix, the ideas on identity and on the topics from the earlier chapters can be synthesized into a proposal of six goals that teachers can hold for their students when they teach with the multicultural spirit. The six goals for multicultural education are summarized in Table A.1. These goals are presented here with a description of the theory that underlies the goals, a tie-in to the previous chapters of this text, and descriptions of some sample activities that could be used in the classroom to meet those goals.

Goal 1: Students Will Gain an Awareness of Their Own Cultural Backgrounds

The idea that students should gain an awareness of their own cultural backgrounds is of crucial importance in multicultural education. In fact, that is why this book started with the study of culture and the effects of cultural background on our perceptions of the world. Multicultural education cannot be effective if the students are not first drawn into the subject and the issues with an understanding of what their views are and how those views were formed.

Banks (2006) further describes the importance of students' understandings of their own cultural backgrounds in his Principle 6.0:

> The multicultural curriculum should provide students with continuous opportunities to develop a better sense of self. . . . Students should be helped to develop accurate self-identities. Students must ask questions such as who am I? and what am I? in order to come to grips with their own identities. . . . Students should develop more sophisticated understandings of why they are the way they are, why their ethnic and cultural groups are the way they are, and what ethnicity and culture mean in their daily lives. (pp. 320–321)

Table A.1 Goals for a Multicultural Education Classroom

Goal 1: Students will gain an awareness of their own cultural backgrounds.

Sample Activities

1. Cultural background pie
2. Cultural silhouette
3. Create a class quilt, with background of children's books
4. Students' personal and cultural knowledge about a topic

Goal 2: Students will gain an understanding of different perspectives on life in the United States.

Sample Activities

1. Immigration through children's books
2. Immigration through examining different media sources
3. Examine an issue or one specific group through different newspapers

Goal 3: Students will gain an understanding of the cultures of specific groups

Sample Activities

1. Comparison of themes and values of folktales from different cultures
2. Focus on a single culture through a collection of stories from that culture
3. Themes and topics of importance to a specific culture

Goal 4: Students will learn how to reduce stereotyping, prejudice, and racism within themselves and within society.

Sample Activities

1. Critical media analysis
2. Linguistic and social history of terms

Goal 5: Students will develop the skills needed to take social action to eliminate social injustice.

Sample Activities

1. Mathematical presentation of data to encourage social action
2. Environmental racism simulation

Goal 6: Students will gain a recognition and understanding of global issues.

Sample Activities

1. Search the Internet for issues of concern to different countries
2. Examine the role of science in creating and solving global issues
3. Examine global issues through children's books

This focus on personal identities and cultural backgrounds lays the groundwork for further multicultural study. It helps students understand that there are different perspectives of the world, that there are different patterns of communication, that there are different traditions, and that all people have important cultural background factors that play a crucial role in who they are. As described in the Preface to this textbook and throughout chapter 1, our identities that have developed over a lifetime may be deeply woven into our personalities, and without studying those we may not realize the effects that these beliefs and attitudes have on our daily actions and practices. It is important, then, for communication and understanding, that students are drawn into the field and the issues of multicultural education by tying it to their own identities.

Sample Activities

1. Have students create cultural background pies of themselves. You did this activity at the beginning of chapter 1, and it might be useful for you to look at that pie again to see if it has changed in any respects. With a clear understanding of your own cultural background pie, you will be able to guide students to examine their own cultures to gain an awareness of their cultural background.

2. Have students create cultural silhouettes of themselves. In this variation of the background pie, students would have a physical representation of themselves through a paper cutout, but they would also write things about their background on the back of the silhouette. They may write about such questions as where they are from, their favorite activities, and perhaps what issue in the world they wish they could help improve. This would involve art and language arts, and could be adapted to virtually any grade level.

3. Create a class quilt, either with material or with paper. Students can bring to school something that comes from their homes or something that they have made at school. Example items would be material, photographs, artwork, or writing. As a class, the students can make a quilt by connecting each person's patch. An important part of this activity would be that the students would share what their item means to them. A number of multicultural children's books could be used in conjunction with this activity. *The Patchwork Quilt* is a story from the African-American community in which a sick grandmother gains strength by working on a quilt with her family and especially her granddaughter. In *The Weaving of a Dream*, a book that retells a traditional Chinese tale, a beautiful tapestry woven by a poor woman is stolen, and her family learns lessons as they seek to retrieve it. The importance of a quilt in keeping a family's traditions over generations is portrayed in *The Keeping Quilt*, in which a Russian family has used and passed on a quilt for four generations. And finally, *Sweet Clara and the Freedom Quilt* tells of the role of a quilt in the route of the Underground Railroad. When

slaves were escaping from slavery, they would sometimes see a quilt on a barn that had woven within it the path to freedom.

4. Find out from students what knowledge they have about a particular subject or topic. We may have learned information or attitudes from our families and communities. We may have learned information or stereotypes from the popular media that are presented within our culture. Before beginning a new topic, find out from students what they know and how or where they learned it. This will give students the opportunity to recognize that their knowledge arises within the context of their own cultures, and it will validate their beliefs that their culture has important information to contribute to society. Table A.2 presents a possible questionnaire form, which can be modified to be appropriate for your own setting.

Table A.2 Students' Personal and Cultural Knowledge of a Topic

---

What do you know about the subject of _____?

Describe how you learned this information. What information about this subject did you learn from:

Your family or neighborhood: _____

_____

The media (television, movies): _____

_____

School: _____

_____

Goal 2: Students Will Gain an Understanding of Different Perspectives on Life in the United States

As discussed consistently throughout this text, there are many perspectives on life in the United States, perspectives that are formed by individuals' cultural or ethnic backgrounds. The experiences that a member of one culture has had within the United States will be different from people of different cultures. The perspectives about life in the United States will arise out of these different sets of experiences. In this second goal of multicultural education, the teacher should move the class from the recognition that there are different perspectives toward an understanding of those perspectives. In particular, the multicultural teacher will ask students to look at different perspectives on a particular event or issue. As Banks (2006) writes, "The way that individuals perceive events and situations occurring in the United States is often influenced by their ethnic and cultural experiences" (p. 332). Therefore, Banks continues, "the teacher should try to help students understand how each group may view a situation differently and why" (p. 332). This approach, Banks argues, will help our students "understand that almost any event or situation can be legitimately looked at from many perspectives" (p. 322).

Sample Activities

1. A good way to gain an understanding of different perspectives on life in the United States is to engage students with a specific issue within society. For example, immigration is a topic that is seen through widely different perspectives by people who have widely different experiences with immigration. Here are two suggestions for sets of classroom experiences that would engage students in the understanding of different perspectives on immigration.

   (a) A number of multicultural children's books have been written that describe the experience of recent immigrants to the United States. In *Molly's Pilgrim*, a girl makes a Russian doll that represents her personal and family history of being a "pilgrim" to the United States. Through this book, children learn that pilgrims are not only people from England who came to this land a long time ago via the Netherlands, but rather that pilgrims today come from many countries and have many traditions that are brought with them. In a similarly current look at immigration, the book *How Many Days to America?* follows a family as they make their way from their home country to the United States. In a biographical children's story about immigrating from Japan to the United States, *Grandfather's Journey* describes the "homesick" feeling that a Japanese American feels for each of his countries. In children's books that address the language differences of recent immigrants, *I Hate English* is written from the perspective of a girl who thinks in Chinese and would like to speak in Chinese but is constantly pushed to speak and listen only in English. The book *I Speak English for My Mom* is written from the perspective of a girl who speaks English but whose mother speaks no English. The girl describes her translation activities for her mother, from answering the phone to going shopping.

   (b) For older students, a study of different perspectives on immigration could be undertaken by asking each student or group of students to study immigration through a different media source. For instance, one group could read articles in the mainstream newspaper within the town. Another group could read articles from a local Latino or Asian newspaper. One group could watch the local TV news reports. Another group could tune to a national news station. The letters to the editor could be read, and recent immigrants could be interviewed. The guiding question through this study is how do different people perceive the topic of immigration in the

United States? Further, are those perceptions based on actual experiences or on personal opinions.

2. Assign students the task of reading the newspapers from different parts of the United States or the world. This activity may involve a field trip to the nearby university library, or it may involve getting a subscription to several different newspapers. The types of stories included in the paper, the way that the stories are written, the photographs used in the paper—these will all vary from city to city. For instance, an issue affecting the daily lives of some students is an increased presence of security on their school campuses, in the form of security guards, metal detectors, or security cameras stationed throughout their schools. In some city newspapers, the opinion may be that this extra security is needed. In others, there may be a feeling that this is excessive monitoring of students. And in still other cities or town newspapers, the issue may not even be addressed at all. For this activity, the students could examine several items. They could pick an issue and note the different types of coverage from different locations. Or they could pick one racial or ethnic group and see how they are portrayed in the different articles. Is only one group included within a story about a problem?

Goal 3: Students Will Gain an Understanding of the Cultures of Specific Groups

The key theoretical foundation for this goal is the concept of cultural pluralism. In a society in which members of groups are allowed or encouraged to continue their culturally based ways of life, it is important for students to begin to understand what those different cultural ways of being entail. This will go beyond the surface approach in which students learn only about the foods, festivals, famous people, and fashion of a particular culture. This goal, instead, goes to the deeper cultural significance such as feelings and understandings of the world.

Banks (2006) describes the type of study needed in order to understand the cultures of specific groups:

> The curriculum should help students understand the significant historical experiences and basic cultural patterns of ethnic groups, the critical contemporary issues and social problems confronting each group, and the dynamic diversity of the experiences, cultures, and individuals within each ethnic group. (p. 322)

In this type of multicultural education experience in the classroom, concepts such as those described in chapter 1—communication, organization, and intellectual styles of different groups—will be the focus. Additionally, study of the historical development of groups such as that described in chapter 3 will help students understand the cultural experiences and understandings of specific groups.

Sample Activities

1. Do a comparative study of folktales and stories from different cultures. Ask students to discover what values are clearly represented in the stories. What are some of the differences across cultures? What are some of the similarities found within the stories? What do the structures of the stories, the characters and their actions, and the morals of the stories indicate to us about the traditions and values of the culture? How are the stories affected by the cultural values of that culture? A story that is fairly easy to find different versions of is the story of *Cinderella*. The story itself is common to many cultures, in the United States and around the world. But it is the differences within the stories that indicate the cultural values of that culture. Table A.3 gives an example of the kind of analysis that can be done of different Cinderella stories and of what that analysis can tell us about the cultures of specific groups.

Table A.3 Studying Cinderella Stories

Example Cinderella Stories from Different Cultures

Cinderella—The European version. When the king announced that the prince would find a wife at a great dance, the mean sisters and women in the kingdom dress beautifully for the dance. A fairy godmother appears and helps the nice sister have beautiful clothing and transportation. At the dance, the nice sister loses her glass slipper, and the prince vows to find the woman who fits the slipper. When he finds her, they are married.

Mufaro's Beautiful Daughters—A tale from Africa. When the king announced his intention to find a wife, the mean sister hurriedly went to visit the king. Along the way, she encountered people who needed help or who gave advice. She ignored them all and was scared away from the king's residence by a large snake monster. When the nice sister went to visit the king, she helped the people along the way and followed the advice of those who wanted to help. When she got to the king's residence, the king told her that he was actually all those people and that she was good-hearted and would become his wife.

Sootface—A tale from the Ojibwa people. A great warrior announced his intention to find a good-hearted and kind woman who would be his wife. But he was invisible to all people except for his future bride. He tested the women by having them describe his magic bow. The mean women in the village tried but could not see him or his bow. The nice sister, who was allowed by a birch tree to use its bark for a new dress, was able to see the warrior and his bow and became his wife.

(continued)

Table A.3 Studying Cinderella Stories (continued)

Additional Cinderella stories:

Adelita: A Mexican Cinderella Story—a story from Mexico

The Rough-Face Girl—a tale from the Algonquins.

Yeh-Shen—a tale from China.

Commonalities

- *Main character:* A young man or woman is treated unfairly by some of his or her family members.
- *Guidance or assistance:* The main character receives help from sources unknown to others, usually in the form of a magical or spiritual being.
- *The test:* The hero or heroine is tested in some way.
- *Ending:* A person of higher rank or status recognizes the inner strength and beauty of the hero or heroine, and a marriage usually ensues.

Differences Indicating Values and Traditions of the Culture

	Cinderella	*Mufaro's Beautiful Daughters*	*Sootface*
Helper	A magical person	A person who changed into other people and animals	The girl's inner strength
The test	Fitting in a slipper	Kindness to strangers and to plants and animals	Seeing an invisible bow
What was needed to pass the test	Physical beauty and kindness	Kindness	A good and kind heart

2. Students can learn to understand the cultures of specific groups by reading collections of stories written from within that culture. Examples include *The People Could Fly: American Black Folktales, A Rainbow at Night,* that is a collection of Navajo children's writings and drawings, and *Native American Animal Stories.* The book *The Circuit: Stories from the Life of a Migrant Child,* by Francisco Jiménez, is a collection of 12 short stories documenting the life and experiences of a Mexican-American family of migrant farm laborers, and is narrated by one of the children of the family. While reading these collections, students should draw out consistent themes that indicate the values, traditions, and understandings of the specific cultures. The teacher's guide for *Native American Animal Stories,* for instance, guides the teacher to recognize and to draw out from the writings the cultural themes of the particular tribe from which the story comes.

Sleeter and Grant (1993) suggest a series of topics that can frame the study of specific cultures. The topics are those that are important to the historical development of specific cultures and that help frame the contemporary concerns and life of people within those cultures. Table A.4 (on pp. 190–191) lists these suggested topics. Through studying these types of topics, students learn not just surface information about a cultural group but also the underlying roots—the understandings and values of the culture.

Goal 4: Students Will Learn How to Reduce Stereotyping, Prejudice, and Racism within Themselves and within Society

As discussed in chapter 2, the results of stereotyping, prejudice, and racism within society can be devastating for the individual and can limit the opportunities for a society to grow. When an individual is commonly and consistently bombarded with prejudice toward himself or herself or toward his or her group, that person's sense of identity and self-esteem is lowered. Some people react by rejecting their own identity group; others react by rejecting other identity groups. In either case, the results are lack of discourse with and understanding of others. To revisit a quote by Charles Taylor (1994), "Due recognition is not just a courtesy we owe people. It is a vital human need" (p. 75).

In encouraging students to reduce stereotyping, prejudice, and racism, the teacher can arrange for students to examine the nature of society and how it allows prejudice and racism to develop and continue. As a continuation from goal 1, students should first understand how they are affected by prejudice and racism. Students can then study how prejudice has developed historically in relation to the political economy, the social attitudes, and the prevailing practices of particular periods. And finally, the emotional impact of prejudice and racism on individuals can be examined as an additional base for beginning to reduce stereotyping, prejudice, and racism. Activities addressing goal 4 center on helping students recognize the stereotyping, prejudice, and racism within society, and to come to understand the feelings involved in situations involving prejudice and racism.

Sample Activities

1. Have students undertake a critical analysis of media representations of different cultural and racial groups. Students may start by keeping a record of how often people of different races and genders are included within the media. But in addition, they should document the roles that the different people are asked to portray. Table A.5 (on p. 192) is a worksheet of some beginning ideas for undertaking a critical media analysis.

2. Students can examine the linguistic and social history of terms or phrases used to describe groups of people. Why, for instance, is there a controversy over whether to use the term Hispanic, Latino/Latina, or Chicano/Chicana? What is the history behind the shifts in preferred names? Why have certain characteristics been stereotyped as belong-

---

Table A.4 Central Themes for the Study of Specific Cultural Groups

The themes suggested below are important to the lives of many students, both to gain a better understanding of the historical development of a particular culture and to gain an insight into the contemporary perspectives held by members of the culture. Lists such as these can be studied for any selected culture after a gathering of perceptions of which topics are of particular importance to that group.

Hispanic American Studies

- Ancient Central and South American civilizations (especially Mayan, Aztec, and Incan) were highly developed
- Blending the cultures of indigenous Americans, Africans, and Europeans was often a violent process, but it yielded vibrant cultures
- U.S. conquest of northern Mexico and of Puerto Rico; how the process of colonization worked
- The Catholic Church: an institution of colonialism or liberation?
- Latino labor in the United States: resisting institutionalized impoverishment by American agribusiness
- Language, literature, and philosophy; how the Spanish language encodes meaning, identity, and worldview
- La familia y el barrio: social organization; personal identity as inseparable from group membership
- Puerto Rico: statehood or independence?
- Immigration in the 1980s and 1990s from Central and South America; how U.S. immigration policies silence Latinos
- Current political and cultural issues of Latinos

Women's Studies

- Gender differences and gender inequality: What is actually fair and what isn't?
- How biology is used as a control mechanism; to what extent are the sexes innately different, and to what extent does biology determine destiny? Physically, what are women capable of?
- The private sphere (the home, dominated by women) versus the public sphere (dominated by men): How does the private sphere limit women's access to the public sphere, and why is the private sphere regarded as "out of bounds" for critique?

(continued)

- Impoverishment of women; physical and psychological violence against women, processes used to exclude and devalue women from economic and political activity in the public sphere
- Gender as a cultural construct; how each sex, and how sex itself, is represented in the media, arts, etc.
- Creative capacities of women and expressions of women's voices in the arts and domestic arts
- Work women do in producing and educating the next generation
- Women as racially, ethnically, and culturally diverse
- Women as social activists

African American Studies
- Ancient Egypt, the cradle of civilization
- Other precolonial African kingdoms
- Colonization and enslavement
- Building the church: the emergence of African-American institutions
- Resisting the yoke of slavery
- Reconstruction
- The Harlem Renaissance
- The Civil Rights movement
- Black nationalism in Africa, the Caribbean, and South America
- Creators, thinkers, and builders today

Native American Studies
(These are a suggested sequence of courses for Native American Studies.)
- Prehistory of the United States
- North American Indians
- American Indian art
- Introduction to literature of the American Indian
- Major works in American Indian literature
- The American Indian in literature and film
- American Indian history
- Contemporary issues in Native American societies

Source: *Making Choices for Multicultural Education,* by Sleeter/Grant © 1993. Adapted by permission of John Wiley and Sons, Inc.

Table A.5 Worksheet for Critical Media Analysis

For this analysis, select three racial, ethnic, or gender groups to consider within a movie, a television show, or a several-hour period of television programming.

Name of Movie, Television Show, or Time Period of Television Programming:

_____

	Group 1	*Group 2*	*Group 3*
Number of times a person from this group is on screen			
Length of time a person from this group is on screen			
Role of people from this group in relation to the lead character			
Actions taken by members of this group in the shows			
Characteristics portrayed by members of this group in the shows			
Are these roles and characteristics reinforced in society?			

---

ing to specific racial and cultural groups but not others? With an understanding of the linguistic and social history of a phrase, people can more easily adapt their language to weed out stereotypical, oppressive, and offensive terms.

Goal 5: Students Will Develop the Skills Needed to Take Social Action to Eliminate Social Injustice

This goal is based on the foundations of the democratic society and on goal 4, the recognition of, and desire to eliminate, prejudice and racism. In using this goal, teachers encourage students to develop critical thinking skills, reflective decision making, and personal and civic action. In addition, students would need to develop an understanding of the causes of oppression and inequality in the United States.

Sample Activities

1. In Mathematics class, working with data that indicates inequities within society, ask the students to prepare a set of data for presentation that has the purpose of convincing a legislator to change a policy. Examples of data could be the salaries or wages for people of different races and genders. Or it could be the price of housing in a community compared to the average salary or wage of the community member. In preparing the data for the purpose of taking social action, students could present the data in graph form, in a Venn diagram form, in mathematical equations, or through some other visual display. The key would be to present mathematical information in a way that would convince someone to take action to eliminate social injustice.

2. Conduct a simulation on environmental racism. Have students first gather information on the race and gender of the members of their town's governing council and then gather the same information on the owner, CEO, or ruling body of a particular corporation that might choose to place a toxic dump within their community. Form student groups that will have the role of representing different interests within the community: local residents (indicate the races of the residents), local businesses, local government, local schools, political or social action groups, the local or national press, and so on. In conducting the simulation, the issue of lack of political power for poor and minority groups will likely be emphasized. The students should gain an understanding of how decisions are made within a community and of how local groups can contribute to the process.

Goal 6: Students Will Gain a Recognition and Understanding of Global Issues

The focus in the first five goals has moved from an understanding of self, to an understanding of other cultures, to the actions of reducing prejudice and racism as well as eliminating social injustice. In this sixth goal, the emphasis moves to the global level. This goal encompasses a number of inter-related sets of knowledge, including an awareness of conditions throughout the world, e.g. population growth, migrations, economic conditions, political systems and their changes, inter-nation conflicts, as well as the impact of the policies of the U.S. on the rest of the world.

Sample Activities

1. Have students go on the Internet to explore the issues of concern to different countries. Each student could select one country and research what current issues are being addressed by the government or the people of that country. Depending on what the students find, they could then be asked to compare the types of concerns globally with concerns in the United States, or within their state, or within their

local community. In addition to discovering the types of concerns that people hold, students can discover methods of addressing issues that are used by people from different countries or cultures.

2. In Science class, students can be asked to research and discover the role of science and technology in the study of global issues. A few examples of global issues include the destruction of the rainforest, nuclear development and testing, hunger, and so on. The focus questions would be: What role has science played in contributing to this global issue? How has this global issue affected the different peoples of the world? What role can science play in the study of solutions or alternatives to this global problem? The focus would thus be on understanding the scientific principles involved in the development of global systems, with the additional focus on the social implications of that type of development.

3. Some children's books have been written that address global and social issues, including the following three books that deal with environmental issues. The book *Why the Sky Is Far Away* is a tale that has been passed down in Africa. It tells about how the sky once was very close and was made of all the food that people needed to live. But in their greediness, the people took too much of it, and now the sky is far away and unattainable. Two children's books that also address the loss of natural resources both are about the loss of the forests. *The Lorax* is a popular Dr. Seuss book, with an accompanying animated movie, in which a character called the lorax watches in vain as the last trees are cut down. And in the similar theme, but this time a true story, *The People Who Hugged the Trees* chronicles the efforts of one woman to stop the destruction of a forest. She won her battle and is now recognized as a hero in the stopping of forest destruction.

One Last Suggestion for a Multicultural Classroom Activity

This activity may be done with children in a classroom. It is probably a good idea to undertake the activity as teachers or future teachers as well, in order to learn more about the community and to be able to later guide children in classrooms to undertake the activity.

Brainstorm to develop a list of ideas about how you could learn about your current community. What would you ask about your community? What types of things would you be able to learn? The following are some ideas to begin your project. You can add many additional ideas that arise within your particular community.

- Old newspapers
- Museums
- Events or activities in the community
- City charter

- Businesses, and the opening and closing of businesses
- Schools, and the opening and closing of schools over time
- School and college yearbooks over time
- Architectural significance of the buildings in town
- Theaters
- Social services resources
- Religious affiliations

After you have brainstormed ideas for what resources you might check in the community, share your ideas with a small group in class. Once a complete list is developed, assign each person in the group a set of community resources to examine. What have you discovered that is multicultural about your community? Or that is based solely on the middle-class European American culture? Where did the architectural styles come from? What cultural information is shared in museums? What groups have lived in your community in the past, and how is that changing currently?

Two resources may be of use in this project. One is a computer program with booklet and video called *Cultural Reporter,* in which groups of high school students actually did projects like the one suggested here. A second is a young adult book called *Come Home with Me: A Multicultural Treasure Hunt.* This is a book in which teenagers learn about their communities by documenting places and events that are important to the different people in their communities, such as churches, stores, agencies that provide transitional services, and playgrounds. The students wrote descriptions and took photographs of these places. This type of learning process is suggested for this preliminary activity.

Table A.6 Bibliography of Multicultural Children's Books Referenced in Appendix

---

Goal 1

Sweet Clara and the Freedom Quilt by Deborah Hopkinson (New York: Alfred A. Knopf, 1993).

The Keeping Quilt by Patricia Polacco (New York: Simon and Schuster, 1988).

The Patchwork Quilt by Valerie Flournoy (New York: Dial Books for Young Children, 1985).

The Weaving of a Dream by Marilee Heyer (New York: Viking Kestrel, 1986).

Goal 2

Grandfather's Journey by Allen Say (Boston: Houghton Mifflin, 1993).

How Many Days to America? by Eve Bunting (New York: Clarion Books, 1988).

I Hate English by Ellen Levine (New York: Scholastic Inc., 1989).

I Speak English for My Mom by Muriel Stanek (Morton Grove, IL: Albert Whitman and Company, 1989).

Molly's Pilgrim by Barbara Cohen (New York: Lothrop, Lee, and Shepard Books, 1983).

Goal 3

A Rainbow at Night by Bruce Hucko (San Francisco: Chronicle Books, 1996).

Adelita: A Mexican Cinderella Story by Tomie De Paola (New York: G. P. Putnam's Sons, 2002).

The Circuit: Stories from the Life of a Migrant Child by Francisco Jiménez (Albuquerque, NM: University of New Mexico Press, 1997).

Mufaro's Beautiful Daughters by John Steptoe (New York: Lothrop, Lee, and Shepard Books, 1987).

Native American Animal Stories by Joseph Bruchac (Golden, CO: Fulcrum Publishing, 1992).

Sootface by Robert D. San Souci (New York: Delacorte Press, 1994).

The People Could Fly: American Black Folktales by Virginia Hamilton (New York: Alfred A. Knopf, 1985).

The Rough-Face Girl by Rafe Martin (New York: G. P. Putnam's Sons, 1992).

Yeh-Shen by Ai-Ling Louie (New York: Philomel Books, 1982).

Goal 6

The Lorax by Dr. Seuss (New York: Lectorum Publications, 1993).

The People Who Hugged the Trees by Deborah L. Rose (Emeryville, CA: R. Rinehart, 1994).

Why the Sky is Far Away by Mary-Joan Gerson (Boston: Little, Brown, 1992).

Final Activity

Come Home with Me: A Multicultural Treasure Hunt by Aylette Jenness (New York: New Press, 1990).

Cultural Reporter by Lisa Falk (Washington, DC: Smithsonian Institution, 1995).

Bibliography

Aaronson, Elliot, Wilson, Timothy D., and Akert, Robin M., *Social Psychology* (4th ed.) (Upper Saddle River, NJ: Prentice-Hall, 2002).

Abeel, Samantha, "Reach for the Moon," in *American Voices: Webs of Diversity,* eds. Elizabeth Quintero and Mary Kay Rummel (Upper Saddle River, NJ: Prentice-Hall, 1998), 138–142.

Access USA, Inc., *The Complete Guide to Immigration and Successful Living in the United States* (Millington, NJ: Access USA, 1994).

Adorno, Theodore W., Frenkel-Brunswil, Else, Levinson, Daniel J., and Sanford, R. Nevitt., *The Authoritarian Personality* (New York: Harper and Row, 1950).

Allport, Gordon W., *The Nature of Prejudice* (Garden City, NY: Doubleday Anchor, 1958).

Anderson, James A., and Adams, Maurianne, "Acknowledging the Learning Styles of Diverse Student Populations: Implications for Instructional Design," *New Directions for Teaching and Learning,* (49) (1992): 19–33.

Anderson, James D., *The Education of Blacks in the South, 1860–1935* (Chapel Hill, NC: University of North Carolina Press, 1988).

Anderson, James, "Cognitive Styles and Multicultural Populations," *Journal of Teacher Education, 39* (1) (1988): 2–9.

Appleton, Nicholas, *Cultural Pluralism in Education* (New York: Longman, 1983).

Arendt, Hannah, *The Human Condition* (Chicago: University of Chicago Press, 1958).

Association of Teacher Educators, *21st Century: Restructuring the Education of Teachers,* (Reston, VA: Association of Teacher Educators, 1991).

Axtell, James (ed.), *The European and the Indian: Essays in the Ethnohistory of Colonial North America* (Oxford: Oxford University Press, 1981).

Banks, James A., *Multiethnic Education, Theory and Practice*, 3rd ed. (Boston: Allyn & Bacon, 1994).

Banks, James A., *Teaching Strategies for Ethnic Studies,* 6th ed. (Boston: Allyn & Bacon, 1997).

Banks, James A., *Cultural Diversity and Education: Foundations, Curriculum, and Teaching,* 5th ed. (Boston: Allyn & Bacon, 2006).

Barton, Paul E., *Parsing the Achievement Gap: Baselines for Tracking Progress* (Princeton, NJ: Educational Testing Service, 2003).

Beck, John M., and Saxe, Richard W., *Teaching the Culturally Disadvantaged Pupil* (Springfield, IL: Charles C. Thomas, 1969).

Bennett, Christine I., *Comprehensive Multicultural Education: Theory and Practice,* 3rd ed. (Boston: Allyn & Bacon, 1995).

Bennett, Christine I., *Comprehensive Multicultural Education: Theory and Practice,* 6th ed. (Boston: Allyn & Bacon, 2006).

Bernstein, Nina, "Overhaul of Immigration Law Could Reshape New York," *New York Times,* (May 30, 2007).

Bowles, Samuel, "Unequal Education and the Reproduction of the Social Division of Labor," in *Schooling in a Corporate Society: The Political Economy of Education in America,* ed. Martin Carnoy (New York: David McKay, 1975).

Brown, Bettina L., "Teaching Style vs. Learning Style. Myths and Realities." (ERIC Document Reproduction Service No. ED482329, 2003).

Browning, R. Stephen (ed.), *From Brown to Bradley: School Desegregation 1954–1974* (Washington, DC: Jefferson Law Book Company, 1975).

Browning-Aiken, Anne, "Border Crossings: Funds of Knowledge within an Immigrant Household," in *Funds of Knowledge: Theorizing Practices in Households, Communities, and Classrooms*, eds. Norma González, Luis C. Moll, and Cathy Amanti (Mahwah, NJ: Lawrence Erlbaum, 2005), 167–181.

Bullard, Robert D., Mohai, Paul, Saha, Robin, and Wright, Beverly, *Toxic Wastes and Race at 20: 1987–2007* (Cleveland, OH: The United Church of Christ, 2007).

Burbules, Nicholas C., and Rice, Suzanne, "Dialogue across Differences: Continuing the Conversation," *Harvard Educational Review, 61* (4) 1991: 393–416.

Carlson, Dennis, and Schramm-Pate, Susan L., "Risky Business: Teaching about the Confederate Flag Controversy in a South Carolina High School," in *Beyond Silenced Voices: Class, Race, and Gender in United States Schools*, revised ed., eds. Lois Weis and Michelle Fine (New York: State University of New York Press, 2005), 217–231.

Cass, Vivienne C., "Homosexual Identity Formation: A Theoretical Model," *Journal of Homosexuality, 4* (3) (1979): 219–235.

Castellano, Olivia, "Canto, Locura y Poesia," in *Race Class and Gender: An Anthology,* 3rd. ed., eds. Margaret L. Andersen and Patricia Hill Collins (Belmont, CA: Wadsworth, 1998), 341–349.

Chavez, J. M., and Roney, C. E., "Psychocultural Factors Affecting the Mental Health Status of Mexican American Adolescents," in *Ethnic Issues in Adolescent and Mental Health*, eds. A. R. Stiffman and L. E. Davis (Newbury Park, CA: Sage, 1990), 73–91.

Checkley, Kathy, "The First Seven . . . and the Eighth: A Conversation with Howard Gardner," *Educational Leadership, 55* (1) (1997): 8–13.

Chu, Harold, "Multiculturalism," in *Dictionary of Multicultural Education*, eds. Carl A. Grant and Gloria Ladson-Billings (Phoenix, AZ: Onyx Press, 1997), 182–183.

Cisneros, Sandra, *The House on Mango Street* (New York: Vintage Contemporary Books, 1989).

Citykids Staff, and Mitchell, Carolyn B., *City Kids Speak on Prejudice* (New York: Random House Books for Young Readers, 1994).

Cleary, Linda Miller, and Peacock, Thomas D., *Collected Wisdom: American Indian Education* (Boston: Allyn & Bacon, 1998).

Cochran, Floyd, "How Hate Groups Recruit Our Young People," *Montana Schools* (Nov/Dec 1992): 10–11.

Coleman, Michael C., *American Indian Children at School, 1850–1930* (Jackson: University Press of Mississippi, 1993).

Cook, Joan, *Foundations of Instructional Computing,* packet of course materials (Bozeman: Montana State University, 1997).

CREDE (Center for Research on Education, Diversity and Excellence), "Various Reports." (Santa Cruz, CA: UC Santa Cruz, 2004). Retrieved from the CREDE Web site at http://www.coe.uh.edu/crede/synthesis.html

Cross, William E., Jr., "The Negro-to-Black Conversion Experience: Toward a Psychology of Black Liberation," *Black World, 20* (9) (1971): 13–27.

Cubberly, Ellwood P., *Changing Conceptions of Education* (Boston: Houghton Mifflin, Company, 1975).

Cummins, Jim, Bismilla, Vicki, Chow, Patricia, Giampapa, Frances, Cohen, Sarah, Leoni, Lisa, Sandhu, Perminder and Sastri, Padma, "Affirming Identity in Multilingual Classrooms," *Educational Leadership, 63* (1) (2005): 38–43.

D'Andrea, Michael, and Daniels, Judy, "Exploring the Different Levels of Multicultural Counseling Training in Counselor Education," *Journal of Counseling and Development, 69* (2) (1990): 78–85.

"Defects of Irish Immigrants, 1851," *The Massachusetts Teachers* (1851): 289–291.

Delpit, Lisa, *Other People's Children: Cultural Conflict in the Classroom* (New York: W. W. Norton, 1995).

DeMarrais, Kathleen Bennett, and LeCompte, Margaret D., *The Way Schools Work: A Sociological Analysis of Education,* 2nd ed. (New York: Longman, 1995).

Donahue, David M., and Flowers, Nancy, *The Uprooted: Refugees and the United States: A Multidisciplinary Teaching Guide* (New York: Amnesty International, 1995).

Dunn, Rita, and Dunn, Kenneth, *Teaching Secondary Students through Their Individual Learning Styles: Practical Approaches for Grades 7–12* (Boston: Allyn & Bacon, 1993).

Dunne, Joseph, *Back to the Rough Ground: Phronesis and Techne in Modern Philosophy and in Aristotle* (Notre Dame, IN: University of Notre Dame Press, 1992).

Durkheim, Émile, "Definition of Education," in *Schools and Society: A Reader in Education and Sociology,* ed. J. H. Ballantine (Palo Alto, CA: Mayfield, 1985), 19–22.

Eckert, Penelope, *Jocks and Burnouts: Social Categories and Identity in the High School* (New York: Teachers College Press, 1989).

Eder, Donna, "Book Review of *Subtractive Schooling," Bilingual Research Journal, 23* (2–3) (1999).

Educational Research Service, *Culturally Sensitive Instruction and Student Learning* (Arlington, VA: Educational Research Service, 1991).

Elkins, Stanley M., *Slavery* (New York: Grosset and Dunlap, 1963).

Erikson, Erik H., *Identity and the Life Cycle* (New York: International Universities Press, 1959).

Erikson, Erik H., *Childhood and Society,* 2nd ed. (New York: Norton, 1963).

Escalante, Jaime, and Dirmann, Jack, "The Jaime Escalante Math Program," *Journal of Negro Education, 59* (30) (1990): 407–423.

Evans-Winters, Venus E., *Teaching Black Girls: Resiliency in Urban Classrooms.* (New York: Peter Lang, 2005).

Feagin, Joe R., and Feagin, Clairece B., *Racial and Ethnic Relations,* 7th ed. (Englewood Cliffs, NJ: Prentice-Hall, 2003).

Fellenz, Robert A., and Conti, Gary J., *Self-Knowledge Inventory of Lifelong Learning Strategies (SKILLS) Manual.* Bozeman, MT: Center for Adult Learning Research.

Fine, M., Weis, L., Centrie, C., and Roberts, R., "Educating Beyond the Borders of Schooling," *Anthropology and Education Quarterly, 31* (2) (2000): 131–151.

Fisher, Margaret, "Equal Protection Under Law: Access to Public Education" (Washington, DC: Office of Juvenile Justice and Delinquent Prevention, 1995).

Fiske, Susan T., and Taylor, Shelley E., *Social Cognition* (New York: McGraw-Hill, 1991).

Franklin, John Hope, and Starr, I. Sidore (eds.), *The Negro in 20th Century America: A Reader on the Struggle for Civil Rights* (New York: Random House, 1967).

Frost, Joe L., and Hawkes, Glenn R., *The Disadvantaged Child* (Boston: Houghton Mifflin, 1966).

Fuchs, Lawrence H., "The American Civic Culture and an Inclusivist Immigration Policy," in *Handbook of Research on Multicultural Education,* eds. James A. Banks and Cherry A. McGee Banks (New York: Macmillan, 1995), 293–309.

Gadamer, Hans Georg, *Truth and Method* (New York: The Seabury Press, 1975).

Gadamer, Hans-Georg, *Truth and Method,* 2nd ed. (New York: Continuum Publishing, 1993).

Gardner, Howard, *Frames of Mind: The Theory of Multiple Intelligences* (New York: Basic Books, 1983).

Gardner, Howard, *The Unschooled Mind: How Children Think and How Schools Should Teach* (New York: Basic Books, 1991).

Genovese, Eugene D., *Roll Jordan Roll: The World the Slaves Made* (New York: Random House, 1976).

George, Phil, "Name Giveaway," in *Tongue-Tied: The Lives of Multilingual Children in Public Education*, ed. Otto Santa Ana, (Boulder, CO: Rowman & Littlefield, 2004), 31.

Giroux, Henry A., "Insurgent Multiculturalism and the Promise of Pedagogy," in *Multiculturalism: A Critical Reader,* ed. David Theo Goldberg (Blackwell, 1994), 325–343.

Golombek, Silvia Blitzer, *A Sociological Image of the City: Through Children's Eyes* (New York: Peter Lang, 1993).

Gougeon, Thomas D., "Orienting New Professionals to Small Isolated Communities," in *Issues Affecting Rural Communities (II). Proceedings of the International Conference [on] Rural Communities and Identities in the Global Millennium*, eds. Jim C. Montgomery and Andrew D. Kitchenham (Nanaimo, BC, Canada: Rural Communities Research and Development Centre, Malaspina University College, 2000).

Gregorc, Anthony F., "Learning/Teaching Styles: Their Nature and Effects," in *Student Learning Styles: Diagnosing and Prescribing Programs*, ed. National Association of Secondary School Principals (Reston, VA: National Association of Secondary School Principals, 1979), 19–26.

Gruwell, Erin, *The Freedom Writers Diary: How a Teacher and 150 Teens Used Writing to Change Themselves and the World Around Them* (New York: Broadway Books, 1999).

Gutierrez, Ramon A., "Ethnic Mexicans in Historical and Social Science Scholarship," in *Handbook of Research on Multicultural Education* (2nd ed.), eds. James A. Banks and Cherry A. McGee Banks (San Francisco: Jossey-Bass, 2004), 261–287.

Hale, Janice E., *Learning while Black: Creating Educational Excellence for African American Children* (Baltimore, MD: The Johns Hopkins University Press, 2001).

Hall, Edward T., *The Hidden Dimension* (New York: Doubleday, 1966).

Hanvey, R., *An Attainable Global Perspective* (New York: Center for War/Peace Studies, 1975).

Heath, Shirley Brice, "What No Bedtime Story Means: Narrative Skills at Home and School," *Language in Society, 11* (1) (1982): 49–76.

Heath, Shirley Brice, *Ways with Words* (Cambridge: Cambridge University Press, 1983).

Helms, Janet E., "Considering Some Methodological Issues in Racial Identity Counseling Research," *The Counseling Psychologist, 17* (2) (1989): 227–252.

Helms, Janet E., *Black and White Racial Identity: Theory, Research, and Practice* (Westport, CT: Greenwood Press, 1990).

Hernandez, Donald J., "Children and Youth in Immigrant Families: Demographic, Social, and Educational Issues," in *Handbook of Research on Multicultural Education* (2nd ed.), eds. James A. Banks and Cherry A. McGee Banks (San Francisco: Jossey-Bass, 2004), 404–419.

Hernandez, Leonardo, and Carlquist-Hernandez, Karen, "Humanization of the Counseling–Teaching Process for Latinos: Learning Principles," *Journal of Non-White Concerns, 7* (1979): pp. 150–158.

Hilliard, Asa G., "Behavioral Style, Culture, and Teaching and Learning," *Journal of Negro Education, 61* (3) (1992): 370–377.

Hoare, Carol H., "Psychosocial Identity Development and Cultural Others," *Journal of Counseling and Development, 70* (1991): 45–53.

Howey, Kenneth R., *A Conceptual Map to Guide the Great City Universities Urban Educator Corps Partnership Initiative* (2001). Retrieved from The Great City Universities Web site at http://www.gcu-edu.org/conceptualframework.doc

Hytten, Kathy, "The Promise of Cultural Studies in Education," *Educational Theory, 49* (4) (1999): 527–543.

Igoa, Christina, *The Inner World of the Immigrant Child* (New York: St. Martin's Press, 1995).

Irvine, Jacqueline Jordan, and York, Darlene Eleanor, "Learning Styles and Culturally Diverse Students: A Literature Review," in *Handbook of Research on Multicultural Education*, eds. James A. Banks and Cherry A. McGee Banks (New York: Macmillan, 1995), 484–497.

Jackson, Philip W., Boostrom, Robert E., and Hansen, David T., *The Moral Life of Schools* (San Francisco: Jossey-Bass, 1998).

Jeffries, Dexter, "Who I Am," in *Identities: Readings from Contemporary Culture*, ed. Ann Raimes (Boston: Houghton Mifflin, 1996).

Jones, Melinda, *Social Psychology of Prejudice* (Upper Saddle River, NJ: Prentice-Hall, 2002).

Jussim, Lee, and Fleming, Christopher, "Self-Fulfilling Prophecies and the Maintenance of Social Stereotypes: The Role of Dyadic Interactions and Social Forces," in *Stereotypes and Stereotyping*, eds. C. Neil Macrae, Charles Stangor, and Charles Hewstone (New York: The Guilford Press, 1996), 161–192.

Keefe, James W., and Languis, Marlin (untitled article), *Learning Stages Network Newsletter, 4* (2) (1983, Summer): 1.

Kim, Heejung S., and Markus, Hazel Rose, "Speech and Silence: An Analysis of the Cultural Practice of Talking" in *Beyond Silenced Voices: Class, Race, and Gender in United States Schools*, eds. Lois Weis and Michelle Fine (Albany: State University of New York Press, 2005), 181–196.

Kimball, Stephanie, and Garrison, James, *Hermeneutic Listening and Multicultural Conversations*. Paper presented at the 1994 Annual Meeting of the American Educational Research Association, New Orleans.

Kimball, Stephanie, and Garrison, James, "Hermeneutic Listening: An Approach to Understanding in Multicultural Conversations," *Studies in Philosophy and Education, 15* (1996): 51–59.

Kipp, Darrell Robes, Fisher, Joe, and Native Voices Public Television, *Transitions: Destruction of a Mother Tongue* (videotape) (Bozeman, MT: Montana Public Television, 1991).

Kluger, Richard, *Simple Justice* (New York: Alfred A. Knopf, 1976).

Kolb, David A., *Experiential Learning: Experience as the Source of Learning and Development* (Englewood Cliffs, NJ: Prentice-Hall, 1984).

Kozol, Jonathan, "Still Separate, Still Unequal: America's Educational Apartheid," *Harper's Magazine*, 311 (1864) (2005).

Kroeber, Alfred Lewis, and Kluckhohn, Clyde, *Culture: A Critical Review of Concepts and Definitions* (New York: Vintage Books, 1963).

Kronenwetter, Michael, *United They Hate* (New York: Walker and Company, 1992).

Ladson-Billings, Gloria, "Culturally Relevant Teaching: The Key to Making Multicultural Education Work," in *Research and Multicultural Education: From the Margins to the Mainstream*, ed. Carl A. Grant (Washington, DC: The Falmer Press, 1992), 106–121.

Larson, Colleen L., and Ovando, Carlos, J., *The Color of Bureaucracy: The Politics of Equity in Multicultural School Communities* (Belmont, CA: Wadsworth, 2001).

Lazear, David, *Eight Ways of Teaching: The Artistry of Teaching with Multiple Intelligences* (Arlington Heights, IL: SkyLight Professional Development, 1999).

Lee, Carol D., and Slaughter-Defoe, Diana T. "Historical and Sociocultural Influences on African American Education" in *Handbook of Research on Multicultural Education* (2nd ed.), eds. James A. Banks and Cherry A. McGee Banks (San Francisco: Jossey-Bass, 2004), 462–490.

Lehman, P. R., "The Emotional Challenge of Ethnic Studies Classes," *College Teaching, 40* (4) (1993): 134–137.

Levinson, Natasha, "Beginning Again: Teaching, Natality, and Social Transformation," in *Philosophy of Education 1996,* ed. Frank Margonis (Urbana, IL: The Philosophy of Education Society, 1997), pp. 241–251.

Lewin, Kurt, *Resolving Social Conflicts* (New York: Harper, 1948).

Lindborg, K., and Ovando, C. J., "School and Community," in *Bilingual and ESL Classrooms: Teaching in Multicultural Contexts,* 2nd ed., eds. C. J. Ovando and V. P. Collier (Boston: McGraw-Hill, 1998), 269–318.

Locke, Don C., *Increasing Multicultural Understanding: A Comprehensive Model,* 2nd ed. (Thousand Oaks, CA: Sage, 1998).

Logan, Richard D., and O'Hearn, George T., "Thought-Style and Life-Style: Some Hypothesized Relationships," *Science Education, 66* (4) (1982): 515–530.

Lomawaima, K. Tsianina, "Educating Native Americans," in *Handbook of Research on Multicultural Education,* eds. James A. Banks and Cherry A. McGee Banks (New York: Macmillan, 1995), pp. 331–347.

Long Standing Bear Chief, a.k.a. Harold E. Gray, *Ni-Kso-Ko-Wa: Blackfoot Spirituality, Traditions, Values and Beliefs* (Browning, MT: Spirit Talk Press, 1992).

Lucas, Tamara, "Influences on the Educational Experiences of Immigrant Students to U.S. Schools" (New Jersey: Author, 1997).

Madrid, Arturo, "Missing People and Others: Joining Together to Expand the Circle," in *Race Class and Gender: An Anthology,* 3rd ed., eds. Margaret L. Andersen and Patricia Hill Collins (Belmont, CA: Wadsworth, 1998), 21–26.

Maldonado, Jr., David, "Ethnic Self-Identity and Self-Understanding," *Social Casework,* (December 1975): 618–622.

Marcia, James E., "Identity in Adolescence," in *Handbook of Adolescent Psychology,* ed. Joseph Adelson (New York: John Wiley and Sons, 1980).

Marshall, Patricia, "Four Misconceptions about Multicultural Education that Impede Understanding," *Action in Teacher Education, 16* (3) 1994: 19–27.

Maslow, Abraham H., "A Theory of Human Motivation," *Psychological Review, 50* (1943): 370–396.

Max Inventory of Learning Styles (computer program) (Santa Barbara, CA: Intellimation Library for the MacIntosh, 1991).

McIntosh, Peggy, "White Privilege: Unpacking the Invisible Knapsack," in *Sources: Notable Selections in Multicultural Education,* ed. Jana Noel (Guilford, CT: Dushkin/McGraw-Hill, 2000), pp. 115–120.

McLaren, Peter, *Life in Schools: An Introduction to Critical Pedagogy in the Foundations of Education,* 4th ed. (Boston: Allyn & Bacon, 2002).

Meier, Matt S., and Rivera, Feliciano, *The Chicanos: A History of Mexican Americans* (New York: Hill and Wang, 1972).

Merton, Robert K., "The Self-Fulfilling Prophecy," *The Antioch Review, 8* (1948): 193–210.

Moll, Luis, Amanti, Cathy, Neff, Deborah, González, Norma, "Funds of Knowledge for Teaching: Using a Qualitative Approach to Connect Homes and Classrooms," *Theory Into Practice, 31* (1992): 132–141.

Mura, David, "Strangers in the Village," in *American Mosaic: Multicultural Readings in Context*, eds. Barbara Roche Rico and Sandra Mano (Boston: Houghton Mifflin, 1995), 696–708.

Murrell, Peter, *The Community Teacher: A New Framework for Effective Urban Teaching* (New York: Teachers College Press, 2001).

Myers, Linda J., Speight, Suzette L., Highlen, Pamela S., Cox, Chikako I., Reynolds, Amy L., Adams, Eve M., and Hanley, C. Patricia, "Identity Development and Worldview: Toward an Optimal Conceptualization," *Journal of Counseling and Development, 69* (2) (1990): 54–63.

Newman, William A., *American Pluralism: A Study of Minority Groups and Social Theory* (New York: Harper and Row, 1973).

Nieto, Sonia, *Affirming Diversity: The Sociocultural Context of Multicultural Education*, 2nd ed. (New York: Longman, 1996).

Nieto, Sonia, *Affirming Diversity: The Sociopolitical Context of Multicultural Education*, 4th ed. (Boston: Pearson, 2004a).

Nieto, Sonia, "Puerto Rican Students in U.S. Schools: A Troubled Past and the Search for a Hopeful Future," in *Handbook of Research on Multicultural Education* (2nd ed.), eds. James A. Banks and Cherry A. McGee Banks (San Francisco: Jossey-Bass, 2004b), 515–541.

Nisbett, Richard, and Ross, Lee, *Human Inference: Strategies and Shortcomings of Social Judgment* (Englewood Cliffs, NJ: Prentice-Hall, 1980).

Noel, Jana R., "Physical and Cultural Dimensions of Horizon," in *Philosophy of Education 1996,* ed. Frank Margonis (Urbana, IL: The Philosophy of Education Society, 1997), pp. 307–314.

Noel, Jana R., "Multicultural Teacher Education: From Awareness through Emotions to Action," *Journal of Teacher Education, 46* (4), 1995a: 267–273.

Noel, Jana R., "Preparing Teachers for Diversity through Critical Conversation," *Journal of Professional Studies, 3* (1) 1995b: 69–73.

Noel, Jana R., "Self, Community and the Overcoming of Prejudice," *Studies in Philosophy and Education, 15* (1996): 131–137.

Noel, Jana R., "Integrating a New Urban Teacher Education Center into a School and Its Community," *Journal of Urban Learning, Teaching, and Research, 2* (2006): 197–205.

Novak, Michael, *The Rise of the Unmeltable Ethnics: Politics and Culture in the Seventies* (New York: Macmillan, 1971).

O'Hair, Mary John, and Odell, Sandra J. (eds.), *Diversity and Teaching: Teacher Education Yearbook 1* (New York: Harcourt Brace Jovanovich, 1993).

Oakes, Jeannie, "More than Meets the Eye: Links between Tracking and the Culture of Schools," in *Beyond Tracking: Finding Success in Inclusive Schools,* eds. Harbison Pool and Jane A. Page (Bloomington, IN: Phi Delta Kappa Educational Foundation, 1995), pp. 59–69.

Oakes, Jeannie, *Keeping Track: How Schools Structure Inequality,* 2nd ed. (New Haven, CT: Yale University Press, 2005).

Oakes, Jeannie, and Lipton, Martin, *Teaching to Change the World* (3rd ed.) (Boston: McGraw-Hill, 2007).

Oakes, Jeannie, Rogers, John, and Lipton, Martin, *Learning Power: Organizing for Education and Justice* (New York: Teachers College Press, 2006).

Ogbu, John U., "Class Stratification, Racial Stratification, and Schooling," in *Class, Race, and Gender in American Education,* ed. Lois Weis, (New York: State University of New York Press, 1988), 163–182.

Ogbu, John U., "Adaptation to Minority Status and Impact on School Success," *Theory into Practice, 31* (4) (1992): 287–295.

Ogbu, John U., "Collective Identity and the Burden of 'Acting White' in Black History, Community, and Education," *The Urban Review, 36* (1) (2004): 1–35.

Pai, Young, and Adler, Susan A., *Cultural Foundations of Education*, 4th ed. (Columbus, OH: Prentice-Hall, 2006).

Parham, Thomas A., "Cycles of Psychological Nigrescence," *The Counseling Psychologist, 17* (2) (1989): 187–226.

Parks, Rosa, with Haskins, Jim, *Rosa Parks: My Story* (New York: Dial Books, 1992).

Parsons, Talcott, "The School Class as a Social System: Some of Its Functions in American Society, in *Schools and Society: A Reader in Education and Sociology*, ed. J. H. Ballantine (Palo Alto, CA: Mayfield, 1985), 179–197.

Peréz, Lisandro, "Growing Up in Cuban Miami: Immigration, the Enclave, and New Generations," in *Ethnicities: Children of Immigrants in America*, eds. Rubén G. Rumbaut and Alejandro Portes (Berkeley: University of California Press, 2001).

Pettigrew, Thomas, "The Ultimate Attribution Error: Extending Allport's Cognitive Analysis of Prejudice," *Personality and Social Psychology Bulletin, 5* (1979): 461–476.

Pewewardy, Cornel, "Learning Styles of American Indian/Alaska Native Students: A Review of the Literature and Implications for Practice," *Journal of American Indian Education, 41* (3) (2002): 22–56.

Philips, Susan U., *The Invisible Culture: Communication in Classroom and Community on the Warm Springs Indian Reservation* (New York: Longman, 1983. Reissued: Long Grove, IL: Waveland Press, 1993.)

Phinney, Jean S., "Ethnic Identity in Adolescents and Adults: A Review of Research," *Psychological Bulletin, 108* (3) (1990): 499–514.

Pollock, Mica, "Race Bending: 'Mixed' Youth Practicing Strategic Racialization in California," *Anthropology and Education Quarterly, 35* (1) (2004): 30–52.

Portes, Alejandro, and Bach, Robert L., *Latin Journey: Cuban and Mexican Immigrants in the United States* (Berkeley: University of California Press, 1985).

Portes, Alejandro, and Rumbaut, Ruben G., *Immigrant America: A Portrait,* 2nd ed. (Berkeley: University of California Press, 1996).

Poston, W. S. Carlos, "The Biracial Identity Development Model: A Needed Addition," *Journal of Counseling and Development, 69* (2) (1990): 152–155.

Provenzo, Eugene F., Jr., *Teaching, Learning, and Schooling: A 21st Century Perspective* (Boston: Allyn & Bacon, 2002).

Quan, Kit Yuen, "The Girl Who Wouldn't Sing," in *Tongue-Tied: The Lives of Multilingual Children in Public Education*, ed. Otto Santa Ana, (Boulder, CO: Rowman & Littlefield, 2004), 13–21.

Red Shirt, Delphine, "Wasicuia Ya He? Do You Speak English?" in *Tongue-Tied: The Lives of Multilingual Children in Public Education*, ed. Otto Santa Ana (Boulder, CO: Rowman & Littlefield, 2004), 56–63.

Roberts, Kenneth L., *Why Europe Leaves Home* (reprinted in "Kenneth L. Roberts and the Threat of Mongrelization in America, 1922"), in *In Their Place*, eds. Lewis H. Carlson and George A. Colbum (New York: John Wiley and Sons, 1972).

Rolón-Dow, Rosalie, "Seduced by Images: Identity and Schooling in the Lives of Puerto Rican Girls," *Anthropology and Education Quarterly, 35* (1) (2004): 8–29.

Rosenthal, Robert, and Jacobson, Lenore, *Pygmalion in the Classroom: Teacher Expectation and Pupils' Intellectual Development* (New York: Holt, Rinehart and Winston, 1968).

Rothenberg, Paula S., *Race, Class, and Gender in the United States: An Integrated Study,* 2nd ed. (New York: St. Martin's Press, 1992).

Rumbaut, Rubén G., and Portes, Alejandro (eds.), *Ethnicities: Children of Immigrants in America* (Berkeley: University of California Press, 2001).

Ryan, William, *Blaming the Victim* (New York: Vantage Books, 1972).

Rytina, Nancy F., *Refugee Applicants and Admissions to the United States: 2004* (Washington, DC: Homeland Security Office of Immigration Statistics, 2005).

Sadker, Myra P., and Sadker, David M., *Teachers, Schools, and Society* (6th ed.) (Boston: McGraw-Hill, 2003).

Sadnovik, Alan R., Cookson, Peter W., Jr., and Semel, Susan F., *Exploring Education: An Introduction to the Foundations of Education,* 2nd ed. (Boston: Allyn & Bacon, 2001).

San Miguel Jr., Guadalupe, "The Struggle against Separate and Unequal Schools: Middle Class Mexican Americans and the Desegregation Campaign in Texas, 1929–1957," *History of Education Quarterly* (Fall, 1983): 343–359.

Santa Ana, Otto (ed.), *Tongue-Tied: The Lives of Multilingual Children in Public Education* (Boulder, CO: Rowman & Littlefield, 2004).

Schniedewind, Nancy, and Davidson, Ellen, *Open Minds to Equality: A Sourcebook of Learning Activities to Affirm Diversity and Promote Equity,* 2nd ed. (Boston: Allyn & Bacon, 1998).

Schutz, Aaron, "Home Is a Prison in the Global City: The Tragic Failure of School-Based Community Engagement Strategies," *Review of Educational Research, 76* (4) (2006): 691–743.

Shade, Barbara J., and New, Clara A., "Cultural Influences on Learning: Teaching Implications," in *Multicultural Education: Issues and Perspectives,* 2nd ed., eds. James A. Banks and Cherry A. McGee Banks (Boston: Allyn & Bacon, 1993), 317–331.

Shade, Barbara J., "Culture and Learning Style within the African-American Community," in *Culture, Style, and the Educative Process: Making Schools Work for Racially Diverse Students,* ed. Barbara J. Robinson Shade (Springfield, IL: Charles C. Thomas, 1997).

Simon, Julian L., "Immigration: The Demographic and Economic Facts" (Washington, DC: National Immigration Forum, Cato Institute, 1995).

Sleeter, Christine E., "Resisting Racial Awareness: How Teachers Understand the Social Order from Their Racial, Gender, and Social Class Locations," *Educational Foundations, 6* (2) (1992): 7–32.

Sleeter, Christine E., "How White Teachers Construct Race," in *Race, Identity, and Representation in Education,* 2nd ed., eds. Cameron McCarthy, Warren Crichlow, Greg Dimitriadis, and Nadine Dolby (New York: Routledge, 2005), 243–256.

Sleeter, Christine E., and Grant, Carl A., *Making Choices for Multicultural Education: Five Approaches to Race, Class, and Gender* (New York: McGraw-Hill, 1993).

Sleeter, Christine E., and Grant, Carl A., *Making Choices for Multicultural Education: Five Approaches to Race, Class, and Gender,* 4th ed. (New York: John Wiley, 2003).

Smith, Elsie J., "Ethnic Identity Development: Toward the Development of a Theory within the Context of Majority/Minority Status," *Journal of Counseling and Development, 70* (1991): 181–188.

Snipp, Matthew C., "American Indian Studies," in *Handbook of Research on Multicultural Education* (2nd ed.), eds. James A. Banks and Cherry A. McGee Banks (San Francisco: Jossey-Bass, 2004), 315–331.

Sowell, Thomas, *Ethnic America: A History* (New York: Basic Books, 1980).

Spring, Joel H., *The Sorting Machine* (New York: David McKay, 1976).

Spring, Joel H., *The American School: 1642–1990,* 2nd ed. (New York: Longman, 1990).

Stillings, Neil A., Feinstein, Mark H., Garfield, Jay L., Rissland, Edwina L., Rosenbaum, David A., Weisler, Steven E., and Baker-Ward, Lynne, *Cognitive Science: An Introduction* (Cambridge, MA: MIT Press, 1987).

Streitmatter, Janice L., and Pate, Glenn S., "Identity Status Development and Cognitive Prejudice in Early Adolescents," *Journal of Early Adolescence, 9* (1–2) (1989): 142–152.

Swisher, Karen, and Dehyle, Donna, "The Styles of Learning Are Different, but the Teaching Is Just the Same: Suggestions for Teachers of American Indian Youth," *Journal of American Indian Education* (1989): 1–14.

Tajfel, Henri, and Turner, John C., "An Integrative Theory of Intergroup Conflict," in *The Social Psychology of Intergroup Relations,* eds. William G. Austin and Stephen Worchel (Monterey, CA: Brooks/Cole, 1979), 33–47.

Takaki, Ronald, *A Different Mirror: A History of Multicultural America* (Boston: Little, Brown, 1993).

Tamura, Eileen H., "The English-Only Effort, the Anti-Japanese Campaign, and Language Acquisition in the Education of Japanese Americans in Hawaii, 1915–1940," *History of Education Quarterly, 33* (1) (1993): 37–58.

Tatum, Beverly Daniel, "Talking About Race, Learning About Racism: The Application of Racial Identity Development Theory in the Classroom," *Harvard Educational Review, 62* (1) (1992): 1–24.

Tatum, Beverly Daniel, "Teaching White Students about Racism: The Search for White Allies and the Restoration of Hope," *Teachers College Record, 95* (4) (1994): 462–476.

Tatum, Beverly Daniel, *"Why Are All the Black Kids Sitting Together in the Cafeteria?" And Other Conversations about Race* (New York: Basic Books, 2003).

Taylor, Charles, *Sources of the Self: The Making of the Modern Identity* (Cambridge: Harvard University Press, 1989).

Taylor, Charles, "The Politics of Recognition," in *Multiculturalism: A Critical Reader,* ed. David Theo Goldberg (Cambridge, MA: Basil Blackwell, 1994), 75–106.

Taylor, Gary, and Spencer, Steve, *Social Identities: Multidisciplinary Approaches* (London: Routledge, 2004).

Tharp, Roland G., "Psychocultural Variables and Constants: Effects on Teaching and Learning in Schools," *American Psychologist, 44* (2) (1989): 349–359.

The Road to Brown (videorecording) (San Francisco: California Newsreel, 1990).

Tiedt, Pamela L., and Tiedt, Iris M., *Multicultural Teaching: A Handbook of Activities, Information, and Resources,* 4th ed. (Boston: Allyn & Bacon, 1995).

Tönnies, Ferdinand (1887). (Translated by Charles P. Loomis), *Community and Society* (*Gemeinschaft and Gesellschaft*) (New York: Harper and Row, 1957.)

Topaz (videorecording) (Santa Fe, NM: One West Media, 1987).

Tozer, Steven E., Violas, Paul C., and Senese, Guy B., *School and Society: Historical and Contemporary Perspectives,* 2nd ed. (New York: McGraw-Hill, 1995).

Trueba, Henry T., "Culturally Based Explanations of Minority Students' Academic Achievement," *Anthropology and Education Quarterly, 19* (30) (1988): 270–287.

Trueba, Henry T., "The Dynamics of Cultural Transmission," in *Healing Multicultural America,* eds. Henry T. Trueba, Cirenio Rodriguez, Yali Zou, and Jose Cintron (Washington, DC: The Falmer Press, 1993), 10–25.

Tversky, Amos, and Kahneman, Daniel, "Availability: A Heuristic for Judging Frequency and Probability," *Cognitive Psychology, 5* (1973): 207–232.

Tyack, David B., "Constructing Difference: Historical Reflections on Schooling and Social Diversity," *Teachers College Record, 95* (1) (1993): 8–34.

Tylor, Edward B., *Primitive Culture* (London: John Murray, 1871).

Valenzuela, Angela, *Subtractive Schooling: U.S.-Mexican Youth and the Politics of Caring* (Albany: State University of New York Press, 1999).

Valenzuela, Angela, "Subtractive Schooling, Caring Relations, and Social Capital in the Schooling of U.S.-Mexican Youth," in *Beyond Silenced Voices: Class, Race, and Gender in United States Schools*, revised ed., ed. Lois Weis and Michelle Fine (Albany: State University of New York Press, 2005), 83–94.

Vygotsky, Lev, *Thought and Language* (Cambridge, MA: MIT Press, 1962).

Wade, R., "Service-Learning for Multicultural Teaching Competency: Insights from the Literature for Teachers," *Equity and Excellence in Education, 33* (2) (2000): 21–29.

Weinberg, Meyer, *A Chance to Learn: A History of Race and Education in the United States* (New York: Cambridge University Press, 1977).

Weiner, Bernard, *Human Motivation* (New York: Springer-Verlag, 1985).

Weinstein, Mark, *Critical Thinking and the Psycho-logic of Race Prejudice* (Montclair State College, Upper Montclair, NJ: Institute for Critical Thinking Resource Publication, Series 3, No. 1, 1990).

Weis, Lois (ed.), *Class, Race and Gender in American Education* (Albany: State University of New York Press, 1988).

Weis, Lois, and Fine, Michelle (eds.), *Beyond Silenced Voices: Class, Race, and Gender in United States Schools*, rev. ed. (New York: State University of New York Press, 2005).

Williams, Gaye, "Reminiscence of a Post-Integration Kid: Or, Where Have We Come Since Then?" in *Race Class and Gender: An Anthology*, 3rd ed., eds. Margaret L. Andersen and Patricia Hill Collins (Belmont, CA: Wadsworth, 1998), 350–353.

Witkin, Herman A., and Moore, Carol Ann, "Cognitive Style and the Teaching/Learning Processes," Paper presented at the annual meeting of the American Educational Research Association, 1974.

Wong, Pia, and Glass, Ron (eds.), *Interrupting Tradition: Prioritizing Urban Children, their Teachers and Schools through Professional Development Schools.* (Albany: State University of New York Press, In Press).

Wood, George, "Introduction," in *Many Children Left Behind: How the No Child Left Behind Act is Damaging Our Children and Our Schools*, eds. Deborah Meier and George Wood (Boston: Beacon Press, 2004), vii–xv.

Yamato, Jenny, "Something about the Subject Makes It Hard to Name," in *Race, Class, & Gender in the United States: An Integrated Study*, 2nd ed., ed. Paula S. Rothenberg (New York: St. Martin's Press, 1992), 58–62.

Yonezawa, Susan, and Wells, Amy Stuart, "Reform as Redefining the Spaces of Schools: An Examination of Detracking by Choice," in *Beyond Silenced Voices: Class, Race, and Gender in United States Schools*, revised ed., eds. Lois Weis and Michelle Fine (Albany: State University of New York Press, 2005), 47–61.

Young, Iris M., "The Ideal of Community and the Politics of Difference," in *Feminism/Postmodernism*, ed. Linda J. Nicholson (New York: Routledge, 1990), 300–323.

Zhou, Min, "Straddling Different Worlds: The Acculturation of Vietnamese Refugee Children," in *Ethnicities: Children of Immigrants in America*, eds. Rubén G. Rumbaut and Alejandro Portes (Berkeley: University of California Press, 2001), 187–227.

Index